THE HEROIC REVOLUTION

a new agenda for urban youthwork

REV. NELSON E. COPELAND, JR.

TO SOW THE FALLOW SOIL

James C. Winston
Publishing Company, Inc.
Trade Division of Winston-Derek Publishers Group

First printing

Book and cover design by Alec Bartsch

PUBLISHED BY JAMES C. WINSTON PUBLISHING COMPANY, INC.
Nashville, Tennessee 37205

Library of Congress Catalog Card No: 93-60356
ISBN: 1-55523-620-0

Printed in the United States of America

To my sister

Tierah Monyce Copeland

As kids, we were our own self-contained youth group.
Many of my youth skills began with you.
Good luck in college.
Thanks.

table of contents

preface

WRITING THIS BOOK WAS AN INTENSELY CREATIVE PROJECT. THOUSANDS OF hours were spent searching libraries, conducting interviews, testing theories, reflecting upon eight years of experience, checking and double-checking sources, and writing—anywhere from airplanes to Greyhound buses, rural farms to urban housing developments. I must praise God for allowing me to describe the implications of his ministry to urban youth.

Judy Landis and Alayna V. Kirby, my "dynamic duo" proofreading team, deserve special recognition. Also, thanks to Laura Lupton for her professional photography. Special thanks to the Evangelical Association for the Promotion of Education, where, as a volunteer and youth program director for many years, I gained much of the experience I bring to this book. My experience there led to leadership of my own programs with the Christian Education Coalition for African-American Leadership.

I have sought to personalize this book as often as possible with the names of specific persons. Although most of these are accurate, a few have been changed to protect the individual mentioned. Finally, thanks to the thousands of teenagers I know from the city and suburbia. Every page of this book is fragranced by my interactions with you.

As you read, remember six points:

- This book is directed to those who work primarily with adolescents in low-cost housing developments.
- I am a preacher by calling.
- I am an urban youth worker by trade.
- I am a social ethicist and philosopher by training.
- Some of the activities mentioned here will be included in my upcoming book, *Great Games for City Kids II*.
- Often, I bring my own experience as an African American to this book.

introduction

THIS BOOK PROVIDES A GENERAL FRAMEWORK FOR THE FUTURE OF URBAN youth ministry, recognizing that many of its practitioners come not from the city but the suburbs and rural America. View the following chapters as a crash course or basic training to those who want an urbocentric view of the way ministry is to be provided in the city. Newcomers to city ministry often mistakenly and arrogantly believe they are bringing God to the city with them; they "unpack" their ministries as if restoring a previously absent Lord. God was present and active in urban America before they came and will remain after they leave. The object of the newcomer is to seek out God's mission (missio dei), already active in the city, and build from there.

This book is subtitled a "new agenda," but is new only to those unaware of the reality urban ministry faces. Having said this, this book is dedicated to those who want to find Jesus already present in the city and to see urban reality through the oculars of potential, rather than sole depravity. Jesus does weep for the city, but he weeps actively. The good wheat and evil tares "both grow together until the harvest" of God.[1] Let us search out the good wheat growing in the city, and not simply accept that all are tares.

The young people of this nation are a valuable resource. They seek a brighter day, but many cities have failed them. They want hope, but some find only empty promises. The time has come for a heroic new agenda to rise from the soil of every American and international city, an agenda involving courageous youth leadership. The time is now.

Leadership is the strand that weaves every one of the following chapters together. The city cannot be improved without it. The future of any youth program that is to make a real difference is grounded in its investment in creating leaders. Yes, create them! Rarely are leaders born—they are made.[2] No urban teen should be so undervalued as to assume he or she lacks positive leadership ability.

Leadership begins with vision. Urban youth ministry in this land must work to open the eyes of every blinded Saul and help them become a Paul.[3] Teens want a better future and will often wait for a mentor to provide them with a dream to pursue. Refuse this offer. Instead, provide them with the dignity needed to create their own dreams and aspirations. They must then lead themselves in order for the vision to become reality.

Leadership continues with introspective power, which is nothing more and nothing less than creative self-discipline. It is the power to lead others by leading oneself. A good external leader must simultaneously become an internal one, because introspective power is a holistic process that is increased by choosing to organize oneself from within.[4] Simply put, self-discipline is the power to lead.

Leadership is directed toward reproduction. Genuine leadership is rarely satisfied by the act of leading. Pleasure is found in raising up others, because no leader will last forever. Any urban community that has hope for tomorrow is reproducing its leaders today, in an act of love rooted in the desire to see teens maximize their potential.

Let us set about the business of creating leaders who desire social, economic, and spiritual transformation. The problems facing us in urban areas are far from impossible to conquer, as long as adults and youths are willing to work, pray, and struggle together to create for themselves a new agenda that will focus the city on God. The Salvation Army song provides an image of the impact Christian leadership can have in the city. Let us apply this same philosophy to urban youth culture.

The Army is coming—amen, amen!
To conquer this city for Jesus—amen!
We'll shout "Hallelujah!" and praise his dear name,
Who redeemed us to God through the blood of the Lamb.
The sound of its footsteps is rolling along;
The kingdom of Satan, triumphant so long,
Is shaking and tott'ring and downward shall fall
For Jesus, the Savior, shall reign over all. . . .
The sound of salvation shall float on the wind—
Through street, court and alley its way shall it find,
The stubborn to break, and the broken to bind,
For Jesus is mighty, yet gentle and kind.[5]

introducing
the new agenda

URBAN YOUTH MINISTRY DEMANDS A SPECIALIZED PARADIGM. IT IS A UNIQUE ministry profession which must seek solutions to its ills from within its specific context. Urban and suburban youth ministry have notable differences, yet the tools of urban youth workers are borrowed from their suburban counterparts. It has become clear that the resources which serve the city youth pastor must come primarily from an urban source.

Working with both urban and suburban adolescents provides a constant reminder that what works well programmatically in the suburbs, and with middle-class teens, may have little or no effect in the city without great translation. Mainline urban youth workers have eagerly utilized the resources and training materials of suburban youth ministry, only to realize that the problems facing them in the city were qualitatively different and required new solutions. Urban youth ministry cannot substantially build upon the techniques of suburban youth ministry. An urbocentric approach is needed, one which assures that the youth program is rooted in and arises from the experiences and circumstances of the city.

I am occasionally confronted by people who insist, "Teens are teens! You do not need a different method for the city than the suburbs." This statement is undoubtedly true when applied to relational ministry, but the issue here is programmatic planning. City teens have an atypical subculture, with substantially different rules, mores, and folkways than that of suburban teens. They have different dress codes, slang, music, hairstyles, even expectations concerning what a good youth group should be. The time has come for the urban youth group to reflect programmatically the young people it serves.

By the time the Cakchiquel Indians were being evangelized in Latin America, they already had a detailed and unique cultural ethos and language. They were taught the scriptures not by imposing the Vulgate Latin version of the Bible upon them, but by translating it to their vernacular so that everyone could read the scriptural text themselves. Later, one of the Cakchiquels, having read over the biblical text for the first time, said with great delight, "This is wonderful! God speaks our language!"[1] In a similar fashion, youth programs should be presented in a language urban youth can decode.

MINISTRY DOUBLE-DUTCH STYLE

The game called "double dutch" describes a typical lower-economic teenager's life. It is similar to jump-rope except there are two ropes turned simultaneously by two people, one clockwise, the other criss-crossing counterclockwise. The object is to see who can remain in the center the longest without getting the ropes entangled around their feet.

Daring anyone to try, the rope turners begin the game with the phrase, "Challenge! Challenge!" When a challenger feels confident, he or she lunges into the ropes while they are turning. If the jumper successfully makes it in, everyone begins to count aloud "One, two, three, four, five..." as the person hops, continuing until the player either tires or miscalculates the ropes and gets entangled. Whoever remains within the ropes longest is the winner.

This is the story of the myriad of inner-city adolescents who feel they must navigate the "ropes" of society every day. They must overcome every obstacle that comes their way, with little time to think. They never have a chance to respond proactively, only reactively. Since the ropes outlast any individual, even the strongest fall and the finest stumble, leaving a wasteland of the former dreams and hopes of any who can survive long enough for a chance at life.

The weak fade away into apathetic despair, wondering if anyone could ever survive; the strong try again, like Camus' Sisyphus, forever pushing a heavy rock up a slope despite knowing it will roll back again each time it reaches the peak. "He knows that he shall never win his hill, yet he refuses to allow his rock to remain at the bottom of the slope." His persistence allowed Sisyphus to keep a "hold on his human dignity in the face of an absurd world"—yet even he understood the futility of his efforts.[2]

Many young people living in cities are searching for *someone* who can help them survive the ropes of poor education, joblessness, inadequate healthcare, single-parent homes, political and economic disenfranchisement, violence, sexual diseases, and gangs. They are searching, yet no one has stood the test. The apparent permanence of these "ropes" will cause even the most determined youth or youth worker to cry as did Habakkuk:

> How long, O Lord, must I call for help,
>   but you do not listen?
> Or cry out to you, "Violence!"
>   but you do not save?
> Why do you make me look at injustice?
>   Why do you tolerate wrong?
> Destruction and violence are before me;
>   there is strife, and conflict abounds.
> Therefore the law is paralyzed,
>   and justice never prevails.
> The wicked hem in the righteous,
>   so that justice is perverted.

> Habakkuk 1:2–4

Many have come to these teens with good ideas and approaches, which over time have failed. Others have taught training seminars and positive-thinking classes which allow young people to survive for longer periods of time. Not many, however, have answered the more fundamental question, "Who is able to cut the ropes?"

Urban teenagers do not want ropes at all. Ropes entangle their potential. Teaching them how to avoid them is not enough—they will eventually get caught. Instead, youths need to realize that Jesus Christ is the only double dutch champion. He will not only jump with them as they face daily trials, he will *cut the ropes* for those who trust in him. With women and men this is impossible, but "with God all things are possible" (MATT. 19:26).

FOUR PRONGS OF THE NEW AGENDA

Reflecting upon conversations and personal experiences with urban youth pastors and youths across this nation, four essential issues become apparent.

The primacy of the salvation of the teens. The highest goal of every Christian youth group is the conversion of its teenagers to Christianity. Do not forget this; I have often had to remind myself of this crucial point. It is easy to turn ministry into social work, and outreach into benevolent acts of goodness, but the urban youth pastor serves an even higher role—calling teens to a commitment to Christ.

This goal needs to be overtly structured into the youth program, to allow those adolescents who are moved to accept Christ to do so in an open and relaxed fashion. What I fear most are those youth workers so pinned-down in the problems of their adolescents' lives that they forget the message of "good news" they were sent to bring. How can young people caught within the urban predicament call on the one they have not believed in? How can they believe in the one of whom they have not heard? How can they hear without someone preaching to them? And how can they preach unless they are sent? It is written, "How beautiful are the feet of those who bring good news!" (ROM. 10:14–15.)

The primacy of evangelism from the teens. One of the most significant things any youth pastor can do is involve youths in evangelism (see Chapter 9). Some ministry organizations view evangelism as the exclusive domain of the youth worker. This is inaccurate. Evangelism is an act all Christian adolescents and adults can take part in. By involving young people in evangelizing their peers, the Gospel message is broadcasted directly by those who represent the first fruits of what the others can become. If the adolescents become active agents of evangelism, God's power working in and through them will result in the growth of the youth group, becoming a point of celebration as the Lord adds to it weekly (cf. ACTS 2:47).

Evangelism takes many forms. Some might argue for an incarnational model while others will desire a more aggressive format. Both can bring blessed results. Be open to the Spirit of God moving in this process. City youths will often know of contextual ways to preach to their peers that may go far beyond what the youth pastor can understand.

For example, rap music is a medium most urban teens can relate to. It is a style and art form that uses specific rhythmic patterns and poetic prose to connote an exact message that often only a rap-conscious audience can decode. Not just anyone will be accepted as a rapper, however. M. C. Ran (Ryan Morris), for example, is an evangelist of a new sort. Active in the Boston Urban Youth Foundation program, he uses rap music as a testimony and instrument of God's goodness in his life. This is the sort of evangelistic message that should be included in tracts to hard-core urban teens:

> I was raised in the city, the ghetto and all,
>> Where some stood low and some stood tall.
> Back in the days it used to be fun—
> But now people run when gangs pull out guns.
> In the city it's not hard to enter,
>> Not going to tell a lie,
>> I was a gang member.

Rolling in a car and warring high,
>   Pulling out guns and doing drive-bys.
My head was in the freezer, cold as ice,
>   Then I took my head out and went to Young Life.
One day I got jumped by some guys I hate,
>   They beat me up bad so I retaliated.
I went to get something, let me give you a clue,
>   It wasn't my 9, it was my 32.
I was real upset, didn't approach a smile.
The talk of the court: M. C. a juvenile.
So I got my gun and I was on my way,
>   But what do you know? I see my brother and Jay.
They said, "Ran, if you do that, you might fail,
>   I'll see you in twenty years, when you get out of jail."[3]

The primacy of social action from the teens. Teenagers must participate in the ongoing work of God. Whenever Christian young people rise up for that which is right, victory may be close at hand. Encourage your teens to feed the homeless, go to a nursing home, or visit a crack-baby ward. Have them write periodically to the local congressperson and evaluate his or her performance in the community.

Social action, like evangelism, must be performed by the teens themselves. Young people are never the same after they allow God to work through them. The saved adolescent is a docking pier for the Kingdom of God, to be evidenced "on earth as it is in heaven" (cf. MATT. 6:10). What good is the salvation of adolescents if they seek not good for others and society?[4] Walter Rauschenbusch put it eloquently: "God wants to turn humanity right side up, but needs a fulcrum. Every saved soul is a fixed point on which God can rest his lever."[5]

Calvin, at fourteen, was skeptical about going to feed the homeless. He kept asking, "What good is this going to do? We can't feed everyone!" I consistently led him back to the point that inactivity is the same thing as apathy. While we could truly neither feed nor help everyone, the Christian is never called to be successful—only faithful.

As he pondered this, we walked the night streets of downtown Philadelphia with three others, giving away our bagged dinner sandwiches to accepting transients. With one bag left, we spotted a man stretched out in an alley, looking as if he were dead. As we slowly approached him, I could see this man was indeed breathing, but asleep. I gave the bag to Calvin and whispered, "Put it beside him." He nodded and did so.

As we tiptoed away from the alley we noticed the man was waking, so we quickly hid behind a wall where we could see him but he could not see us. As he opened his eyes, he saw the bag lying beside him, looked up to heaven, and smiled.

Calvin immediately retorted snootily, "It looks like he thinks God did it!" I responded, "He did, but it was through your hands." From that evening on, Calvin never questioned the usefulness of social action and requested that at least one of our yearly projects be to feed the homeless. We must provide ample opportunities for God to work his saving, revolutionary power through our youths to affect positive social transformation. "God is the substance of all [positive] revolution."[6]

The primacy of empowering teens. Teenagers from the city feel they have no power over their own destiny. They desire empowerment. Urban youths need opportunities for ownership in their neighborhoods and youth groups, which may translate into sending teams of adolescents to community meetings so they can know and respond to the decisions being made over them, or giving more leadership to youths in the youth group. After all, the best youth leaders lead least, because they empower their members to lead (see Chapters 3 and 5).

Empowerment is crucial to harmony in the city. Whenever there has been unrest, it has come on the coattails of a group of people realizing they have not the power over their own destiny that is due them. Those persons entrusted to do ministry with city youths should give them power! It is a disservice and a lie to tell teenagers to come to a "youth group" which in reality is not guided by them at all. It would be better to call it a "youth pastor group."

Teenagers will obtain the power due them one way or another, whether negative (joining a gang, being profitable in the drug market, acting disorderly in the youth group, or in a riot) or positive (excelling in sports, music, drama, academics, and youth group leadership). Urban youths deserve the opportunity to utilize their God-given skills and control some of the institutions that affect their lives. The youth group is one conduit through which urban youth empowerment can be expressed. It is dangerous to disempower youths, because it makes celibate their aspirations, bankrupts their hopes and defers their dreams. Poet Langston Hughes knew the consequences of "a dream deferred:"

> What happens to a dream deferred?
> Does it dry up
> Like a raisin in the sun?
> Or fester like a sore—
> And then run?
> Does it stink like rotten meat?
> Or crust and sugar over—
> Like a syrupy sweet?
>
> Maybe it just sags
> Like a heavy load.
>
> *Or does it explode?*[7]

building
cultural selfhood

2

COMING TO TERMS WITH ONE'S ETHNIC BEAUTY IS IMPORTANT AND unavoidable. Culture is a part of who and what we are. In the city, minority youth are often discouraged from learning about their history. Once they do, however, they discover the value, elegance, and royalty in their culture. Building cultural selfhood provides a methodology of self-identity that one can be proud to live by.

All youth are made in the image of God, yet developing selfhood among city youth is a constant battle. One day they feel good about who and what they are; the next, they feel maimed by God. Youth is a time for developing selfhood. It is a time to choose an identity for oneself and give it personality and depth.

When speaking with people involved in urban youth ministry, I am amazed at how many youth workers overlook the crucial element of culture when attempting to build a young person's self-image. The ethnic culture to which a youth belongs establishes the image that God has created for this teen. It is this image he or she must have pride in and rally around. We must begin not by teaching adolescents to forget about their cultural identity, but to consider it a source of inner strength. Not only are we created *in* God's image, we are created *with* his image. To focus upon the inner spiritual self is not enough—youth must be guided to see God's image in both their inner character and their outer characteristics. True cultural selfhood comes from honoring who you are both inwardly and outwardly. A *good* self-image can be obtained without a sense of culture. A *positive* self-image cannot survive without culture.

BUILDING THE CULTURAL SELF

When I worked for the Evangelical Association for the Promotion of Education in Philadelphia, I dedicated my efforts toward finding a way to give city youth a sense of identity based on more than my positive statements of affirmation—something internal instead of external. I wanted the young people I influenced to have a sense of dignity not contingent upon what I thought of them, but rooted in the ethnic cultural heritage they were created into by God—their cultural self.

Many urban teens have an empty understanding of their role as a cultural contributor to society and to the Kingdom of God, due partly to their alienation from knowledge of their own ethnic heritage. For example, I once quizzed a group of thirteen African-American eighth and ninth graders about great heroic figures of their culture. What I found was startling. I began by asking, "Who was Harriet Tubman?" They hesitated. Finally one boy responded, "I know, she was a conductor." Puzzled by his response, I asked him what he meant; he elaborated, "She was a conductor of a train railroad." No one argued, because they did not realize Harriet Tubman was a participant in freeing slaves through the "underground railroad." This, of course, had nothing to do with operating trains.

Dismissing this occurrence as coincidence, I proceeded to ask another question. "Who was Frederick Douglass?" I received no intelligent response, confusing me a bit as I assumed eighth and ninth graders should know this. I continued by asking, "Can anyone tell me who invented peanut butter?" The response was similar.

By this time I had had enough. I decided I would ask an easier question, one that they had to know. I inquired, "Can someone tell me anything about Martin Luther King, Jr?" I received two responses. "Wasn't he the man who went to sleep and had a dream?" Secondly, "He was shot because he was nice."

At this point, I was mentally ready to switch gears. I decided to use this opportunity to teach these students about their ignorance of their own history. I asked, "Who was George Washington?" Not surprisingly, every hand went up. Most said, "He was the first president." Others stated, "He never told a lie." I then asked, "Does anyone know what Betsy Ross did?" Most affirmed she was known for making flags during the colonial period. Only two didn't know her.

We moved on to "Who was Abraham Lincoln?" The dialogue had begun. This group knew not only that Abraham Lincoln was the sixteenth president, but one youth yelled, "He freed the slaves by signing the Emancipation Proclamation in 1863!" I must admit this blew me away.

I posed a question: "Why do we know so much about this history and so little about the other?" They honestly didn't understand their failure to grasp anything about African-American history, except for one fourteen-year-old girl who said, "Well, Nelson, I guess the reason we don't know our history is because we never learned it." Precisely.[1]

The urban metropolis has failed to teach cultural history to its children and adolescents. The strong cultural self confronts this situation by requiring that the books they read and the history they are told connote ethnic worth instead of inferiority. Urban youth (particularly minority youth) view their culture as leprous, and fail to see the source of religious strength that lies therein. This cannot happen!

Christ is the center of building a youth's cultural identity. He is the pinnacle of culture. Our teens must discover that Jesus does not reject their culture, he embraces it. Not only can self-identity be found culturally, Jesus himself can be enjoyed culturally.

The following approach will teach youth to see themselves not as a problem, but as a solution. Complementing the Afrocentric concept of *"Nija,* the ideology of victorious thought," it promotes the strength of inner identity over that defined by others.[2] To build cultural selfhood in youth, there are three steps of affirmation that must be built upon: the affirmation of self, culture, and others.

Paul Johannes Tillich, in his book *The Courage to Be,* formulates an ideology of self-affirmation that seeks to synthesize Christianity and modern existentialism. Self-affirmation, a crucial first step in building the cultural self, entails two important qualities: courage in-spite-of and vitality in-spite-of.[3]

Courage in-spite-of. Urban youth are constantly being told they cannot make it in this society. They don't have the right skills, the proper education, the correct communication skills to become any-thing of worth. This prophecy often becomes reality. Inner-city teens must be taught to affirm the core of what they were created to be by God, to have the courage to say "I am somebody!" no matter what confronts them.

Youth must be encouraged to realize they are special not because any particular person or group says so, but because their uniqueness is founded in the image of God. God made them who they are and they should never be ashamed of it. They must be willing to have faith in their own self-worth when no one else does. The poet Ruyard Kipling put it well in this excerpt from his poem, "If":

> If you can keep your head
> When all about you are losing theirs
> And blaming it on you.
> If you can trust yourself
> When all men doubt you
> But make allowance for their doubting too.[4]

As youth workers, teaching city teens to have the courage to be what they are, regardless of others, is difficult. It is not easy telling a nerdy youth, "You are made in God's image and he is pleased." Or telling a heavy teen with low self-esteem, "Look on the bright side, Jesus thinks you are great." All of life is a processing of who you are. In order for such advice to make any sense within the auspices of urban youth ministry, the courage to be oneself cannot be separated from the necessity of viewing oneself as a wonderful creation of God.

Toya is an excellent runner, nationally ranked among ninth graders. She has one of the strongest personalities I have ever known a teen to have. Normally spirited, she seemed somewhat reserved during senior high youth group one evening. Later, as I was driving the teens home, I intentionally dropped her off last so I could find out why she was not herself.

She told me she had a running injury that would keep her off the track for at least a month. I asked, "Is this why you are down?" Toya said, "No. I can accept the injury. It's just that many of the people I thought were my friends are treating me like some kind of traitor." I asked why. "Because I'm one of the two best runners, and the big end-of-the-season relays are coming up." She continued with a raised voice, "The coach is not speaking to me, friendly, like he used to. I thought if I could count on anyone, it would be him. Well, I guess I found out all he really wanted out of me were the points I could get him."

I suggested she go to the coach and tell him how she felt. Clearly he wanted her to feel guilty so she might decide to run in the big relay, giving him a chance at winning the meet. Toya's response reflected the strength of her character. She stated, "I'm sick of having people talking behind my back, like something is wrong with me. I refuse to be pressured into running for the sake of the team, and injure myself in the long run. I know I am the best on the team. Everyone I respect tells me that with training I could make the Olympics. That goal is more important than running one little race and damaging myself permanently." I interjected, "You're right!" Toya continued, "I know I am—I'm determined! God has given me a lot of talent, and I want to use it for him. I'm just a ninth grader! If I ruin myself now, I'll never have a chance. I'm not going to run until I'm ready. In all my running I want to give God the glory, and this is not giving him glory." Toya had enough bravery to see her self-worth in Christ beyond her coach, her teammates, and me.

To have courage is to have joy. I dropped Toya off at home, and although her problem was not solved, the decision she had made led her to rejoice.

Vitality in-spite-of. Vitality gives courage meaning—the two are directly related. Tillich tells us, "Diminishing vitality consequently entails diminishing courage. To strengthen vitality means to strengthen the courage to be."[5] A Christian teen in the city is not necessarily bored, but full of life, because the teenager's sense of self is rooted in a commitment to Jesus Christ.

We must communicate to the youth of the world that courage is inextricably tied to vitality. Hardship is everywhere, and is particularly acute in urban areas. The youths that arise victorious from such hardship tend to act in one of three ways:

WITH COURAGE BUT NO VITALITY. These teens believe in who they are, but fail to express themselves with excitement, so that others may realize the strength of their personality. They are often quiet, conversationally unexciting, and wise—good listeners who do not waver easily from decisions. They are faithful background supporters who do not desire leadership.

WITH VITALITY BUT NO COURAGE. These are the loud-mouths of the group. Although often providing a good percentage of the morale of the youth group, there is not much depth to their character. They must have fun at all times or they are bored. Usually boisterous and emotional, they need constant attention, make statements ungrounded in reason, and can be swayed from decisions easily. If given a task, they perform it conditionally.

WITH COURAGE AND VITALITY. These adolescents have a strong sense of individuality and are full of self-esteem. Willing to stand up to anyone for what they believe is right, they are a joy to be around. They are strong-willed, faithful and thoughtful, giving and loving. Balancing rationality and emotion well, these youth usually ascend to leadership.

Where there is vitality, life and joy are present. Young people living in the city need this element added to their lives and their characters. Without it, spiritual death is inevitable and true courage cannot be realized.

AFFIRMATION OF CULTURE

Affirming an adolescent's cultural and ethnic identity is both an internal and external process: internal because cultural traits are taught; external because cultural features are genetic. Molefi Kete Asante, in his book *Afrocentricity,* describes the usefulness of affirming one's ethnic core.[6] He concludes that individuals must strive to view their culture as beautiful, upholding the philosophy of *Nija*—which he defines as viewing one's culture not with shame, but with dignity. As I travel across the country, I am often disheartened to find the youth of urban America being "miseducated" about themselves by youth workers who color their cultural education with shame and ignorance, rather than pride and dignity.[7] Only the gospel of Satan could make people ashamed of the color of their skin or the regality of their ethnic culture. The affirmation of culture, on the other hand, engenders two positive characteristics: intelligence in-spite-of and boldness in-spite-of.[8]

Intelligence in-spite-of. Knowledge of one's cultural heritage is a must, as one must use intelligence to weather the winds of racial hatred and ignorance. In a heated debate, one can respond to derogatory comments aimed at one's ethnicity with historical prudence instead of flippant half-truths. City teens (particularly minority youth) have to defend their cultural self-worth on a daily basis. Some respond with anger, others with an intelligent sense of self. The youth worker should encourage youths to know their culture so well (including its history, present plight and issues related to that plight, and a good opinion about its future) that they can affirm the beauty and majesty of their cultural wealth in any situation.

Urban youth must be made aware that the cultural issues they need to learn are not being accurately taught in the classroom; they must take up outside study. Some ideas for learning about one's culture are:

- Reading books crucial to its history and survival.

- Attending events that promote its beauty.
- Learning its music and dance.
- Wearing its traditional garments.
- Learning its language.
- Staying up-to-date on issues that concern it, and forming opinions on those issues.
- Having at least six good things to say to someone else about it at all times.
- Having discussions with the aged of the culture for wisdom.
- Observing its holidays.
- Educating others about its beauty.
- Finding ways to be an asset to it today.

Boldness in-spite-of. Intelligence begets bold action. Intelligence about one's cultural attractiveness will manifest itself in cultural self-defense. Whenever it is perceived that one's ethnicity is being degraded, a confrontational self-defense must arise out of intelligence. It is not the power of the fist that will solve an incident, it is the boldness of individual will to affirm the culture in spite of another's subjugation. The goal is not for one group to win or lose, but for both to recognize the worth of the other. Boldness comes to the defense of intelligence when one's worth is not being recognized. Intelligence, in turn, fuels boldness through any and all adversity.

Cultural boldness is not militant, but arises from a genuine appreciation for ethnicity. Some urban teens have little appreciation for their culture; to ask them to be bold would be futile, as they already believe in a lie that will lead to their destruction. When I meet these adolescents, I get the eerie feeling that they suffer from cultural diarrhea—such overeating of another's culture that they under-digest their own, thus rejecting the nutrients theirs has to offer. Poet and writer Langston Hughes provides a classic example of this thinking in a short story about an African-American man who was extremely fair-complexioned, so much so that he could pass for white. The following is an excerpt from a letter this gentleman wrote to his mother:

Dear Ma,

I felt like a dog, passing you downtown last night and not speaking to you.... If I hadn't the [white] girl with me, Ma, we might have talked. I'm not as scared as I used to be about somebody taking me for colored anymore.... Since I've begun to pass for white, nobody has ever doubted that I am a white man.

But I don't mind being "white," Ma, and it was mighty generous of you to urge me to go ahead and make use of my light skin and good hair.... When I look at the colored boy porter who sweeps out the office, I think that's what I might be doing if I wasn't light-skinned enough to get by.

I felt bad about last night.... That's the kind of thing that makes passing hard, having to deny your own family when you see them.

What did you think of the girl with me, Ma? She's the kid I'm going to marry.... I wonder what she would sa[y] if I told her I was colored.... Since I have made up my mind to live in the white world, and have found my place in it (a good place), why think about race anymore? I'm going to marry white and live white, and if any of my kids are born dark I'll swear they aren't mine. I won't get caught in the mire of color again. Not me. I'm free, Ma, Free!⁹

The tragedy of this story is not in this man's intelligence, his awareness of his African descent; it is in his lack of boldness to be as God created him. Ethnicity must be rescued by boldness.

AFFIRMATION OF OTHERS

The final step toward cultural selfhood involves the acceptance of other ethnic groups, without which we would be building the cultural self in vain. God created each ethnic group, and we should celebrate the cultural diversity he has provided.

The Israelites were commanded by God to love outsiders. All aliens were to receive the same respect and honor due any Israelite. The Lord's word is evident in Leviticus 19:33–34, "When an alien lives with you in your land, do not mistreat him. The alien living with you must be treated as one of your native-born. Love him as yourself, for you were aliens in Egypt."[10] It is no coincidence that the Israelites were commanded to love other cultural groups as if they were of their own. To treat someone as if native-born is to recognize their sacredness as the same as your own. Cultural selfhood is reciprocal. To affirm one's own self-worth has no meaning without affirming that of another.

The city is full of diversity, as is the body of Christ. Two ideas are necessary for affirming the importance of others in the development of the cultural self: ethnos in-spite-of and cultural reciprocity in-spite-of.

Ethnos in-spite-of. In the seventh chapter of Revelation, verses nine to seventeen, there is a great multitude in the court of heaven. A tremendous celebration of worship is taking place before the throne of God, to honor Christ the Lamb. The significance of this text for cultural affirmation is found in verse nine: "After this I looked and there before me was a great multitude that no one could count, from every nation, tribe, people and language, standing before the throne and in front of the Lamb."[11]

Notice the scripture illustrates that every culture stands before the Lamb. Interestingly, the word used for "nations" is *ethnos*.[12] These nations are ethnically, not politically, defined—America is not there, nor any form of a national politic. Hispanics, Asians, Africans, Polynesians, Europeans, all ethnicities stand before the glorified Christ as his chosen people. Heaven is not devoid of culture, it is colored by cultural diversity.

Those gathered have all " 'come out of great tribulation' (verse fourteen). No longer on earth, they crowd the throne room of heaven clad in victors' robes and bearing the emblem of festive joy."[13] This harmony among disparate cultures resulted from holding on to cultural identity in the face of great adversity. In heaven, ethnicity will rise to its highest potential and be brought together by Christ. This radical imagery must be understood before urban ministry can adequately progress.

We must teach teenagers that heaven is for them. Jesus has not only prepared a place for their soul, he has prepared a place where their culture will be comfortable. The genius of the Heavenly Father has provided a place both ethnically diverse and spiritually unifying. Our message to youth, then, is that heaven is a place where every culture thrives. The heavenly host is not all European, as many urban youth believe—it is a great festival of the best every culture was created to be.

Cultural reciprocity in-spite-of. The second, more important part of affirming others is the ability to share and give freely with other cultural groups. As humans, we are inextricably tied to one another—this is God's plan. We must depend on each other, giving as much to the construction of other cultural groups as we do our own; this mutual interdependence is called cultural reciprocity. Undeniably, degrading someone else's cultural group for the benefit of your own is not only unconstructive—it is destructive.

City adolescents struggle not only with their own sense of ethnic identity, but also with their attitudes toward other groups. There are four ways in which racial harmony can be realized: cultural assimilation, amalgamation, plurality, and reciprocity.[14] I believe cultural reciprocity is the best approach.

CULTURAL ASSIMILATION. In this scenario, the less dominant culture accepts the ideology of the dominant cultural group and discards its own. In mathematical terms, $A + B + C = A$. Urban teens of color constantly fight against being assimilated into the larger American culture—resisting not out of hatred, but self-preservation. I have met very few teens who want to discard their cultural richness for the jewels of another.

CULTURAL AMALGAMATION. Amalgamation is equivalent to the "melting pot" theory, in which all cultural differences melt together to create a new culture independent of its constituent ethnicities. Thus, $A + B + C = D$. This philosophy denies cultural individuality in an attempt to create an equal society, ordering that ethnicity must be forgotten. What this theory lacks is the notion of a society being equal *with* color.

CULTURAL PLURALITY. Imagine a society where all ethnic groups exist as separate, thriving units cooperating with one another—that is, $A + B + C = A + B + C$. At the outset, this approach looks supportable and many champion it; after all, plurality is a form of togetherness that operates with respect for others. It is a good option. It alludes, however, to an urban form of segregation in which people live and relate only in their own "neighborhoods." Cultural plurality promotes every group as a needed part of the society, but only to the degree that it retains its separateness. Booker T. Washington encapsulated this idea in his 1895 Atlanta Exposition speech: "In all things that are purely social we can be as separate as the fingers, yet one as the hand in all things essential to mutual progress."[15] The ultimate end of plurality is to be "separate but equal."

CULTURAL RECIPROCITY. I have found this approach to be best. When teaching the importance of ethnic togetherness to urban youth, strive to inspire them to give as much to another cultural group as they do their own. God intended that we share each other's expertise to create a good society "on earth as it is in heaven," one in which people give to and receive from one another. In short, $A \times B \times C = ABC$. Cultural reciprocity does not add our likenesses—it multiplies them. We become "one in Christ" without trampling the essence of individual cultures.[16] Reciprocating allows society to work beyond the potential of each distinctive cultural group, providing an atmosphere of affirmation in which cultural selfhood can survive.

The ideal of cultural reciprocity must be communicated to youth. It is a viable alternative to cultural plurality that goes a step beyond assimilation and amalgamation. For this endeavor to be successful, urban youth workers must be willing to go beyond societal expectations of cultural togetherness, promoting a model that is godly, yet obtainable in the context of our urban youth groups.

PROGRAMMING CULTURAL ESTEEM

Turning the theory of building cultural esteem into a real program is an arduous process. Consider the following four methods for providing your youth program with a cultural emphasis.

Method 1: Structured cultural programming. This type of pro-gramming focuses solely upon building cultural self-worth. Often intense, these programs have a clearly defined goal and meet with regularity. Their overarching purpose is to teach youth the impor-tance of their ethnic inheritance while preparing them to encounter the everyday world. Here are two examples:

The *Simba Wachanga* program, Swahili for "young lions," is oper-ating in several American cities. Its mission is to train young African-American boys to become men dedicated to the purposes of their cul-ture, while giving them the balanced cultural perspective needed to operate in the world. Skill development, cultural history, recreation, adult role models, learning cultural rites of passage, and harmonizing cultural tradition with contemporary reality are all parts of this intri-cate program.[17]

Beginning a program like Simba Wachanga requires a sixfold approach. Although this program is designed for young men, its principles can also be applied to all-female and coeducational groups.

- Organize a group of men in the cultural group willing to par-ticipate in the program.
- Develop study sessions with these men, discussing the history of the culture and male development. Read significant books on these topics.
- Identify the location, frequency, and length of the youth meet-ings. Target an age range.
- Objectives of the program should include skill development, history education, male socialization, recreation, and a "Big Brother" plan.
- The weekly structure consists of a field trip and other sessions concerning cultural history, skill development, and "rites of passage" (male socialization).
- Field trips should include visits to a prison, drug-abuse center, teenage pregnancy center, public hospital emergency room on a Saturday evening, top high-school honors class, stock mar-ket, campground, and a computer-oriented business.[18]

The second model is one I created for a series of youth meetings concerning cultural selfhood. This plan, outlined below, structures a four-week series of youth group sessions that provides the teen with an opportunity to gain a stronger sense of cultural self-esteem and identity.[19]

I. OPENING (ten minutes)
   Open with prayer, receive prayer requests and concerns, sing or play a game.

II. AFFIRMING SELF (ten minutes)
   Week 1: *Great gifts and talents I possess.*
           A writing activity that will encourage teens to reflect on what they are good at.
   Week 2: *If I were Jesus, why would I love me?*
           Begin by telling youth about Jesus' love for everyone. Then have them list at least seven reasons why they believe Jesus loves them.
   Week 3: *Affirming my self-worth when no one else does.*
           Encourage teens to think about what they consider valuable about themselves, including those qualities not recognized by others.
   Week 4: *Proof that I am somebody special.*
           Acting as attorneys, have the youth write a rebuttal to convince the court that they are a precious, godly commodity.

III. AFFIRMING CULTURE (thirty minutes)
   Adolescents will come to appreciate different aspects of their culture. In many cases they will become deeply involved in the issues facing their ethnic group, often bringing to light new concerns that need to be focused upon. Become proactive and pass on your conclusions to an organization equipped to represent them, even if it is the Supreme Court. The weekly themes are:
   Week 1: *History and accomplishments.*
   Week 2: *Contemporary issues concerning the culture.*
   Week 3: *Music and stories of the culture.*
   Week 4: *Twenty-five reasons God created our culture.*

IV. AFFIRMING OTHERS (twenty-five minutes)
   This section will explore the significance of other cultural groups. Each week, a speaker will represent their ethnic group, sharing and answering questions that will enhance the teens' understanding of that group. Use any ethnic groups you see necessary. A typical series I would use for Hispanic youth is:

Week 1: *The beauty of our Native-American brothers and sisters.*
Week 2: *The beauty of our Italian sisters and brothers.*
Week 3: *The beauty of our African brothers and sisters.*
Week 4: *The beauty of our Asian sisters and brothers.*

V. AFFIRMING ONE ANOTHER (ten minutes)

This ends as a time of sharing, where the activity will provide the opportunity to build someone else's esteem. The first week, ask each youth to share something they appreciate about others. By the final week they should have to bring a gift that expresses the worth of the other person to them. *Note:* The atmosphere here must be one of unthreatening intimacy or some teens will not willfully participate.

VI. CLOSING (five minutes)

Announcements, closing words, and a prayer.

Method 2: Integrated cultural programming. This method attempts to integrate cultural exposure into an existing youth group format. The goal is to introduce adolescents to cultural topics on a consistent basis, adding a dimension that will lead teens into a better understanding of who they are ethnically. This can be accomplished in a number of ways:

- Each week, ten to fifteen minutes can be devoted to discussing significant topics concerning the culture.
- Have a weekly "History Moment." Each week a teen will be assigned a person to research and will prepare to talk for at least two minutes about that person. As an extra incentive, every volunteer can receive one to five dollars off their next field trip.
- Invite monthly speakers from various cultural groups to come to the meeting and explain the history of their culture.
- One week every month can be designated "Our Culture Week," which will break the normal club routine and focus on some aspect of cultural pride (such as food, music, dance, art, drama, literature, relationships, history, great leaders, actors, and significant firsts, to name a few ideas).

Method 3: Cultural imaging. One climactic issue of the 1989 movie by Spike Lee, *Do The Right Thing,* concerned an Italian restaurant owner named Sal who solicited his business in an African-American neighborhood. This by itself was not the problem—tension arose because the community at large did not appreciate that every picture on the walls of his restaurant was of a great Italian leader or figure. Since his clientele was African-American, many believed his restaurant should at least reflect some of that culture on the walls. Sal never changed the pictures, and a resulting boycott eventually led to a riot that wiped him out completely.

Urban youth workers must be conscious of the images and pictures they present to their youth groups. Presenting images youth feel comfortable with—images that reflect their own, strictly for the purpose of outwardly affirming who they are—builds cultural selfhood.

In the Vieux Carre of New Orleans there is a tremendous Methodist youth community center called Saint Marks. When I visited this ministry, I was amazed at the images presented on the walls. Every place I looked, there was a mural or painting reflecting African Culture. The imaging of cultural greatness was unavoidable. Yet, a few blocks away you could easily find billboards that had pictures with negative connotations. Pictures tell what is beautiful to the designer. Hang images and artwork that oppose the decadent caricatures urban teens have become accustomed to.

Method 4: Cultural role modeling. Any youth program seeking to teach cultural significance should seek to provide *live* representatives of your teens' culture. Role models should be people directly involved in the program; if this isn't possible, at least cultivate a small group of people willing to participate with the group as often as possible. Invite members of different ethnic groups to share themselves with the youth. What it means to be Japanese cannot be adequately taught by a Hispanic—it must be taught by someone who is Japanese. The reality of urban youth ministry is that much of our programs are being led by persons not of the youths' ethnic group, which causes a problem in teaching cultural issues.

In Philadelphia during every Black History Month, I was concerned that my staff consisted mainly of middle-class European college-aged students. I knew that although they could teach the culture historically, they could not teach it experientially. Surrogate role models should be avoided in cultural education, in order that the information presented is pure and drawn from experience. Cultural role models are precious to any program lacking ethnic staff balance—don't forget it!

WARNING: CULTURE WORSHIP

In your excitement to implant models of cultural selfhood in your youth, do not make your ethnic group the zenith of your religious program. Many lead their program into a form of totemism or idol worship. Do not let this happen. Worship the creator, not the created. Youth must be proud of who and what they are, but not to the extent that they lose sight of who created them.

Secular culturalism, in which the collective harmony of the group is an end in itself, is rampant. This philosophy is not that of a Christian. Let your message be, "Your heritage is something special to me, but more importantly, you need Jesus! It is he who has created your ethnic elegance and it is to Christ that all honor is due."

youth gangs and leadership

3

GANGS CAN BE GOOD OR EVIL, AND CAN BE FOUND WITHIN ALL SOCIETIES. As children become teens, they seek to create options for themselves that society neglects to offer. They seek togetherness. In doing so, youth can exhibit tremendous leadership ability and a binding cohesiveness.

When I was a young boy growing up in Baltimore, my closest friends and I would express this bond by declaring ourselves "blood brothers,"[1] thereby completely dedicating ourselves to mutual protection and friendship. We supported each other through fun times and mischief. Everyone had their niche, making them crucial to the group. We were "The Gang of Flannery Lane."

We were good boys. The most we did was attempt to smoke a cigarette—which all swore to never do again. Our time was spent playing games together. One day, however, we noticed that another gang of kids had moved in down the alley. They were bigger than all of us, but we were more intelligent. As the leader of the group, I had to devise a plan that would rid us of this menace. Not only were they threatening our "turf," they had most of my gang afraid to go outside. I was determined to put this group in their place.

I came up with a three-part strategy, which the gang approved. Operation One was the "egg attack." We took two eggs a piece from our parents' refrigerators and quietly made our way down the alley to where we knew our opposers would be. Just when we were at strategic readiness, I yelled, "Attack!" We all pelted them.

Operation Two was "the tease." After egging the enemy, three of my gang ran down the alley to prepare for Operation Three. Meanwhile, the others and I were teasing the egged gang, attempting to get them mad enough to chase us home. They took the bait. As they were chasing us, I waited until we were close enough to home and yelled, "Dog attack!"

The final operation was now underway. Our dogs tore off in their direction and stopped them in their tracks; they were crying as the dogs surrounded them, screaming, "Please! Don't let them kill us!" I responded calmly, "No. Not unless you all never come back down our alley again." They were all in obvious agreement. We pulled back our dogs and told them they had twenty seconds to be out of our sight or their fate would be worse. Those boys never did come back down our part of the alley unless they were with their parents. We had won! Our dogs had given us an advantage over their physical strength and peace was once again restored.

YOUTH GROUPS AND GANGS

Youth create gangs for unity and protection. These purposes are innocent—it is when they are taken to extremes that they become detrimental. In the urban context, a significant minority of youth go to extremes to terrorize their community, reinforcing the negative opinion most people have about all youth gangs. In the larger sense, however, a gang is simply a group of youths dedicating their loyalties toward a common purpose, which teenagers join out of a need for social development.[2] The task of the urban youth worker is to encourage the growth of good gangs.

In the 1970s, Walter B. Miller, a researcher for the federal government, studied nine hundred American cities for youth gang involvement. He found 105,000 noticeable gangs operating in these cities, with a membership of 1.6 million youths. Totaling the top six cities of Chicago, Detroit, Los Angeles, New York, Philadelphia, and San

Francisco, he estimated that between 760 and 2,700 gangs were operating, with between twenty-eight and eighty-one thousand members.[3] Although gangs have grown larger and become more violent since this study was performed, it provides a basis with which to consider the challenge before us.

There are solutions to the evils of urban gang involvement, and Christianity is one of them. The task of urban youth ministry is to redirect teens involved in gangs for the benefit of Jesus. We not only want to save the gang member, we want to save the gang. To undertake this process accurately we must be familiar with youth gang theory and leadership, the ethnic groups involved, and available alternatives.

YOUTH NEED GANGS

Frederic Thrasher, in his 1927 sociological classic *The Gang,* provides an insightful study of 1,313 Chicago gangs. His greatest contribution was to recognize that youth need gangs. Among youth aged eleven to seventeen, there is an elemental desire for gang membership.[4] A gang can be as innocent as a group of kids hanging out on a street corner or as destructive as a complex drug-selling organization. Youth join gangs because they see something of what they want in life present in those gangs.

Gangs are life—rough and untamed.[5] Many people give up on gang members, believing them to be beyond rehabilitation. They are not. Each street gang is full of "life" waiting to be directed, a rough crust that can be smoothed. A gang is not a bad thing; it is neutral until influenced. A group of teens telling jokes on the street corner every evening is a gang that has not been influenced. My task is to influence them to join a positive organized gang (my youth group) before they are influenced to join an organized community with adverse intentions.

Youth gangs will not stay neutral. We must get them involved with issues concerning Jesus instead of those that concern Satan. A gang is a bundle of potentialities waiting to be realized. In many urban communities there have been more bad options for youth than good ones.

Interestingly enough, most youth do not join organized criminal gangs—they form small groups of friends seeking solace from the streets. They create for themselves an option unavailable in the community, choosing life over the extinction that so many street corners produce. Their gangs exist as an attempt to fight boredom.

Urban youth workers need to create options that dispel boredom from the streets of the city. Gangs become bad when there is no guidance leading to constructive excitement, generating life. Guidance must be deliberate, in order that the energy in the gang be used for good.

Gangs are conflict groups. Our youth groups need to reclaim the notion of conflict. Conflict is not a bad thing. Gangs thrive on conflict. City adolescents live in a situation where conflict is ever-present. Most gangs, although forming spontaneously, develop through strife and warfare.[6] To adequately entice gangs off the streets we must provide opportunities for conflict and warfare within our youth groups.

I have seen many youths leave gangs because their desire for warfare was satisfied on the basketball court. Recreation is a form of conflict that can both drive away boredom and create the feeling of controlled warfare.

Another option is to confront a social problem. Social analysts noticed gang membership dropped tremendously in the sixties because those who would have taken part in the warfare of mischief were absorbed instead by the warfare of the civil-rights movement.[7] Go to mass rallies with your youth, help lick envelopes for a political candidate, feed the homeless, collect trash, plant trees in the community, picket a local business that is ripping off the neighborhood, march for godly causes.[8] The inadequacy of our profession in offering opportunities for positive conflict to urban youth is the noose that hangs us in our attempts to reach gangs effectively.

Gangs give youth what society does not. Youth involve themselves in negative gang activity because of a lack of options. The gang provides the option that was desperately lacking within the social structure. Urban teens want their talents to be utilized, but can find no place to apply them other than within the context of a gang.

Thrasher points out that youth gangs are a "spontaneous effort to create a society where none adequate to their needs exist."[9]

Urban underclass adolescents need space to be creative. In suburban contexts youth have a better opportunity to satisfy their creative needs; working with both urban and suburban youth has taught me this lesson. My suburban teens have many options to quench their creative desires, while the city teens do not. Urban youths must create their own excitement, since it is not provided by the society at large. The gang, good or bad, replaces missing institutions.

Gangs utilize the talents of all their members, and youth groups must do the same. Everyone should have an investment in the group. There are no unused persons in a gang; the same should be true of all youth groups. Teens will then know their importance as a member of the group, and we will be able to offer what urban society does not—a need for youth.

FOUR DESIRES YOUTH MUST SATISFY

In his book *The Unadjusted Girl,* William I. Thomas attempted to learn the reasons some problem girls were unable to adjust to society. Studying pregnant girls, prostitutes, and disturbed females, he looked for something missing from their societal development which might have led them down these paths. He discovered these girls were unadjusted primarily because they lacked the ability to adequately satisfy four desires: the desire for new experience, security, response, and recognition.[10]

I have observed within the field of urban youth ministry that youth join gangs because their needs are not being satisfied in one or more of these areas. Teens have left my youth group for the same reason. A successful youth program must creatively satisfy all four of these desires.

The desire for new experience. Teenagers are adventurers. They need to go places, see things, and "boldly go where no man has gone before." When they can't, they become restless and seek to quench this desire elsewhere. Gangs offer adventure.

Thomas notes that anger motivates this desire.[11] When a youth does not have adequate opportunity to capture new experience, the side effect is anger. Throughout my urban experience, I have met many teenagers who are angry with the world. They are usually bright individuals who feel pent-up in their community and will seek any way to escape. These adolescents are the best type to invite to an adventurous activity. If we offer programs known for adventure, youth will come.

I am amazed at the reasons city kids love amusement parks. Every time I go, I see them waiting in line for sometimes up to two hours for a two minute ride. I always ask them why, and the response is always the same: "Because of the adventure!" Only at an amusement park can a teenager be thrown upside-down, spun around, whipped, bumped, crashed and still be alive to tell the story. Teenagers need the risk of new experiences to break the monotony of everyday existence.

The desire for security. New experience risks, security does not. Although teens thirst for new experience, they also want to be secure—that is, they fear the unknown. Thomas finds that although their pursuit of new experience pulls them in the direction of death, their fear of death seeks out security.[12]

Taking city adolescents on a night hike in the woods makes for great observation. On a retreat with teenagers, I love doing night hikes because of the element of fear. Urban youth are afraid of the night, dark places, and open spaces; when you mix those three, you have the desire for security and new experience balanced.

During a night hike, youths stay close to each other because of their fear of the unknown. In all reality, they are very much afraid. Any unidentified noise is imagined to be *Friday the Thirteenth's* Jason or *Nightmare on Elm Street's* Freddie Krueger. At a certain point they become petrified, and all seek each others' support to keep an eye out for anything that might be of harm to them. I often ask, "Why did you come if you are afraid?" Their response reflects that they want the new experience it will bring, but only within the security of the group.

Gangs offer security to their members as they undertake new risks. A gang member knows that no matter how fearful a situation is, the group is their security. Let us transplant this quality to our youth clubs, securing the fears of our youth with the strength of the groups' backing.

The desire for response. This desire is founded upon our need for love. Many urban youth I come in contact with, however, often lack the knowledge that someone loves them.

Youth gang members care about each other, responding to one another with a genuine concern wrought from conflict with others. Through thick and thin, they appreciate each other. In the words of the song "You've Got a Friend," "Winter, Spring, Summer, or Fall, all you have to do is call, and I'll be there, yes I will. You've got a friend."[13] Members realize that their compatriots are also their best friends, and are often the only people that care about them. When a youth pastor comes along and actually puts his or her arms around these youth and shows genuine care and appreciation, they will come to see that person as a true friend and mentor.

Derrick was sixteen. He involved himself with a small gang of boys that came to senior high club mainly to start trouble. I liked Derrick because, away from his peers, he was sensible and open. I would take him and his best friend out and around town with me, trying to influence them positively. Derrick got tossed out of his high school and began to attend another.

One day he participated in stealing a car with some friends and, somehow, word got back to the police that he was involved. By this time Derrick had been downtown so often he was sentenced to a reform school for a year and a half, so he could finish high school. Once there, I wanted him to know I still cared about him and wanted to come visit. I wrote him a letter. Two weeks later I received:

To Nelson,

You know I did something wrong. I'm trying to get better, not worse. I would like to apologize for what I did. I hope God forgives me and you will pray for me. I wish I could pay you back for all you did. You were like a brother to me. I respect you for that and hope we can stay in touch. I'll be up here for about a year, but I think this will help me out.

Derrick

There are many promising young people like Derrick that need us to respond to them with love. Unless we unconditionally love teens, their gangs will give them the response they should have received from their youth group.

Desire for recognition. Adolescence is a time to perform recognizable achievements. Instead of being recognized for their abilities, however, teens are often ignored. We must make a more determined effort to acknowledge and appreciate youth accomplishments. Youth have an insatiable desire to be recognized, which must be fulfilled by the youth worker before it is fulfilled by the gang.

Thomas discovered that this desire is closely related to the fear of failure.[14] Urban youth are often afraid their life will amount to nothing. Therefore, they fight self-extinction at any cost. Their eyes have seen too many carcasses of lost dreams and aspirations scattered about their communities to want to consciously follow that path. They seek to be successful at something that will bring them recognition, whether it is in a gang or the church choir. They yearn to leave their mark.

Gangs recognize and reward the accomplishments of their members. Completing an objective of the gang brings notoriety, respect and prestige. In some gangs these involve killing, theft, or robbery, while in others the fittest is the most recognized. Those that successfully perform are treated as heroes by the group.

Urban youth ministry should be in the business of creating occasions for youth to be recognized. We need to praise adolescents for their positive accomplishments, no matter how small, and encourage them to be their best. We must not let the youth of the city be recognized with more worth by those who are evil than those who are good.

MINISTRY TO THE STAGES OF GANG DEVELOPMENT

Over time, gangs develop into hierarchies or organizational units. They mature and develop a focused purpose. The manner in which we are to minister to youth involved a gang depends heavily upon its developmental stage. Up to this point, I have used "gang" to refer to both unorganized and organized associations of teens.

Frederic Thrasher, the historical sociologist of gang theory, and Barbara Wade, Miami police gang information coordinator in 1986, have both contributed to our understanding of gang development and reform.

Stage 1: The diffuse type. The most basic form of a gang is a group of teenagers which formed because the members have fun with each other. The solidarity of such a group is insecure. The bond between members is not necessarily criminal; it is based on their common experience in the world. If they get into trouble, there is no structure for organized retaliation. There is no formalized leadership present, and any mischief carried out is not very organized.[15] During my time in Philadelphia, there was a small gang of three pre-teens from a neighboring community that would throw rocks and jump on vehicles. They became a consistent menace. What puzzled us was that we knew each of these young people. Individually, they were easy to rehabilitate and talk to, but together they became a problem. They eventually stopped this activity and became active in the program. Although a menace, they were never a fearful threat.

Barbara Wade believes these are the type of kids that can be influenced most easily. They can be led in any direction. Not hardened by skepticism, they are just having fun.[16] The urban youth ministry program must target these youth for redemption. These teens are the easiest to get off the streets and involve in constructive programs.

Stage 2: The solidified type. This group of teens has become an organized base of activity. It has a purpose, goal, and mission—usually to do harm or damage. Within this group, "a high degree of loyalty and morale and a minimum of internal friction contribute to a well-integrated fighting machine, by means of which the gang presents a solid front against its foes."[17]

Getting these youth involved in the youth group takes a lot more effort. They feel they do not need your group because they are securely affirmed by their gang structure. They already have leadership and are needed there. They know if they attend the youth group they will be viewed as "sinful" or a "problem child."

Wade points out that it takes extra time to get these youths involved. They often have many psychological and emotional needs.[18] Youth involved with drug gangs almost always do not fit into the regular youth group crowd. One great way to get them involved is through a sports league. Gangs enjoy sports—remember that.

One summer I directed a sports program that included a significant number of known drug dealers among its members. Since their involvement with drugs was mainly in the evenings, many openly expressed that playing basketball was day recreation for them. It was interesting seeing these youth having to learn scriptures by day in order to play in the league. In their eyes, joining this league was penance for their "night job." Though often invited, they never considered joining the youth group, believing it was too holy for their sins.

Stage 3: The conventionalized type. On the tail end of an engagement in Honolulu, a friend gave me a tour of a few housing developments in the Kalihi part of town. I was amazed at the obvious presence of formal gangs. Evidence of their activity was everywhere. Most of these gangs were Asian or Polynesian; those involved were extremely hard-core and had no intention of leaving. Ministry is difficult in this situation, because the problem is no longer people—it is the gang machine that consumes people. The top leaders of these gangs are not teenagers, but adults aged twenty to thirty-five. Teenagers provide the major means of operation, however, because they are "juveniles under the law" and therefore cannot be incarcerated quickly.

Attempting to reform this kind of machine is tiring, because it is an entrenched evil. Police have found it similar to an octopus: if one tentacle is taken out another soon appears.[19] I believe it is useless to attack the machine as a whole through youth ministry; instead, true ministry should target *persons* reachable within the machine.

Our youth groups should deliberately reach out to youth involved in gangs, just as gangs actively recruit the membership of good teens. Ask your teens if there are any young persons involved in a gang that they believe "want out" or can be reached. Target these youth, and attempt to coax them into a safe relationship with the youth group.

Rehabilitating youth involved in systematic gangs is often more of a task than the youth pastor is trained to do. Seek professional help. Salvation comes not only through prayer and faith, but also through leading these teens to the professional services they may need to be freed from gang involvement.

YOUTH GANG LEADERSHIP

Sociologist William Foote Whyte, in his 1943 masterpiece *The Street Corner Society*, writes from three-and-a-half years of experience living in an Italian poverty community he calls Cornerville. His work is significant because of his personal understanding of how one ascends to leadership within organized and unorganized gang groups.

The leader. The leader is the focal point of any gang. Every decision must be made by the leader and executed by the followers. The more organized the gang, the more powerful the leader. In most groups, without the leader "there is no common activity or general conversation."[20] The leader is the hub of all liveliness.

Among youth gangs the leader can be easily recognized as the person who asks all the questions and makes any needed threats. Providing a ministry to a youth gang leader is hard, because the leader has everything he (or she) wants within the context of the gang. Not many with any sensibility would leave their leadership position to be an average member in your youth group. Their position has been won over time, and has been earned; giving it up would be like pulling teeth. "In some gangs the leader is determined through physical prowess, aggressiveness, combativeness, and toughness; in others the leader is simply the most persuasive or perhaps the oldest or most affluent member."[21]

Asking a gang leader to come to the youth group alone is threatening. Invite him to come with some of his members. During that time, focus on changing the attitude of the leader. If the leader has a good time, the "posse" will also. Another way to get gangs involved (through the leader) is with a negotiated settlement. For example, you get word to the leader that your church will fund a summer basketball league for every member of the gang, as long as they begin faithfully attending youth group. Any slip-ups and they will have to create their own recreation. Obviously their motives for coming are wrong, but it allows the opportunity for great things to happen. Gang leaders have all the qualities needed to lead a youth group. The youth pastors' leadership threatens their ability to lead. If their negative direction can be channeled towards Jesus instead, they can do wonders for the leadership of the group.

The follower. In Whyte's assessment, the followers within a gang are easiest to reform because they have no lasting need to the leader. They are expendable and can be replaced. Only the loss of the leader's main officers can cause the gang to ripple.[22] These teenagers are the easiest to get involved in your youth program because they have the least to lose by leaving the gang. Breaking away in some cases can be dangerous, but is less so for teens involved in diffused or solidified gangs.

Many teens have membership because it gives them clout in the neighborhood or because a bond has formed between them and the leader. The most important means of involving adolescent youth gang members is to find out what their function was in the gang and transfer it to the advantage of the youth group.

Change in leadership. Urban youth gangs have a propensity for leadership disputes and changes. These typically take one of four directions:

UPRISING. This scenario occurs when there is dissatisfaction with the leader and opposition results. Members often become jealous and seek to usurp the power of the leader politically, usually not through "an uprising of the bottom men, but by a shift in the relations between men at the top of the structure."[23]

JAILING. Many teens involved in gang leadership have a long record of incidents with the law. If successfully prosecuted for a serious crime they can be jailed, rendering them inoperative in the leadership of the group.

DEATH. I am associated with one community in which drug gang leadership changes, on average, twice a year. Gang members in pursuit of power often kill each other or are killed by police. If the prime leader is killed, the gang's entire structure shifts. If a minor leader is killed, someone is promoted from the lower ranks to take his place.

QUITTING. Often the pressure of leadership becomes more than the leader can handle. He feels he must constantly "watch his back" and protect himself. This teen can be helped. Every once in a while a youth gang leader will quit. To do so he might need to relocate for safety. His decision is usually made because of either a newfound religious decision or fear of death.

ETHNIC GANGS

Most youth gangs tend to be ethnically defined. Rarely is there a mixture of cultures within a gang. Edward Dolan and Shan Finney, two journalists from California, did a significant amount of research on the characteristics of criminal ethnic youth gangs in America.

African-American gangs. According to their 1984 study, forty-seven percent of America's youth gangs are African-American. Most of their crimes are committed against the local community, and lean heavily toward thefts, burglaries, protection rackets, and the sale of drugs. Members are paid with a pre-negotiated share of the bounty. The execution of the gang's goals is carefully planned and funded from its treasury. Each member is given a task in the operation.

Turf control and violence are considered necessary if an incoming group does not heed warnings. There is no turf sharing—the area staked is to be completely controlled by the gang and nothing short. Some gangs are known by the colored scarves they carry, others by their caps or jackets. I have seen some instances where the gang was recognized by the color of tape used to seal drugs sold on the street.[24]

Hispanic gangs. Thirty-five percent of the nation's youth gangs are Hispanic. Characteristic of these youth is a tremendous appreciation for their turf and community. Territory is worth fighting for; it is more important than the individual. Training younger children to be capable of defending and dying for this turf is highly esteemed in the gang. As a result, a large number of youth are killed each year.

Membership for an outsider is extremely difficult. Loyalty must be pre-tested. *Machismo* (manhood) is a driving factor with the teen. The need to defend honor and prove courage causes a vicious circle of retaliation and re-retaliation. Gangs are often distinguished by a particular bandanna or tattoo.[25]

Asian gangs. This group's national total is 7.5 percent and increasing. Asian gangs can be further divided into specific nationalities, often rivaling one another. The youth involved are sometimes sponsored by adult organized gangs. Conflict among gangs typically consists of continuing scrimmages from the native countries.

Each group's crime is focused. Chinese gangs are cited for gambling and prostitution, while Koreans target robbery, burglary, and the protection racket. Filipino gangs specialize in illegal drugs, burglaries, and muggings, and the Japanese also have a targeted ring. Asian gangs tend to be secretive.[26]

European-American gangs. These constitute ten percent of the national average. Dolan and Finney found that these teens are more interested in rebellion than in killing. Tending to be from suburban backgrounds, they have little interest in protecting turf. Interests are in drunkenness, drug abuse, wild parties, negative rock music and anti-social behavior. Little detailed research exists in this area, which may contribute to Dolan and Finney's limited findings.

European-American gangs are, therefore, reduced to three categories: punks, outlaws, and supremacists. Punks seek anti-cultural values. Alcohol and drug abuse are prevalent among members, along with a taunting disgust in the American value system evident in their hairstyles and music. The outlaws are limited to motorcycle gangs that resort to criminal activity for the advantage of brotherhood. Supremacist gangs are usually founded by adult organizations, such as the Ku Klux Klan, American Nazi Party, or the Supreme White Power groups.[27]

ALTERNATIVE GANGS

If we are to succeed at our task in urban youth ministry, we need to offer and be knowledgeable about alternatives to gang activity that will maintain the solidarity of the gang, yet include an ethic of morality among its operating objectives. We will look at some examples of both reformed gangs and counter-gangs.

Reformed gangs. Reformed gangs have made a decision to turn their ways around and become a positive force in the same communities they once terrorized. I will highlight two such gangs as examples of the promise this type of gang can demonstrate.

SAINT SINNERS. This Los Angeles Mexican gang exists for graffiti. Not very violent, it has made a conscious decision to stick to spending more time practicing rockabilly dance steps than wielding a spray can. Its members, therefore, have managed to stay out of jail. The *placa,* the symbol that marks the gang's territory, is extremely important to this group. These symbols send messages to other gangs; what is communicated depends on what is sprayed.

Today, the members have become born-again Christians and have begun to take their graffiti to the canvas instead of the wall. Rather than aerosol cans, it is now the brush that does what is needed. In addition, they have redirected their energies in positive directions that benefit themselves and their community.[28]

YOUNG DILLINGERS. This Washington, D.C.–based African-American gang used to boast that it never lost a fight. In 1980, its members decided to wage war against the same evils they had once perpetuated. Initially, they were praised with open arms, and had a board of directors with prominent community and political leaders. However, their method of justice became suspect when four members were killed during gang-related activity. Different from other reformed gangs in this respect, they would often beat captured drug dealers, drawing much criticism.

Their methods caused many of their supporters to abandon them. The tragedy of this gang lies—more than in its tactics—in the board's failure to foster a more ethical approach to justice. We must learn the lesson that a gang which earnestly tries to do good, and is rejected, is less likely ever to attempt good again. This reality is best expressed by the co-founder of the gang: "We've been accused of being vigilantes all along, which we weren't, but maybe that's what we should become."[29]

Counter-gangs. The primary purpose of a counter-gang is to fight evil without participating in it, operating on the principle of non-violent self-defense. Their actions are based on love and a desire to protect the people and community for good. This was the goal of Superman, Wonder Woman, and Spiderman—the only difference is that they had super powers. These teens have will, morals, and determination. Here are two examples.

GUARDIAN ANGELS. This is the most notorious counter-gang in the country. Curtis Sliwa, a high school dropout from the Bronx, grew up witnessing many muggings and killings. After some time he dedicated himself to doing something about them. At twenty-five, he founded a group called "The Magnificent Thirteen," which patrolled subways. This group expanded to become the Guardian Angels, a nationwide organization with members in New York, Los Angeles, Miami, Boston, San Francisco, and Newark.

This group, known for wearing a matching red beret and T-shirt, made significant inroads in securing safety and capturing the trust of crime communities. The Angels have had an uncanny ability to inspire a spirit of volunteerism in many gang-related youth looking for a better option to champion. The group operates as a conventionalized gang would—the difference is that its motives are for good. It has tough entry and membership procedures. No Angel can be caught smoking or behaving uncouthly. Members must be holding down a job or enrolled in school; if they fail to uphold any of these regulations they are stripped of their beret and shirt.[30] Sliwa explains:

> Survival is predicated on the bad guys knowing we're not cops. We don't bother people smoking, drinking, dealing in dope, even

carrying illegal handguns. But if we see anyone being harassed, assaulted, robbed, raped or savaged, we'll get in-between the two parties like peanut butter between two slices of bread. If we have had visual contact with the crime being committed, we'll grab the assailant, make a citizen's arrest, check for witnesses, and call the police.[31]

A MODEL FOR CHRISTIAN GANGS. Youth need Christian gangs in urban communities. Our youth groups should operate with the same confrontational intensity and cohesive unity as a gang, with love for each other and sacrifice as their principle ideal. Let us learn a lesson from those we have so often misunderstood: gangs form to meet missing needs. We must take up where society leaves off and construct thorough programs that urban teens *need*. Here are three such models

Jesus' Gang. The twelve disciples were an interesting group. Jesus sought to mold them into people capable of changing the world. The gang became a caring community in which the gifts of each disciple could be brought to fruition. These people did not initially believe they could change the world—it was their leader who fostered this belief in them. Everyone in the group was needed and was recruited for a purpose by the leader. Each had gifts crucial to the leader's objectives.

The disciples went through extensive training and preliminary missions to prepare them for the task ahead. They became so trusting of one another that the leader could call them "friends," even though one member would drastically recant membership. Their solidarity grew out of the adversity they faced together.

On the evening the leader knew the group would disband, he held a ceremony which was to become a tradition in which all future members would take part. Those members could thus remember the originator of the group "as often as possible," and rely on this tradition as the basis for all future fellowship.[32]

This was the first Christian gang—Jesus' gang, whose members, through their love and loyalty to their leader, could face the world and indefatigably change it despite his physical absence. Our youth groups must follow this pattern; they should be communities of care, in which each person is needed by the group. The solidarity that is formed will train youth to face the world in the absence of the leader.

The Hebrew Boys Gang. Shadrach, Meshach and Abednego were a gang of three that stood firm against societal conformity, refusing to bow to the totem of King Nebuchadnezzar. Their behavior angered the King, who insisted they either bow before him or be punished with death by fire. They refused, telling Nebuchadnezzar they would not conform because Yahweh was "able to deliver" them—and even if he did not, they were not to bow. This gang stood together with the knowledge that none of them would face this ordeal alone. As a result, God provided safety for them so that they could serve as an element in the King's salvation.[33]

Teenagers must learn a lesson from these three: it is better to take a stand together than alone. The quirks of city life can be dealt with much more easily if one stands against injustice as part of a group, rather than as an individual. Strife fuels a gang's ability to resist. Christian gangs are held together by outward adversity.

Basis for Christian urban youth gangs. It is imperative that our youth groups operate as a positive gang. They must lure our youth with the same intensity as do negative gangs. We must offer safety, security, identity, intimacy, the feeling of being needed, and, most of all, Christ. All gangs offer five qualities salvageable for the Kingdom of God which can provide a basis for a successful urban youth group.

The first is *non-conformity.* The youth group must understand that to be Christian is to be deviant from the ways of the world. Deviance is defined as consciously turning away from "normal" behavior. To be a Christian non-conformist is to refuse to be "conformed to the pattern of this world, but [to] be transformed by the renewing of the mind. Then you will be able to test and approve what God's will is."[34] A Christian gang will exhibit this characteristic as a response to living the Christian message.

Gangs draw attention because of their non-conformity. Youth often don't understand that non-conformity to the world's standards means conformity to Jesus' standards. To choose this path means to do whatever Jesus would do if he was in our situation, with guidance from prayer, his word, and his gang (other Christians).[35] Urban youth groups must, above all else, present a model that opposes Satan's Kingdom and is in prayerful alignment with God's.

The second objective is *moral discipline*. Most gangs do not behave morally; Christian gangs do. Some urban areas lack ethical standards among their operating principles, and Christian teenagers can unknowingly reflect this gap. The purpose of the gang is to encourage a discipline of moral traits required for membership. Morality should be practiced in four ways:

- *Prudence* is inner integrity: facing your outer influences and not allowing them to control you, having the courage for non-conformity and the intelligence to know why.
- *Temperance* applies to anything that hampers a personal commitment with Christ. It means not over-doing anything.
- *Justice* is desiring fairness for everyone, and more importantly, acting fairly toward everyone. Be truthful, fair, equal and desire good for others.[36]
- *Fortitude* is having the courage to live by and defend Christian convictions.

These are basic steps (cardinal virtues) that can lead non-Christian teens to bring the higher traits of faith, hope, and love into their lives.

Third, the concept of *protection* must be reclaimed. Gang members protect each other—they refuse to let harm come to any member without resistance. Our youth must learn the art of protecting others, which in turn brings about stability. Unlike most gangs, which use protection hurtfully, the Christian gang must protect non-violently.

There are two varieties of non-violence: removing yourself from a violent situation or delving into a violent situation to stabilize it.

Christian gangs sponsor the latter. Protection must be both physical and spiritual.

Urban youth face dangerous physical situations. To survive, most learn to fight at a young age. No teen in your youth group should ever be in a fight without the Christian gang responding to both parties; this response is based on a reconciliatory care for both. Violent situations are confronted to bring harmony, not discord. We cannot allow one of our members to be harmed without bringing both sides into accountability.

The gang must also protect its members spiritually, as youth is a time of spiritual warfare. The gang helps its members through this time of manifold problems and temptations. Prayer is the key here—teach youth to pray for each other and concern themselves with the burdens of others. They protect each other by "carrying one another's burdens; and by doing this they fulfill the law of Christ."[37]

The fourth quality that can be gained from gangs is *camaraderie*. Gang members constantly have a sense that they are cared for by the group. When I work with youth, I often hug them and treat them like family, because that is what they are: a group that consistently shares common experiences. This familial feeling is the glue that should keep your youth group coming. I would like to think my youth come because of dedication to me. They don't—they come because of the camaraderie they experience between all members.

Camaraderie develops over time. I was involved in a senior high group that included teens from six different housing developments. At first it seemed too risky, but over three years, through trips, retreats and shared experiences, kids from neighborhoods once in conflict now visit each other's communities regularly, regardless of the program.

The last crucial element of a Christian gang is *confrontation*. None of the others make sense without it. To confront an issue is to recognize its reality. Urban youth gangs thrive on confrontation, such as mugging, gang war, and fighting. It is confrontation that makes them believe in the worthiness of their cause. The Christian gang must fight a war of flesh and spirit. We must confront issues as a gang.

The best way to do this is to stay on the front line. The Guardian Angels succeed with urban underclass youth because they are on the front line of crime fighting. Get teens active in an issue and they will perform. In a ten-month tutoring program in Philadelphia, the notion of recycling and neighborhood beautification was introduced to youth in five communities. By the program's end, they had collected a total of six hundred pounds of aluminum and seven thousand pounds of glass. Confront an issue with your gang—the results will be incredibly unifying.

disciplinary
integrity

THOSE NOT WILLING TO DISCIPLINE ARE NOT WILLING TO HAVE A GOOD youth program. Discipline provides integrity and a code of expected behavior within any group. The purpose of a youth group is to give honor to God; any behavior that does not must be checked.

Discipline is a problem in urban America. The educational system has gone to incredible lengths to understand the relationship between youth, self-control and discipline. Most educators have concluded that discipline is necessary to the development of self-control.

THE GREAT DEBATE

There are two general approaches to discipline within the context of urban youth ministry: one which makes teens the primary educators of their own discipline, and another which places this responsibility on the youth worker. The first is generally supported by youth workers who have come into urban ministry with a suburban background, the second by indigenous youth workers who have risen directly out of urban life. Each has a convincing basis for its disciplinary procedure.

Train up children in the way they should go. Those holding to this philosophy are against authoritarian methods of discipline, believing discipline should be learned over time through the youth team's effort. Their groups tend to be laissez-faire, giving teenagers many opportunities for freedom of expression and dialogue. The purpose of this approach is to have the youth exhibit self-discipline independent of that imposed by the youth worker.

Youth are treated as adults-in-training and are rarely spoken down to. Any discipline problems are confronted in a dignified manner. To embarrass teens or strip them of their freedom of speech and expression is unjust. Youth is a time of self-expression that must be lovingly nurtured. Youth workers view their relationship to the youth as that of a big brother or sister. They spend time with the teens and encourage them along whatever path they choose.[1]

Spare the rod, spoil the child. Many urban programs are strict. Because the city is a dog-eat-dog place, many youth workers are unwilling to give their teenagers full responsibility for their own freedom. Freedom, instead, is permitted within limited boundaries. It is not worth the risk to have teens learn by experience, because they might end up dead. Youth must strictly adhere to pre-determined guidelines of behavior or face unfavorable consequences.

Discipline is the reason for good behavior. The teens know that if they "mess up," they will be temporarily removed from the program. This method is often used in highly structured and organized youth programs that offer something teenagers want, such as a sports league, computer, drama, or music program. Strictness results from expecting excellence and having something of dignified worth to offer the community.[2]

Disciplinary integrity. The method I believe most appropriate is that of disciplinary integrity. It involves both love and justice. To curtail discipline problems, we must be willing to allow youth to let their behavior determine their restrictions. Freedom is allowed in proportion to the self-discipline shown by the individual.

I remember my first urban youth group well; it was a group of about fifteen junior high teenagers from a housing development in south Philadelphia called Passyunk Homes. Three others and I, most of us new to youth ministry, were responsible for running it. These youths had never taken part in a youth group before, making it initially difficult to maintain constructive control. Some were disrespectful, others talked constantly or had bad attitudes toward us. The core was genuine, however—the youth wanted to be there. After a while we realized we were having a lot of fun with these kids, but were not sure how to handle the behavior problems. We were afraid that if we began to set a standard of discipline, they would leave the group.

It became clear, however, that without establishing consequences for behavior we would never accomplish our goals. After much discussion, we concluded that discipline was essential to the integrity of the group—and soon discovered that the few teens we lost would be replaced by others. I learned an important lesson from this situation which I continue to impress upon those in a similar predicament, and which underlies the concept of disciplinary integrity: it is better to have a code of discipline and a small group than to have a large group that is uncontrollable.

Disciplinary integrity can be distilled into three principles:

- To love is to discipline.
- To love God is to have discipline.
- Discipline behavior, counsel people.

To Love is to Discipline

Love and discipline are interrelated. Love is caring deeply about another's well-being; discipline is the restraint applied to loved ones when their own self-control fails. Those who do not love their teenagers will not discipline them—those who do, will.

Discipline also manifests love because allowing teens to freely experiment in their environment can be dangerous—especially in some cities. When I was a teenager, my mother placed restrictions on my freedom because she understood the potential danger of our community. Restraints were necessary for my survival. She always said, "I love you too much to allow you to face a potentially dangerous situation." When I broke the rules, the punishment I incurred resulted from love, not anger.

In urban ministry, there will always come a time when a particular teenager's behavior seriously jeopardizes the progression of the youth group. Consequences must ensue. Teenagers must understand that urban ministry is concerned with training disciples, not doormats. I have seen youth workers who allow their youth to control them; as a result, they feel like a hostage and love does not result.

The form of discipline I support comes from the Latin word *disciplus,* which means the *act* of disciplining. It is "a system of rules and regulations exemplified by the leader, that motivates—not forces—the followers to model their behavior."[3] The biblical account often alludes to God as a parent who disciplines out of love. The proverbial writer, for example, pronounces, "My son, do not despise the Lord's discipline and do not resent his rebuke, because the Lord disciplines those he loves, as a father the son he delights in" (PROV. 3:11–12). Job 5:17 advances this point, "Blessed is the man who God corrects; so do not despise the discipline of the Almighty."[4] Since God cares enough to discipline those he loves, so should we.

To Love God is to Have Discipline

Jawanza Kunjufu, an educator and lecturer on urban youth issues, once wrote, "I feel there is an inverse relationship between God and discipline problems; a decrease in respect for God creates an increase in behavioral problems."[5] This statement speaks to all of us involved with adolescents. The teenager who has a genuine relationship with Jesus will develop the characteristics of self-discipline.

Evangelism must teach teens that accepting Christianity means living a life of manifest discipline. Their love of God will allow the Holy Spirit to work in their lives and constrain them to proper behavior. It is amazing how far a little discipline will go.

M. Scott Peck, in his book *The Road Less Travelled,* describes four elements of discipline applicable to those who desire a well-disciplined Christian life.

DELAYING GRATIFICATION. This is the first, most difficult step for youth—putting off fun until they have performed a needed, less-gratifying task. When youth practice this form of discipline, they have acknowledged that God's objectives for them are more important than their own.

ACCEPTING RESPONSIBILITY. Responsibility is accepting the consequences of one's actions. Learning to be responsible is often a milestone in a teenager's development, because the normal teen's defense mechanism accepts responsibility but denies involvement in any wrongs that result. Christian youth fully accept responsibility both for their actions and for the consequences of their actions.

DEDICATION TO TRUTH. The disciplined youth follows the paths of rightness and righteousness. This aspect of discipline depends upon the youth's perception of God as the source of all truth; teens who maintain this belief are motivated by the pursuit of truth rather than their own will. God is love and that's the truth.

BALANCING. One must be able to harmonize all that one does and says for the benefit of Jesus Christ; otherwise, order and self-control will be lost. Christian teens who seek balance find freedom of mind and spirit, and stamina in daily life. They neither overdo nor underdo—they do what is needed in accordance with their commitment to Jesus.[6]

DISCIPLINE BEHAVIOR, COUNSEL PEOPLE

Punishing people for their behavior is a common, but incorrect, disciplinary tactic. Behavior needs discipline, but people need counseling. We cannot truly discipline someone when we take their behavior personally. Individuals' actions, good or bad, reflect their decisions on the best way to respond to external stimuli. Bad decisions must be corrected through discipline. However, the discipline should be directed at the behavior, not the individual.

Keep this in mind when dealing with youth. We cannot adequately discipline without also counseling the person with the behavioral problem. We place restraints on teens to keep them from repeating bad behavior until they can correct it on their own; heart-to-heart counseling, however, is necessary to help them do so. We must act as a helper, not a warden—restraining behavior in the best interest of the youth. These seven helping skills are essential for a youth director seeking to help teens overcome their discipline problems:

Listening Skills

Attending—noticing verbal and nonverbal signals.
Paraphrasing—responding to basic messages.
Clarifying—self-disclosing and focusing discussion.
Perception-checking—determining the accuracy of information.

Leading Skills

Indirect leading—getting started.
Direct leading—encouraging and elaborating discussion.
Focusing—controlling confusion, diffusion, and vagueness.
Questioning—conducting open and closed inquiries.

Reflecting Skills

Reflecting feelings—responding to feelings.
Reflecting experience—responding to total experience.
Reflecting content—repeating ideas in fresh words or for emphasis.

Summarizing Skills

Pulling themes together.

Confronting Skills

Recognizing feelings in oneself—being aware of your own experience.
Describing and sharing feelings—modeling feeling expression.
Feeding back opinions—reacting honestly to others' expression.
Meditating—promoting self-confrontation.
Repeating—tapping obscure feelings.
Associating—facilitating loosening of feelings.

Interpreting Skills

Interpretive questions—facilitating awareness.
Fantasy and metaphor—symbolizing ideas and feelings.

Informing Skills

Advising—giving suggestions and opinions based on experience.
Informing—giving valid information based on expertise.[7]

Beneath their tough exterior, urban adolescents are fragile and delicate. Discipline must strive to restore teenage behavior into what Jesus would be pleased with, without destroying self-esteem.

MODELS FOR SUCCESSFUL URBAN DISCIPLINE

Disciplining urban youth is difficult. There is no one way to discipline, as every group responds to restraints in different ways. The youth worker knowledgeable in the following theories and models, which have proven successful in guiding youth behavior, will be able to achieve a happy medium by using any or all of them at his or her discretion.

Successful theories. The following four theories are extremely useful to urban youth ministry. As theories, they must be considered incomplete; finding the best approach to a particular situation will require trial and error.

The first is communication theory, which strives to help the teen "connect behavior with articulation."[8] Teenagers often will behave inadequately because they feel they cannot communicate; younger children will sometimes do the same. When young people cannot articulate what they are feeling, they will try to express it through a change in behavior. "Bad behavior" never means "bad person"—it is simply an expression of uncommunicated frustration.

I once tutored a young girl named Sheila, who was full of life and enthusiasm. One of her problems, however, was that she would get frustrated easily and often would stomp off crying or refuse to listen. For quite some time, I asked her (in a private counseling atmosphere) to tell me what she was feeling. Although she would try, she could not, and would become even more frustrated.

Once I realized that the cause of her frustration was her poor communication skills, my next step was to determine how to better help her communicate. Through tutoring, the nature of Sheila's problem eventually became clear—she couldn't comprehend words. Although she could pronounce them, she couldn't remember what they meant when she needed to use them.

For three months straight, we did creative vocabulary-building activities until I could see an improvement. Her spelling tests, which had rarely been above satisfactory, began to receive excellent marks.

The dictionary became her best friend. Behavior problems reduced significantly simply because she could communicate what she was feeling inside.

The second theory is behavior modification. Burris Frederic Skinner and Albert Bandura, its major exponents, believe that the primary determinant of a teenager's behavior is his or her external environment. According to Skinner, if positive stimuli are given for good behavior, more good behavior will result. He found that negatively disciplining a young person is less effective than praising the teen's positive actions. He would advocate that the youth pastor take notice of the wonderful things the teen does and glorify them, inspiring the teen to seek out the same positive reaction again.[9]

Bandura expanded Skinner's view of behaviorism to include *reciprocal determinism,* which holds that one's behavior is determined both by outer influences and by inner decisions. The disciplinary task, then, becomes one of training a youth to behave, through *imitation, modeling* and *serving* (vicarious learning), rather than forcing them to behave.[10] To discipline is futile if we believe external restraints change internal motives. Restraints do not dispel the cause of an action— they simply prevent it from happening again.

Third is the theory of assertiveness. In eighth grade, I had an English teacher who seemed, on the surface, quite mean. She was a firm, strict woman who never raised her voice. No one bothered her. When she demanded something of you, you did it without question. We walked in a straight line whenever we entered her class because we were afraid of the consequences. Although we would act up in other classes, we never attempted to in hers. I do not remember anyone deviating in any way, ever. Despite its rigidity, I learned a great deal from this class and tried my hardest to live up to the teacher's expectations.

There are over 300,000 teachers throughout this country who use assertive discipline. These educators estimate that using this approach reduces behavior problems by close to eighty percent. In some contexts, it can also be extremely useful for youth workers. If there were a creed to which these teachers subscribed, it would read:

I will tolerate no student's stopping me from teaching. I will tolerate no student's preventing another student from learning. I will tolerate no student's engaging in any behavior that is not in his or her own best interest and in the best interest of others. And most important, whenever a student chooses to behave appropriately, I will immediately recognize and reinforce that behavior. Assertive teachers are the bosses in their classrooms. They have the skills and confidence to take charge.[11]

The last theory is the expectation of self-control. I expect all teens to be able to have enough self-control to handle themselves in public. Therefore, I tell them ahead of time what is expected. Too often we have no preset behavioral expectations for our youth. Teenagers need to know what is expected of them in order to get the most from your group. If your youth know what the leader expects from the beginning, they will also know the consequences of their actions.

What you should expect from teenagers should change as they mature. My expectations for a twelve-year-old are different from those for an eighteen-year-old. The expectations listed below should apply to most urban teens.

Children aged 10–12 should be:
- Ready for leadership.
- Responsible for their own actions.
- Able to express themselves both verbally and non-verbally.
- Able to maintain self-discipline and suggest their own discipline.
- Beginning to ask deep questions about God.

Teenagers aged 13–14 should be:
- Able to clearly understand another's point of view.
- Ready to be disciplined.
- Aware that they are not children anymore and are capable of behaving in a responsible manner.
- Ready to serve others unselfishly.
- Forming practical questions concerning Christianity.

Teenagers aged 15–18 should be:
- Behaving as mature individuals without an outer source of correction.
- Aware of the importance of obtaining work and using money wisely.
- Capable of understanding complex concepts and giving thorough, intelligent responses.
- Ready for intense social action.
- Developing at least two career goals for their life.

Successful models. The following six models are directly applicable to the urban youth group. Unlike theories, models must be put in place for a set period of time in order to work effectively. Theories can be discarded after a few weeks; models cannot. Models can be directly applied to almost any youth situation to promote a code of discipline. To adequately assess their serviceability, they should be implemented for a term of at least four months.

The first of these is the "strike" system, patterned after baseball. Each youth starts with no strikes against them when they enter the group. If an individual misbehaves and does something that warrants correction, he or she will receive a strike. Teens who collect three strikes will face the consequences of their cumulative misbehavior. Depending on the situation, these consequences could be:

- They must leave immediately.
- They will have to sit in a room by themselves until the group is completed.
- A call will be made to their parents explaining their behavior.
- A note explaining their behavior will be written to the parents, which must be signed before they will be allowed to return.
- They will not be allowed to attend the following week.

The strike system gives teens a chance to get themselves in order before it is too late. They will know how far they can take you. Over time this system can have great effects. A reward can be given to those who have no strikes, the "model citizens" of the group.

Another method is the democratic rule election, in which the entire group designs an agreed-upon set of rules that the staff enforces. In this process, which usually takes place on the first day of the group meeting, the youth team and the youth ask themselves two questions: "What rules would we like to have in our group that would give us pleasure and please Jesus?" and "What will we do with those who break the rules?" Typical responses over the years have been:

- No fighting
- No cursing
- Be courteous to each other
- No wisecracks ("bussin'")
- Leave attitudes at the door
- Respect counselors
- Come to learn about God
- Listen
- No talking when someone else is
- Demonstrate self-control
- Rule breakers will miss the next trip
- Rule breakers must write an essay to return

The list is negotiated until all agree it is adequate, and it is then signed by everyone. Newcomers must read the list and sign. This system works well when enforcing rules, because the staff's response can always be, "They are your rules—I'm just following them."

A third method is the point system. Some type of chart is usually posted on the wall with all the teens' names and corresponding dates. Points are given for everything: attendance, participation, praying, volunteering, and overall behavior. Extra points can be given for specific events, such as receiving a good test score, helping to clean up, or leading the Bible study.

When giving out points, it is important to remember that they don't cost you anything. Bestow thousands of points in a day. One summer, a junior high group of mine agreed to see who could earn a million points by the end of the summer. Whoever did so would receive a wonderful gift. In addition, all would receive something just for participating. The point system we used was:

- On-time attendance—20,000 points.
- Courteous behavior—worth up to 10,000 points.
- Participation—10,000 points.
- Recycling—5,000 points.
- Extra credit—odd jobs, cleaning up, and special assignments ranged from 5,000 to 25,000 points, depending upon the task.

On average, a teen could earn 50,000 points a day. The youth enjoyed the challenge of competition and adding up their points. These numbers were larger than anything they had ever experienced in their lives. When a particular teen discovered I had made a mistake in adding up the points one day, he brought his calculator every day from then on to be sure he was getting what he earned.

Another effective approach is to elect a youth council. A youth council provides a structure for better decision-making. Most decisions on the direction of the group, as well as verdicts on disciplinary procedures, should be made within it. The quality of the verdict that can result from teenagers getting together to discuss behavior, with the best interest of the group in mind, has always amazed me. To establish the council, have an election in which the whole group participates. Meet weekly after each youth group to discuss upcoming events and agree on ways to discipline any behavior problems. Implement the council's decisions as binding on the group.

In order for a youth council to be effective it must be allowed to lead, with the guidance of the youth worker. The youth council shares its leadership with that of the youth staff to maintain order and discipline, and plan activities. Decisions made must be followed through in order for the council to recognize its strength.

If the council is to be a good disciplinary unit, it must determine a structure of discipline in advance. One youth council established this set of behavioral rules:

Individual Members

- A first offender receives one warning from a staff person.
- After another offense, the teen is sent home.
- After the meeting, the council will determine the official penalty and call the youth's parent with the verdict.

Council Members

- Any disciplinary action taken against a council member will be determined by a trial of the complete council.

Expulsion

- Expulsion of a non–council member can only be finalized by a majority vote.[12]

If these rules were not followed, the youth would bring up the violation at their weekly meeting and discuss a course of action. As a result, they actually voted members out of the group for a short time because of consistent bad behavior, and even voted irresponsible members off the council.

Involving parents is the fifth method of discipline. Parents, as experienced disciplinarians, are an excellent source of youth correction. They know all the methods—especially what works on their own children. Miraculously, there are many things youth will not do in the presence of a parent. Parents are a vital element in any youth program; here are three suggestions for involving them in the disciplinary process:

- Get parent volunteers either to join the youth team or to periodically help manage the teens in the youth group and on trips.
- Form a parents' discipline committee that will design the disciplinary procedures for the youth group. This process helps establish a consistent form of discipline between the home and the youth group.
- Call a parent and explain the discipline problems you are having with their teenager, asking them to recommend a procedure you can use successfully. Most parents know the type of discipline to which their teens best respond.

The last resort is the use of physical restraint. There may come a time when a teenager is so out of control that physical restraint is needed to bring immediate stability. On many occasions, I have been forced to physically handle teenagers who were endangering the safety of themselves or others. The youth group should be a place of pure safety and respect; anyone taking this for granted must be stopped.

Youth worker physical restraint is required in two situations. First, fights must be stopped at all costs—they destroy youth groups. Much of what the youth team has sought to build over many months can be abruptly destroyed with a fight. Second, an adolescent who refuses to obey a disciplinary command must be removed. In both cases, this disciplinary action should be followed up with a call to a parent or familiar adult, and strict guidelines should be set on how and when the youth can return.

ONE CASE OF DISCIPLINARY INTEGRITY

The events that occurred on the evening of February 20, 1991, at a church in south Philadelphia, will take a lifetime to forget. Two hundred urban senior high youth and staff from Camden, New Jersey and Philadelphia were packed into the church sanctuary. The same group had gathered the previous week and enjoyed a splendid evening, during which many teenagers gave their lives to Christ. All of our defenses were down. We expected the same spirit this evening, but instead were plunged into a youth fight of massive proportions. I learned seven lessons from this experience that solidified my support for disciplinary integrity.

Lesson One: Watchfulness. The theme of the evening was marriage. We had invited married couples to share their experiences with the teenagers. Everything was going smoothly, but I noticed something did not seem right when I broke the teenagers into small groups. I overheard two separate groups of teenagers making threatening statements to each other, like "No one better look at me wrong or I'll punch them," and "All I need is a reason and I'll start something."

As the teenagers were shuffling to their groups, I overheard four girls from opposing communities exchanging nasty words. When they saw me, they went their separate ways. Hearing these remarks concerned me, however, as I could sense evil brewing. Interestingly enough, the director of the other group had sensed the same. Together we decided that we would not have a mass dismissal when the group regathered, but that his teens would be allowed to receive their refreshments and board their busses first.

After the small groups were finished and the teens were filing back into the sanctuary for some wrap-up statements, it happened. Before all the teens could get to their seats, I noticed a large group milling in the back—I knew what that meant. On the microphone, I remember shouting, "Staff, I need you in the back immediately!" and "Everyone get in your seats now!"

It was too late—the fight had begun. It spread like wildfire, starting with four teens and spreading to about sixty, with seventy onlookers and approximately forty who separated themselves completely. The fight escalated into a barnyard brawl. There was mass hysteria: people fighting on pews, throwing chairs, crying, bleeding, and trampling people. A rumor circulated that some teens had guns. Our staff of thirty-five could not control the situation—we had to call the police. The evening street glittered in every direction with the lights of the reported twenty-five police vehicles called in. It took about thirty minutes to bring everything under control. Ultimately, three teens were taken to the police station, while many others mended their wounds.

Lesson Two: Consistency of verdict. The next day, I laid the disciplinary plan of action before the staff. I asked for the name of every Philadelphia teenager present at the church, divided into three categories: fighters, onlookers, and peacemakers. The fighters were not allowed to return until they called to apologize, and were put on a disciplinary contract stating that if they were in another fight of any kind in our programs within the next year, they would be kicked out for six months to a year. I labeled the onlookers "lukewarm" because of their failure to make a stand either way.[13] Most fights last because of the embarrassment of "losing face" before a crowd. Therefore, I was just as hard on these teens: they were not to return until they could give me a call and explain why being part of the crowd is just as bad as fighting. The peacemakers fell into two categories: those who completely separated themselves from the fight and those who jumped into the battlefield in an attempt to bring about peace. Only the peacemakers were allowed back into the youth group. They were the only ones to successfully carry out the principles we had taught. They were our truest disciples. In one week, we went from a group of sixty-five to a group of eighteen. I was not going to budge.

After the Senior High Youth Council approved this procedure, I sent letters to the parents of everyone involved detailing the requirements for readmission—which was hard to do for some teenagers, as I had seen them come a long way spiritually. I firmly believed, however, that if their relationship with God was as strong as I perceived it to be, they would do what they had to do to return. All of them did.

During the final three months of that school year we regained only twelve members. But we did not mind, knowing discipline was being adequately administered. Somehow, going through this trauma gave the staff and teenagers a newfound respect for the integrity of our group.

Lesson Three: Be ready for repercussions. I began to prepare myself to bear the brunt of the disciplinary backlash. Whenever a decision of this nature is made, there is bound to be resentment. Many adolescents were angry and threatening. Many could not understand why they were guilty. Typical excuses were, "I had to give backup to my friends" or "My brother was hit. I'm not letting anybody get away with that"—all good reasons, just not Christian ones. Many in the disciplined group did not speak to me when they saw me; I had to speak first to get a response.

Over the next three weeks, I became so extremely unpopular in one neighborhood that I no longer visited often. Many teenagers, disgusted that I would not let them return, decided they did not want to. My response was, "If we don't stand for something, we will fall for anything." Until they could see the wrongness of their actions, we did not want them. Forgiveness must be sought before it can be granted—that is what I wanted my teens to realize.

The repercussions I faced by following a decision were a minor issue. If I were to bend to the ousted youth, I would have rendered void the noble and courageous acts of the peacemakers. A youth group is to be reverent—a sanctuary that gives God glory. The staff and the Youth Council had decided beforehand that our meetings were to be a place of utmost respect and learning. Behavior detracting from that environment would simply not be tolerated.

Lesson Four: Parents are not always right. I had always been taught that, no matter what they say, parents are always right. One should never correct a parent—especially when it comes to their own children. I beg to differ. Two days after the incident, I called the parents of the teenagers who had received six-month expulsions. Most were understanding; two, however, were extremely bitter.

The first berated me for penalizing her son for defending himself. When I explained that the issue went deeper than that, she refused to listen and continued to reject the decision of the staff and Youth Council. I eloquently told her that her son would not be allowed back regardless of what she believed his penalty should be. Our youth group had a responsibility to maintain safety and her son had constantly infringed the rules; therefore he *would* face the penalty. She further condemned me for my bold audacity and ended the conversation.

The second parent yelled at me for four entire minutes without letting a word in edgewise. When she finished her tirade, I explained the full reasoning behind our decision. Her response was, "You are not his parent—you can't do this." She continued, "If you expel my son, I will take out both my sons." I calmly replied, "Your decision is final at home. My decision is final concerning the youth group. Your teenagers are not the only ones for whom I must ensure safety. I am not picking on your children—I have had to call many parents with the same news, and I refuse to treat your children any differently from theirs. No matter what your decision is, I cannot allow your son to return until September." She hung up and her teens did not return.

Parents cannot be allowed to manipulate the rules of the youth group. Although they are the prime determinants of the adolescents' attendance, they must understand that in order for disciplinary guidelines to be effective, they must be enforced. Many teenagers realized how serious their actions were once they realized that even their parents could not get them back in. As a result, some called and asked for forgiveness.

Lesson Five: Remembering to Discipline Staff. Two weeks later, I received a phone call from a friend who had heard about the incident. She asked me a question I had never considered, inquiring, "Did you discipline your staff?" I asked her what she meant. "Did you hold them accountable for their mistakes that evening?" she clarified. As I thought about it, I realized she was right: I had convicted the youth and let the staff go scot-free. We all contributed to the severity of the fight that night by not foreseeing indicators of tension, allowing youth to make threatening statements without correcting them, not helping break up the fights, and failing to encourage the teens to take their seats. I erred by not letting the staff know I suspected something was wrong. All of us were undeniably guilty for not doing all that we could to prevent this catastrophe. Too many weeks had passed to adequately talk with those staff members in need of confrontation. We were all ashamed we hadn't done more.

Lesson Six: Knowing when to overrule a verdict. There comes a time when, in good conscience, a rule must bend to prevent the destruction of an individual. The integrity of the group is paramount, but not at the expense of a teenager's life. Discipline has a tendency to be overdone. Beyond correcting wrong behavior, alienation from the youth group can mean entrance into a negative group or activity, such as the drug market, prostitution, bad youth gangs, number running, or stealing. Behavior rules must stand firm, yet bend toward justice.

As summer was approaching, I noticed a few of the expelled teens beginning to be seen with the wrong crowd. I knew that if I were to keep them out through the summer, they might become wrongly influenced. This left me with a decision: should I follow the rules and possibly lose them, or should I reduce their disciplinary contract so that they could have the positive influence of the youth group? The decision was easy. I allowed them to return to the program—however, they were not allowed to participate in trips and extra activities until their contract was up. Somehow, it seemed I saved some lives from destruction, yet did not compromise for those youth members who had earned the right to be there.

Lesson Seven: Make peace with the peacemakers. In order to conclude disciplinary integrity, the process must come full circle and befriend those it harmed. Many youths from the group in Camden were peacemakers. The senior high staff figured this group should be the one that would begin to restore peace. We planned a Peacemakers Banquet, an evening honoring all those who made the decision of peace during the fight. We did this up right—it was semi-formal, with a good meal served by the Senior High staff, staff and youth testimonies and a speaker to tie it all together. The most precious result of this successful evening occurred when two Camden youth suggested to some Philadelphia teens that a summer swap program might be a first step to restoration. Other dialogue took off from there.

As I observed the youth talking over dinner, I could not help but wonder whether it was worth the effort to discipline the many for the benefit of the few. I had to answer "Yes!" Those six months of strict discipline did more for the unity of the youth group than all that had been taught in the months before. I remember closing my eyes and meditating upon the truth of Matthew 5:9—"Blessed are the peacemakers, for they shall be called the children of God."

involving older teens

5

Urban adolescents aged seventeen to twenty-one are often abandoned by the cohorts of youth ministry. Commitment to these youths tends to end at age seventeen, when they graduate high school. The existence of a later stage of adolescence, with its own specific needs, is generally overlooked. When planning a wholistic youth program, it is important to construct programs for this older, distinctive phase—young adulthood.[1]

Ministry for the Other Half of Adolescence

Older urban teens tend to drift away from the youth group at about age seventeen, beginning to find its activities a bit immature for their taste. They perceive themselves as having outgrown the other, younger teens in the group. While they do not dislike the program, they feel they are old enough to have greater input in its operation. Ministry to older teens, therefore, requires a specialized approach.

These teenagers are physically and mentally adults. Socially, they are not. They need to test their autonomy in order to reach adulthood. During late adolescence, teens begin to desire:

- Independence from family.
- A career.

- Adult responsibility.
- Closer fellowship with their own peers.
- Power to control the direction of their own life.
- A mate.

Because of these mental and physical realizations, teenagers decide to leave the fun-loving youth group they had known. Targeted to early adolescents, it can no longer meet their needs.

In common among urban organizations and churches is their disinterest in creating programs for teenagers aged eighteen to twenty-one. In all honesty, many are afraid to minister to these teens because they can be the toughest converts to the Christian message. Instead of expanding the focus of the youth program and creating a group that meets the needs of older teens, we consider them full adults and discard them. We asphyxiate these teens by failing to address their interests in a conventional youth group format, forcing them to jump directly from youth to adulthood.

Frederic Thrasher, in his study on gangs, noticed that approximately forty-one percent of the teens he studied who were involved in gang activity were between the ages of sixteen and twenty-five.[2] We must not, therefore, discard older teens—they are within the bounds of youth ministry. The problem is that these boundaries have not often extended far enough.

We must reach out to these youths. Most homicides and other serious crimes are committed by late adolescents; it is imperative that a tough-minded and intelligent approach be directed at them. There is much hurt and anomy within these teens, but beneath the tough veneer and seeming disinterest are young men and women waiting to be guided, matured, and discipled for Godly purposes—to become assets to society rather than perpetuators of the violent, fatalistic cycle of poverty. The church must provide a welcoming context in which older adolescents can relate. Trust me: if it does not, the streets will.

I have seen many teenagers go through my youth program as model youth. Since the program did not extend through the full course of adolescence, however, some were lost to drugs, unplanned parenthood, or apathy, and were left to face the world alone and attempt to do something meaningful with their lives.

I once visited a police substation in a housing development in south Philadelphia, where Officer James Harris and I looked through photographs of teenagers with a record of drug offenses in the community. As he showed me each picture, it was as if most of the youths I had ministered to in that community were passing before my eyes. Out of about forty pictures he showed me, fifteen were of teenagers once diligently involved in youth group. They had all become too old and dropped out.

They began and graduated as good teens. I remember many of them giving their lives to Christ. *What had happened?* I said to Officer Harris, "These teens were very active in my group once." He replied, "It looks like they're in someone else's group now." How true.

THREE DILEMMAS WITH AGES 18–21

We must confront three dilemmas hampering older urban adolescents' involvement in youth groups. The first is a conflict between suburban and urban expectations. When suburban youth reach late adolescence and leave the youth group, societal expectations for them are evident: attending college or securing a "good" job are the expected norms. The teen that chooses neither, out of apathy, is shunned as a derelict of the community.

Underclass city teens often do not have these options, as they cannot see how either one could significantly affect their lives. Worse, there are few voices encouraging them otherwise. If you insist they get a job, some respond, "Why? It takes *work* to find work." Searching newspapers, interviewing, dressing up, and carrying on an impressive conversation entail preparation, thought, and work. Urban youth are not willing to go through that process just to flip hamburgers for minimum wage.

If you attempt to encourage them to go to college and get a good education, you will find that a significant number of urban teens, through defective schooling, have been programmed to believe themselves incapable of entering academia. In elementary school they learn, "I can succeed!"; in Junior High, "I might succeed?"; in High school, "I won't succeed." This mentality is reversible, but cracking through it is a painstaking process. If we want older adolescents from the urban context to be interested in our programs, we must be willing to creatively tear through this type of thinking.

The second dilemma involves the way youth workers relate to and communicate with older teens. I was giving a friend of mine, who was eighteen at the time, directions to a house for an errand. I was speaking to him as if he were thirteen, asking "Do you follow me?" after every statement, and continually asking him to repeat what I had just said. After a while, he abruptly said, "Do you think I'm stupid?!" His remark made me begin to realize that we must communicate with older teens as we would adults. Mentally, they are more than youth—they are young adults.

Youth workers who work with a vast array of teenagers and children can forget whom to treat as a child and whom as an adult. I would get one consistent, simple response from older teenagers I sought to recruit back into the youth group: "I refuse to be treated and spoken to as a child." Even when I guaranteed adult treatment, and held to my promise, many were still extremely uncomfortable. With thought, my problem and its solution became apparent: younger and older teens have different ideas about what makes a "good" youth group.

Younger teens want constant goofy excitement. Older teens desire a close-knit group that creates its own agenda under their own leadership, only partly relying on the expertise of the youth leader. They realize the youth worker has certain skills and resources they can use, and is capable of keeping the group together. The older the adolescents, however, the less they will need an officiator from the church or youth program.

A fundamental change must happen within the power structure of such a group. It is pointless to establish a young-adult youth group without letting its members, themselves, be its leaders and decision-makers. If you are not willing to make this commitment, the group will most likely fail within the first five meetings. There is no other way.

The third dilemma concerns urban youth ministry's ability to realize good programmatic options for older teens. You must ask yourself the question, "Can I, given my resources, time, staff, and money, adequately expand my youth program to meet the needs of older teens?" The answer you give will determine the route to take.

If the answer is "Yes!" you must find a way to integrate and nurture older adolescents within the mission of your entire youth program. If it is "No!" you will need to process them out of your program in a smooth and dignified manner. Consider the following possibilities.

INTEGRATING OLDER TEENS INTO YOUR PROGRAM

When programs for older teens do not already exist, the youth director must create them from scratch. Here are five successfully proven ways to include urban eighteen to twenty-one-year-olds in your youth program.

Young adults' fellowships. These groups, which can exist within both church and para-church organizations, give youths who are ready for adult autonomy a framework for leadership, Christian fellowship, and nurturance, independent of the youth worker. Young adult fellowships have six characteristics in common.

First, they are generally formed by adult organizations. In the early half of the nineteenth century, most organized gangs had youth auxiliaries under teenage leadership. They were deliberately created by the adult leaders, who understood that in order for their regime to continue, they must have a leadership pool to draw upon. Gang auxiliaries taught, through practice, the ropes of being a gang member.[3]

The church must be willing to be intentional in its ministry to older teens. We cannot just put a bunch of young adults in a room together and say, "Form community." The process begins with adult leadership. The concerned youth pastor should begin such a group as a highly involved member. The hard part is knowing when to leave: if adult leadership pulls out too early, the group might flounder and fail; if too late, teen leadership is dwarfed.

The intention is for adult leadership to decrease as youth leadership increases. The ultimate joy of a fellowship group is to have trained the youth so well that no adult involvement is needed at all. The group becomes a self-contained ministry atop the church or para-church rostrum. It must then be held accountable for the image it portrays as an auxiliary group.

Second, fellowship groups meet needs. Young adults have much "personal stuff" that can be dealt with by their peers without adult help. Groups naturally come to the rescue of hurting members. After time, the group should become accustomed to its caring role and respond to the needs of others out of the friendships that have formed within it.

One way to begin this process is to set aside time during the session when sharing and prayer concerns can be expressed. Most city kids, who think it is "uncool" to share, initially hate this opportunity. The secret is to do it long enough for them to see that many of their prayers can be and are answered by Jesus.

If the sharing process can fully mature, it explodes, and the fellowship becomes more than a youth meeting—it becomes a nurturance center, where teenagers are cemented together by overcoming personal problems together in the power of the Holy Spirit. Reaching that level can take some time, primarily because older urban adolescents take time to open up. Young adults, with the correct guidance, can be brought together in fellowship and become a sparkling jewel to their church and community.

Third, these groups must provide *real* responsibility. If the group is part of a large organization, give it a budget or the opportunity to propose one. Most youths aged eighteen to twenty-one are beginning to learn how to be responsible with money. When they are given a real budget, they are forced to learn how to manage it.

I suggest that for the first two years the group should have a set budget. Have the members draw up a one-year plan which shows their objectives clearly, and give disbursements only in the manner in which they were proposed. Thus, the youth will have to devise a spending plan.

The first few times they often make mistakes. *Don't bail them out* without letting their budget be hurt in some way. This lesson is most valuable to learn. By the third year you will have created talented budget analysts who have gained a crucial skill and learned responsibility. The earlier this skill is obtained the better—preferably in early adolescence.

Fourth, all fellowship groups should have a name. Names provide identity and imagery. When the group is mentioned by name, it should identify to others what the group is about in a fun way. Most names should have one to three words; wordiness is cumbersome. It would sound odd to say, "Hey, Rasheeda! Would you like to come to my youth group, The Knights in Christian Armor Seeking Exegetical Approaches to Gaining the Community of the Transcendental Unity of Apperception?" Before Rasheeda would accept, she'd most likely say, "Why didn't you just call it God's Funky Witnesses!"

The fifth common characteristic of successful fellowship groups is the need for an established set of rules. Good groups have already dealt with problems before they arise. They have a framework for discipline and conflict resolution in place, which is necessary to ensure that the actions of others cannot infringe upon the objectives of the fellowship.

These rules should never be created by anyone but the members of the group. They are to be written and submitted to the youth pastor, who has the right to suggest rules or disapprove of certain rules. Young adults must keep in mind, when deciding rules independently, that the ones they accept must please not only the youth pastor, but Jesus as well. I always say, "Don't bring me the rules until you get Jesus' signature." One year I got one back stating:

Dear Nelson,

I've looked over the rules of this group and think you should accept them without any questions.

Love,
Jesus.

Finally, young adult fellowship groups need a mission. Young adults have a desire to do something significant for Jesus, which can be satisfied by feeding the homeless, going to a political rally or on a mission trip, or visiting a nursing home or AIDS clinic for kids. The expertise of the youth director is often helpful here. The primacy of the mission takes the members beyond their own problems into the problems of others.

One day I showed a videotape about the hunger crisis in Africa to a group of young people. Afterward, some were crying, shaking their heads, or silent, in disbelief that people could be that much in need. The young adult officers demanded that we do something to help immediately. Because of this one night, we collected about one hundred pounds of canned goods over the next two-and-a-half months and gave them to the homeless.

Paid staff. We must entertain the idea of hiring community-based young adults as paid staff members, thereby   both creating jobs and providing the opportunity for apprenticeship. I am amazed that some ministry organizations never consider raising up leaders from the communities in which they work. Teens eighteen and older are ready to learn a trade. From a business perspective, involving young adults who know what works and have in-the-field training is more beneficial than importing outsiders. These teens will be more valuable to you than an imported college student seeking "field placement" any day.

Raoul, for example, is an extremely bright, observant twenty-two-year-old Christian who has lived in a large housing development for much of his life. He has a job and a car he's worked very hard for. His heart is in ministry. The youth of the community know and love him, and think of him as a big brother.

Most evenings he can be found with a load of teenagers in his car, just driving around. The conversation is usually fun and encouraging. The youth know that if they have a problem, Raoul cares. He takes the time to visit families—to most, he *is* family. In a word, he's pastoral. He volunteers weekly for the Junior High group in his community, run through a para-church organization.

Raoul is actively involved in recruiting teenagers to attend his church. He stays on them to make sure they come. Overall, Raoul is the most ideal youth worker in the community. He has both a vision for his community and the moral stamina to carry it out. He is the type of young adult you would want to direct your youth programs.

Unfortunately, urban youth ministry has a track record of letting good leaders like Raoul volunteer with their organizations, but not direct them. For some unapparent reason, we would rather pay a graduate student with limited urban experience to solve the problems of a community, instead of someone who is from it. This backward mentality must be remedied.

Volunteers. Raoul observes the ministry organization he volunteers for spending too much of its time recruiting volunteers from around the country, and too little looking for people from his own neighborhood. He makes two convincing points.

First, most volunteer-oriented organizations, which draw their people from the late-adolescent age group, look for these volunteers outside of the actual community in which they will be ministering. This is wrong. Recruitment should begin in the community itself and expand outward if necessary. Every missionary knows that the answers to peoples' problems are found within the people themselves.

Second, a common excuse not to recruit within a community is: "We want born-again Christians running our programs." This assertion insinuates that there are no Christian young adults in the community, which is false. God has people everywhere waiting to be called into service.

In reality, most imported volunteers are no more spiritual than those you could find within the community. I would even contend that those within the community are more effective spiritually, because they are there for the long haul. They will live, work, worship, cry, encourage, play, die, and become a true incarnation of the Gospel message, among their neighbors. That is *pure* volunteerism.

Peer counselors. Another way to get young adults involved in your city program is to make them peer counselors for the younger youth group. Peer counseling programs, which are being attempted in many forms around the country, generally focus on training a small group to be capable of counseling peers through crisis situations.

Counseling programs are ideal for young adults. Many high schools and colleges use them to offset the demands on the psychologist or psychotherapist. If implemented correctly, the youth pastor ends up dealing with only the more serious crises, because his or her network of peer counselors has taken care of the others. This is not a simple program, however: it requires commitment, confidentiality, time, desire, and training. Many resources are available to help you get started.[4]

If all else fails, use recreation. Some youth workers, who cannot effectively reach out to older teens given the time and resources they have, include them on a regular basis via scheduled recreational activities. There are two forms of recreation that have had phenomenal results with urban young adults—trips and sports.

Trips can be an excellent tool for recruiting older adolescents. They can also provide the youth pastor with an excuse to reunite regularly with young adults who grow too old for the youth group. Trips should be considered in the yearly planning so young adults will know they are a part of the church's program, and not just an addendum to what is done with the youth group.

A good sports program can draw young men like a magnet. Teens who would otherwise never consider approaching the church will come if recreation is involved. I have visited churches (with sports facilities), which open their doors regularly to such adolescents and use their interest in sports as a point for ministry outreach.

One such church charges fifty cents admission to all those who come to practice basketball. However, those who attend the Sunday service are allowed a full week of free admission. Another uses its courts for tryouts in a Christian basketball league that requires all members to learn scriptures in order to play in each game. Still another requires one can of food for the homeless for admittance.

Processing Older Teens out of Your Program

Here are four options for youth ministers who, given their overall resource pool, cannot extend a maintained program to older urban teenagers.

Graduation. Every youth program should have a graduation ceremony, which promotes a sense of accomplishment and brings an official end to your services to the graduates. As teens are sent out into the world from the youth program, the graduation affirms your belief that they can make it, and explains what you are willing to do for them once they're gone. A graduation ceremony should make these points clear: first, the former members are now alumni of this program and can return to contribute anytime; second, as they enter the professional world they can call the youth pastor for help with an application or a reference. In addition, fun and serious accomplishment awards should be given and scholarships awarded to those entering college.

Church Membership. For many disadvantaged teenagers, the youth group is the only place where they receive the Christian message and the nurturance necessary to make a decision for Christ. It is a disservice to your teens to set them free into the world without active church membership. Churches take over where the youth group leaves off.

Ronnie is twenty. Living her life in a housing development has been tough for her and her family. She is functionally illiterate and jumps from job to job as she can get them. The school system let her pass through all twelve grades without teaching her to read.

Ronnie was almost an institution in the youth group, heavily involved since the age of eleven. Everyone knew her—whenever the youth group did something, she was ready, eager, and waiting. When Ronnie graduated, I was sure she would leave the group. When she asked to stay, I reminded her that she would not be spending time with anyone of her own age. She did not mind.

After two years, Ronnie came up to me and said, "Nelson, if you don't mind, I'm going to miss next week." Wondering what had produced this revelation, I asked, "Why? Do you not love me anymore?" She responded with laughter and stated, "My sister invited me to her church for a Bible study and I want to go and see what goes on." Selfishly knowing that this might be the opportune time to rid her from my roster, I encouraged her: "Yes! You go and enjoy yourself."

The following week she was absent, as expected—then the next, and the next—until I began to wonder why I had never heard from her. When I stopped by her home one day to ask where she had been, she gleefully told me that she was now a member of the church with the Bible study and didn't think she would be coming back to youth group. Over and over she mentioned that there were people there her age who were "on fire for Jesus."

At this point, I asked her a question that had been on my mind for two years. "Ronnie," I asked, "Why did you stay with us so long? You should have left us two years ago." She said, "I'm a Christian, and Christians need fellowship. The only way I could find that in this project was to stay with the youth group. But now the church I am a member of gives me that, and more. If I'd had this earlier, I would have left earlier." Her response floored me. I didn't know what to say. I felt guilty for not providing options for church membership for her and the other young adults that went before her.

Education, job, or military assistance. There are four honest ways out of a low-cost housing development: the lottery, education, a job, or the military. You can control all but the first. Youth workers who are processing young adults out of their programs should offer information about colleges or trade schools, the job market, and the military, in that order.

Higher education is the most effective method for breaking the chain of poverty. Jobs provide an immediate answer to financial need. The military instills discipline and uproots young adults from their present situation, allowing them to see the world. Encourage those teens who choose the military to do so under the pretense of paying for their education. Invite some of these groups to make presentations to your youth.

Continue relationships. The most lasting contribution you can make, no matter how unresponsive your church or para-church organization is toward teens who become to old for its youth group, is to continue your relationship with these young adults. It will be a strength to your ministry. The objective is not to run programs—they are only a place for ministry to happen. The objective is to meet and share in Christ. If we relate with teens for the sake of having a big youth group and impressing the pastor, we ought to resign. Our prime purpose is to "meet" and share with others the wealth of life and dignity Jesus can give. In the words of the Hasidic Jewish philosopher Martin Buber, "All real living is meeting."[5] Relationships should be continued throughout life, even when programs end.

the urban youth intellectual

THE MIND IS A POWERFUL INSTRUMENT. IT CAN DREAM AND CAUSE OTHERS TO dream, think and cause others to think, envision hope for today and tomorrow. The mind is the most puissant instrument that may be utilized by Jesus in an urban teenager's life. Adolescents who use their minds to their fullest potential will transform themselves into critically active, precision tools capable of rectifying the wrongs that confront them; those who let their minds atrophy will reduce themselves to superficial shadows of what they might have become.

The theme of the United Negro College Fund, "A mind is a terrible thing to waste," is by far the greatest truism that should guide your youth group. Our profession must consider a young person's intellect to be his or her greatest gift. Unless comatose, every teenager has the ability to think constructively on any and every issue. There is no such thing as an uneducable young person.

Even physically challenged youths have no excuse. I have seen young people do tremendous things with intellect considered underdeveloped by society's standards. Intellectual ability has nothing to do with academics, proficiency tests, or degrees. It relies on the process of keeping one's mind *active* on whatever level of cognition one can obtain. Nurturing an active mind is the goal of the urban youth intellectual.

Expect thinking out of teenagers and you will receive it in return. For some, it will take prodding. To the lazy mind—especially one which has received a sub-education—analytical thinking may be a wrenching ordeal. College is not an option for a host of urban youth not because they cannot achieve, but because they have been systematically convinced that their minds are incapable of collegiate excellence. This is one falsehood I seek to destroy.

Urban teens have the brightest minds in America—they need only to be cultivated. The cultivated mind from the underclass is better able to lead this nation's businesses, schools, and industries than most, because it has lived through injustice and societal persecution and can more accurately determine appropriate solutions to the problems it confronts.

We will discuss below some obstacles to intellectual progress, as well as the desirable attributes of the urban youth intellectual.

OBSTACLES TO INTELLECTUAL PROGRESS

There are many hindrances in the city that can cause youths to come up short on their intellectual potential, many of which are imposed upon them by their families, schools, and even youth groups. Five are mentioned here.

Personal inferiority. Many urban adolescents do not believe in their capabilities. When asked to tough-mindedly approach an issue, they may shy away, assuming that someone else is better qualified to answer. Such behavior results from a fundamental sense of inferiority. It is a tragedy to witness young people who have active, fertile minds, afraid to use them because they have been taught that they have no operative opinion. Overcoming adolescents' feelings of inferiority involves teaching them to:

- Realize God has given them a mind with which to think.
- Realize their opinion has worth, regardless of what another thinks.
- Realize that study, whether academic or experiential, enhances their mind's effectiveness.
- Never accept another's imposed opinion without first critically questioning and validating it.

- Never stop asking questions.
- Never accept superficial answers.
- Avoid giving superficial answers.

Feelings of inferiority can be quickly sensed when seeking insight from city youth concerning an issue. Ask them this question: "What do you think about a social system where some have sufficient resources to live and others do not? Must this reality remain unchanged, or *do you see* a way to enhance society so that all can have what is needed to live?" The first response you will receive is, "Huh?" and the second is, "I don't know." Never accept either.

Every living person has an opinion, even if it is half-baked or cannot be communicated adequately. You will find that almost all teens have in-depth knowledge on every issue that concerns their existence. They have never been forced to realize, however, that their opinion on an issue will determine whether or not they are controlled by it. It is always better to stand for something than to fall for anything. Personal inferiority makes people believe that someone else is inherently better than they are, which can lead them to accept unjustifiable situations that otherwise should have been questioned.

Clinical psychologist Na'im Akbar applies the term "plantation ghost" to people so dehumanized and psychologically torn from belief in their own mental capacities that they become brainwashed into thinking they are still a slave, when actually free.[1] These individuals roam through life seeking the mentally safe bondage of the plantation, where someone else thinks for you and tells you when to come and when to go. We must convince urban teens that it is better to face the fear that comes with freedom of thought than to have someone else tell them what their opinion must be. We will not win this struggle until some youths begin to realize that it is not worth conforming to the mental processes of a world which intellectually incarcerates them. They must transform themselves into thinking persons by renewing their minds, that they may prove *with their own thoughts* what is that good, acceptable, and perfect will of God.[2]

Nutrition and hygiene. Another obstacle to intellectual progress is inadequate bodily maintenance. Anyone who works with young people from the city (particularly in impoverished communities) will notice their poor diets, health, and hygiene. Failure to maintain oneself in any of these areas can deeply effect thinking ability.

I encourage four basic health practices crucial for allowing good cognitive ability:

GET ADEQUATE REST. Some teenagers believe they can go to bed at two A.M., wake at six in the morning, and not be mentally affected. They're wrong. The body and mind are like a battery that must be recharged. At least six to eight hours of sleep are necessary for one's thinking ability to be at optimum level. I travel a lot and often brag that I need only four hours of sleep to be my best. In reality, though, my body may be operating, but my mental capacities are not. My mental speed is significantly reduced, and simple deductions will take me a while to process.

Inadequate rest will hamper your teenagers' ability to succeed in school. If you find this hard to believe, visit any high school. It is easy to pick out the students who are not getting enough rest—they are drowsy and forgetful, slur their speech, need questions repeated, and have lapses in attention, to name just a few symptoms. Benjamin Franklin was right: "Early to bed, early to rise, makes a body healthy, wealthy, and wise."

KEEP YOUR BODY CLEAN. The rudimentary acts of washing, brushing teeth, and caring for skin often reflect the way people think about themselves. People who think well of themselves, clean themselves. The adage "Cleanliness is next to Godliness" has an element of truth to it, as self-esteem is partially related to one's cleanliness. I have met many teenagers who neither wash nor brush regularly. Besides being teased by peers for their noticeable smell, their self-esteem is often low.

A person's self-worth does not depend on the number of times he or she washes, but on the individual's ability to feel clean. Severely impoverished people, who may not be capable of cleaning themselves regularly, must have a normal laundering ritual established *by them* so that they may feel they have kept clean to the best of their ability. We must teach this lesson to some urban youngsters.

Booker T. Washington writes on the greatest lesson he learned as a student at Hampton Institute in Virginia:

> I sometimes feel that the most valuable lesson I got at Hampton Institute was in the use and value of the bath. I learned there for the first time some of its value, not only in keeping the body healthy, but in inspiring self-respect and promoting virtue. In all my travels in the South and elsewhere since leaving Hampton I have always in some way sought my daily bath.[3]

GET ADEQUATE HEALTH CARE. City teens receive and expect inadequate health care. One reason is their fear of possible expenses incurred by a visit to the doctor. As a result, health problems are abundant. Many families seek to doctor their own health, and by the time they get to the hospital, it is via the emergency room. In the long run, natural death rates are much higher.

State and Federal programs have been constructed that allow those on public assistance to receive basic health care. The hard part is getting young people to actually get their health checked. Many wait until they have problems too serious to correct. Encourage your teens to follow these guidelines:

- Your body is the only one you will ever have, so take care of it.
- Your body sends signals when something is not right. Tell your parents immediately upon your body's first warning sign, so that they can judge whether a clinic visit is needed.
- If your parents diagnose that everything is fine, but bodily pain persists (or gets worse) over a twenty-four hour period (or less), get to a hospital.
- Get a yearly checkup.
- No one is responsible for your health but you.

In order for urban adolescents to use their minds effectively, their bodies must first be functional.

CUT DOWN ON JUNK FOOD AND ESTABLISH BALANCED EATING. Junk food is one of the primary reasons for ineffective thinking. Teens live off this stuff, their breakfast, lunch and dinner consisting of candy, potato chips, pretzels, onion rings, cookies, cake and ice cream. I know adolescents who spend an average of fifteen dollars a week on junk food. Ultimately, they become junk-food junkies.

A simple activity for teens who constantly eat junk food during youth group is called "Health in the Box." Get two large boxes and place them at the entrance. Label one box "Junk Food," the other "Mind Food." As the teens enter, any junk food they bring with them must be placed in the appropriate box. They must then take a healthy item from the "Mind Food" box, which is a cornucopia of fruit and other healthy items. This activity will at least ensure that their minds are operating on healthy nutrients during the time you are together. It should be used every week.

Most teenagers recognize the correlation between good health and eating right, but like any "junkies," their bodies have developed a continual need for sugar. The mind cannot function properly under these conditions; it must be sustained with good nutrients. A friend of mine who was in charge of snacks in an inner-city tutoring program tried to reduce junk-food intake by serving fruit and other healthy snacks when the kids entered. The result was a noticeable improvement in overall performance during tutoring. These youngsters were no longer bouncing off the walls as they had been when too much sugar-filled junk food was in their systems; attention spans were longer and more focused. Another friend has stated, "Good minds eat good food. We are a tutoring program and want good performance. We may not be able to make them eat right before they get here, but be sure they will when they arrive."

It is also necessary for juveniles to learn the importance of a balanced diet. While most urban teens will agree that a healthy diet is needed, they don't know the how-to's of implementing one. Many of my close friends know I like candy—o. k., a lot of candy. Sugar and caffeine are my "uppers" when travelling. What they ultimately do to my metabolism is force me to *need* them in order to feel productive.

In reality I do not. Therefore, I purposefully limit myself so that I will be mentally effective. We must likewise help city kids shape their diets so that they receive what they need for their minds to function properly.

When helping teenagers improve their nutrition, always teach them these fundamental principles:

- The four basic food groups, with daily requirements, are:

Fruits and vegetables	*2 servings*
Milk and cheese	*2–4 servings*
Bread and cereal	*4 servings*
Meat, poultry, fish and beans	*2 servings*

- Set an alternative. Write down those unhealthy snacks eaten most often and devise a plan that will cut down their intake by ninety percent over five weeks. One method is to follow a chart like the one below. A youth director can provide incentives to youths who uphold their promise to cut down on junk

Junk Food Chart
(numbers indicate servings per day)

	Mon	Tue	Wed	Thu	Fri	Sat	Sun
Week 0 (100%)	5	5	5	5	5	5	3
Week 1 (90%)	4	4	4	4	5	4	4
Week 2 (75%)	4	4	4	3	4	3	3
Week 3 (50%)	3	3	2	2	2	2	2
Week 4 (25%)	2	2	1	1	0	1	1
Week 5 (10%)	1	0	1	0	1	0	1

food, such as money off a trip, or just plain encouragement. Simply cutting down on candy is not enough—as teens cut down on candy, they should simultaneously be turned on to fruits, crackers, and other simple snacks.

- Eat regularly; that is, eat breakfast, lunch, and dinner. Eliminate unnecessary snacks. Breakfast is particularly important—it is the most important meal of the day, and should be eaten in a relaxed fashion. Realistically, city teens eat on the run, but they can at least be encouraged to have:
  — One glass of a fruit drink. *No soda.* If the home has no fruit juice, drink a glass of milk or water instead.
  — Fruit or cereal for simple sugar. If unavailable, substitute two pieces of bread.
  — A high-protein food, such as eggs, bacon, or sausage.

Testing biases. A third obstacle facing urban youth is the cultural bias built into standardized aptitude and intelligence tests. I attended a large African-American high school in Baltimore, Maryland. In my senior year, I scored 900 on the SAT, taking the test only once. I did not understand why my high school made such a tremendous fuss over my achievement, since I knew it was an average score nationally.

As I entered college, however, I came to understand. Although it was an average national score, the average score of my peers was between 700 and 750. Because of my score, a few others and I were considered "the cream of the crop." What I did not fully understand was why I was considered so special, when I knew there were others consistently more intelligent. Could one test be so accurate? Can intellect be tested? Why didn't some of those who were smarter than I do better? These are just a few of the problematic aspects of standardized testing.

On the one hand, there is a need to accurately place people according to their proven intellectual ability; on the other hand, we must ensure that the methods used are unbiased, particularly toward urban youths. Presently, prejudices can be found in most aptitude and IQ tests that favor middle-class Whites.

Some professionals question the tests' overall validity because they use terminology and concepts foreign to many urban Native Americans, Hispanics, African Americans, Asians, even underclass European American youth. For example, for "a child who has never handled money or seen a farm animal [to receive] a question that assumes knowledge of quarters and cows" would not be fair.[4] Professor Patricia Sexton explains, "there is not a shred of proof that the IQ tests are valid measures of native intelligence, and in fact there is much proof that they are not."[5] Further, Dr. Leonard Kornberg criticizes the tests as narrow in scope and unable to measure the "general ability of intelligence." In his opinion, such IQ achievement tests "sometimes seemed to be a middle-class invention."[6]

City youths have brilliant minds. Because of culturally biased testing, however, many of these teens become convinced that they are intellectually primitive—when in reality they are geniuses untapped awaiting tests set upon equal footing, tests which allow them to mentally wrestle on familiar, not foreign, ground. The urban youth minister must recognize that the true ability of these teens is in many cases not being accurately measured, and help urban adolescents realize that standardized tests may not fully express their intellectual and survival ability.

The history of standardized testing began with Alfred Binet and Theodore Simon in 1905, who searched for a way to determine which students would be placed in special classes in Paris schools. Through trial and error, they found that some children were better at "higher" mental abilities (memory, attention, and comprehension) than "lower" ones (reaction time, speed of hand movement), and vice versa.[7] They concluded that higher abilities were more important.

Binet developed the concept of mental age by "measuring the number of items an individual could correctly identify and remember in relation to the number of items that the average individual of a given age could correctly handle."[8] By testing large numbers of people, he formed a bell curve which could be used to determine whether a specific individual was more than or less than average.

This intelligence test was revised at Stanford University and is presently called the Stanford-Binet Test. It has an average score of 100, with 60 defining mental retardation and 156 genius, and may be taken from age two through adulthood.[9] The Stanford-Binet has become the single most utilized intelligence test.

The Wechsler Intelligence Scale for Children and the Wechsler Adult Intelligence Scale (given to older adolescents), created by David Wechsler, are the second most commonly used intelligence tests. Actually consisting of several tests, they determine not only general intellectual ability but an individual's proficiency at specific functions. Given this approach, Wechsler defines intelligence as "the capacity of the individual to understand the world about him and his resourcefulness to cope with its challenges."[10]

The test most crucial to a number of high school students' collegiate options is the Scholastic Aptitude Test (SAT). People of color on average have scored significantly lower on the verbal section of this test than middle-class white students. (Scores on the mathematics section are consistent across cultural groups.) Although there have been many revisions to make the SAT culturally unbiased, specialists still raise many formidable questions.

Those who perform well on the SAT verbal are, first, able to process information quickly and efficiently, and second, can recall significant amounts of data from short-term and long-term memory.[11] The longer one's memory span and the more quickly one can solve a given problem, the greater the individual may perform. In short, the SAT is a speed-processing performance test. If two students were allowed to finish the test *at their own mental speeds,* the slower student might do just as well. Because the test deals with fast processing in limited time, however, the slower student will perform poorly.

Earl Hunt and colleagues have also noted that verbal tests like the SAT accurately reflect only those processes "related to knowledge acquired through experience," and that they record "pure mechanical processes whose operations are independent of the specific information that is processed."[12]

Intelligence tests can give us valuable information about city youths, but they do not paint the entire picture. Even when an urban Puerto Rican adolescent has the quickness of memory and processing needed to perform well on verbal tests, cultural inequality remains. Many of these tests promise universality, but do not deliver it.

There has been a forceful effort to produce culturally unbiased tests, which usually fall into one of three categories. The first is non-verbal testing. The Raven Progressive Matrices Test, for example, tests a person's ability to match items and complete visual relationships of objects. The second category promotes "items that are familiar to people from all socioeconomic and ethnic backgrounds."[13] It relies on common items to form such questions as "What is the relationship between, a tree, water, and soil?" Every item in this question should have been experienced regardless of the test-taker's economic, social, or cultural background.

The third type of test constructs a counter-bias in favor of a specific cultural-economic group. This variety does not test people universally, but tests how well their intellectual ability has allowed them to achieve within their own normative social group. Sociologist Adrian Dove designed the Dove Counterbalance General Intelligence Test (alias the Chitling Test) in the late sixties, as a satirical parody of standard intelligence tests which culturally and linguistically favors African American urban youth. A middle-class white American taking this test may have exactly the same feelings as an urban youth taking a Euro-biased standardized test. Here are a few sample questions from the Chitling test:

1. A "handkerchief head" is:
   (a) a cool cat
   (b) a porter
   (c) an Uncle Tom
   (d) a hoddi
   (e) a preacher.

2. A "gas head" is a person who has a:
   (a) fast-moving car
   (b) stable of "lace"
   (c) "process"
   (d) habit of stealing cars
   (e) long jail record for arson.

3. If a pimp is uptight with a woman who gets state aid, what does he mean when he talks about "Mother's Day?"
   (a) second Sunday in May
   (b) third Sunday in June
   (c) first of every month
   (d) none of these
   (e) first and fifteenth of every month.

4. If a man is called a "blood," then he is a:
   (a) fighter
   (b) Mexican American
   (c) Negro
   (d) hungry hemophile
   (e) Redman or Indian.

5. Cheap chitlings (not the kind you purchase at a frozen-food counter) will taste rubbery unless they are cooked long enough. How soon can you quit cooking them to eat and enjoy them?
   (a) 45 minutes
   (b) two hours
   (c) 24 hours
   (d) one week (on a low flame)
   (e) one hour.

6. "Jet" is:
   (a) an East Oakland motorcycle club
   (b) one of the gangs in "West Side Story"
   (c) a news and gossip magazine
   (d) a way of life for the very rich.

Answers: 1. c, 2. c, 3. e, 4. c, 5. c, 6. c.[14]

The dropout and diploma attainment. A high school diploma is a valuable piece of paper. While it does not measure ability or intellectual stature, it is a symbol of the minimal educational attainment accepted by our society. The twelve-year act of finishing high school provides options in almost every facet of life. According to a 1981 report by the National Urban League, a high school diploma is a "license to life" that becomes a "turning point" that can open many career doors. Without it, one "is virtually assured of membership in the underclass."[15] The only other way out is through entrepreneurial ability (see Chapter 7).

The value of the diploma cannot be overstated, particularly for people of color who would like a fair chance in American society. A diploma is needed to obtain most non–minimum wage jobs, military training, and higher education. Therefore, to fail to earn a diploma is to consign oneself to poverty. Exceptions are those young people who have friends in places of power; urban youth do not often have that advantage.

The Committee on the Status of Black Americans, in conjunction with the Commission on Behavioral and Social Sciences and Education and the National Research Council, has reported that dropout rates at age eighteen are highest at "thirteen percent for white women to about eighteen percent for black men."[16] However, the dropout rate has noticeably decreased historically for many ethnic groups. Among African Americans aged twenty-five to twenty-nine, "high school graduation has grown dramatically and almost continuously, from about fifty percent in 1965 to nearly eighty percent in the early 1980s."[17]

In the city of Philadelphia, only forty-one percent of the class of 1988 received diplomas. Even more staggering, of the 19,362 students in the freshman class of 1984, 31.6% dropped out of the school system—a total of 6,128 students. An additional 5,264 of these freshmen did not graduate because they transferred to another district, were left behind a grade, went to jail, or died. Of the four predominant ethnic groups in Philadelphia, 37.4% of the Hispanic students dropped out, 33.8% of the African Americans, 26.3% of the Whites, and 16.3% of the Asians.[18]

We must attempt to greatly reduce the number of teens who do not complete high school, by encouraging them to finish or receive an equivalent. Each year, 450,000 people complete the General Educational Development Test (GED). Sixty percent are under age twenty-four.[19] Make an issue of those teens that complete high school or finish their GED—these are major accomplishments.

Ministering in low-cost housing developments, I find that a significant proportion of urban adolescents, because of academic detainment, moving, or health, are one or two grades below where they should be for their age. Consequently, I ask teenagers three questions concerning their grade: What grade are you in? How old are you? and Is this the grade in which you naturally belong? Teenagers having an extremely difficult time in life so often want to throw high school out the window. It can seem more reasonable to quit school and help the family in times of crisis (which is a realistic option), but if there is any chance to help teens stay in school, sacrifice yourself to keep them there. I received a letter from a young lady who wrote to me about her high school experiences:

> I am going to check into night school tomorrow with my girl-friend. She's the only person that will talk to me. . . . I was surprised when she said she was eighteen and in the tenth grade. She dropped out of school two years ago and decided to come back. I don't know if I would have the heart to come back. There were times in the past year that I just wanted to throw everything away. I am glad there were many people around like you.[20]

According to James Mackey, there are three primary reasons teenagers choose to drop out of school. The first is a feeling of *personal incapacity,* or accepting one's inferiority and disbelieving in one's own ability to effectively correct educational mistakes. Second is *guidelessness:* a conscious rejection of the rules of the educational process. Last is *cultural estrangement,* which goes beyond the simple rejection of educational rules and regulations. In this case, teens reject the standards of the entire educational structure because they perceive that they have gotten a raw deal.[21] Many times, these dropouts have good reason to reject the education system, but neglect to make one mental deduction—without an education, there is not much they can do about it.

Many situations will drive teens to feel they cannot finish school: pregnancy, the need to raise younger family members while a parent works, illiteracy, and discouragement, to name a few. None should stop a person from receiving a diploma.

An urban youth worker once told me about a young man who dropped out a few times throughout his senior high years, primarily because the work seemed too hard. He had been held back a few times, and was bordering on illiteracy. He went on like this for years, until one day he became serious enough to say to himself, "I have no future without a diploma." For two years past his seventeenth birthday he went to school, admitting that it was grueling—but he didn't give up. Finally, as he approached his twentieth birthday, he received his diploma. Shortly after the graduation ceremony, this young man could be seen walking around his housing development with his cap and gown, excited, festive, joyous, telling everyone, "I did it! I did it! I got my diploma! I did it!"

Ignorant youth workers. The final obstacle lies at our own doorstep. Urban youth workers often display an underlying ignorance of the intellectual potential of their teenagers, an apathetic failure to recognize the mental capabilities of their youth and allow them to challenge the very structure of the youth group with their minds. I believe that youth workers who refuse to allow adolescents to contest them have their own insecurities to blame. It is one thing to tell teenagers to utilize their brilliant minds to affect change in the world; it is another to allow that same free thought to challenge the youth worker. In essence, some youth groups are totalitarian regimes for Jesus, where the youth worker's view cannot be challenged at all.

If ministry is to be ministry, we must be intellectually challenged by our teens, just as we challenge them. This type of ministry is stimulating and reciprocal. We must strive not only to incite urban youth to cognitive excellence, but must likewise expect the same of ourselves.

Many people within this profession believe they have "arrived" at their intellectual best. They have not. Once you have become the best, there is nothing left to learn. The only omniscient mind belongs to God, not to you and especially not to me. May the theme of our youth groups be, "Come let us reason *together*."[22]

ATTRIBUTES OF THE URBAN YOUTH INTELLECTUAL

Up to this point we have focused on the obstacles that can cause metropolitan youths to underachieve intellectually. We will now consider the attributes that the urban youth intellectual needs to be able to overcome those obstacles. Through much observation and reflection, I have determined nine indispensable characteristics. While not exhaustive, these are important defenses against the negative forces acting on the minds of urban adolescents.

Thinking for oneself. The ability to think independently of others is a valuable skill for youths to acquire. Malcolm X had tremendous success recruiting urban teenagers in Harlem because his first challenge to them was that they begin to think independently and learn to rightly weigh the issues of life for themselves. He once remarked:

> One of the first things I think young people . . . should learn is how to see for yourself and listen for yourself and think for yourself. Then you can come to an intelligent decision for yourself. If you form the habit of going by what you hear others say about someone, or going by what others think about someone, instead of searching that thing out for yourself and seeing for yourself, you will be walking west when you think you think you're going east, and you will be walking east when you think you're going west. . . . The most important thing that we can learn to do today is think for ourselves.[23]

There are four active forms of intelligence: creative, recreative, consumer, and inventive.[24] Youths who are creative thinkers rarely subscribe to the ideas and opinions of their peer group without first deciding if they are true and worth imitating. Normally, these adolescents set the trends and have no need to imitate, because their minds are constantly rehashing existing concepts to formulate fresh ways of thinking about issues.

Recreative thinkers reform and reshape existing ideas. They will often clarify the unclear thoughts of creative thinkers, sometimes becoming more popular than creative thinkers because they can take those same ideas to new heights.

Consumer intellectuals neither create nor recreate; they take ideas and put them into practice. Some teenagers will weigh ideas only for their usefulness to a particular situation and will seek strategies to implement them.

Lastly, the inventive thinkers are teens that have all three qualities. They can both create and recreate ideas, as well as invent strategies to set them in motion. Friends, we must teach our teens to think for themselves so that they may begin to pierce the canopy of intellectual mediocrity. Frederick Douglass once mentioned that humanity must begin to think with the front of its head rather than the back in order to achieve true victory.[25] Urban youth groups which inventively practice this thought will strike a victory for urban youth ministry.

Balancing thinking and feeling. City youths must learn to properly relate emotion and cognition. If they don't, they will become ineffective at both. Excessively intellectual urban teenagers, who have detached themselves from the joy of emotion, become both cognitively bankrupt and unable to feel. Occasionally, these teenagers have anger within which has not been successfully dealt with, rendering them incapable of genuine compassion toward others. The ultimate result of all their thinking is emptiness.

Drastically sympathetic teens value emotion over thought, which can lead to unsifted activism accomplishing nothing more than new ulcers. Racing down a blind temperamental road, they are constantly reacting instead of thinking through to the root of a given situation. While extreme intellectuals overrule feeling, sympathetic youths neglect intellect.

Urban teen intellectuals are an energetic combination of both. These youths have successfully and creatively balanced intellect and feeling for the purpose of constructive action, whether it is leadership in the youth group, helping tutor children after school, or extra-curricular activities. Both cognitive competence and emotional sensitivity drive them toward personal excellence.

Pursuing personal excellence. Some urban youth pastors define individual excellence as being the best compared to others. I disagree. Whenever someone chooses this definition of excellence, they automatically set up their young people for failure. It implies that one person possesses skills or gifts greater than another's; inevitably, one is then seen as a greater achiever than another. The *quantity* of ability used is irrelevant, however—what matters is whether the individual is using his or her given ability to the fullest.

Excellence is to answer to oneself, to say "I am doing my utmost to be the best I can be." There are youths who do not perform at the same mental or physical heights as others because of severe handicaps, or psychological and physical problems. They are still capable of excellence, measured not against others, but against themselves. A mentally handicapped teen who pushes herself or himself to learn to write the alphabet is much more an intellectual than the teen who wins an academic prize with little or no cognitive effort.

Failing with dignity. Like excellence, failure is a deceptive word. We must teach urban adolescents that failure is an inner attribute resulting from a cave-in of personal dignity and determination. To fail is to try again, to lose is to start over. Failing with dignity entails recognizing that a lost fight does not equal lost personhood. One has failed only when one has given up.

In tenth grade, I took French. It was grueling. I tried my best to learn the language but made no headway, eventually despairing on ever mastering it and failing that course for the year. I had no feelings toward the class and simply gave up. Worse, I did not care.

In my sophomore year of college, I was required to take a course in poetry. I was convinced I was going to like it—that is, until my first test returned with a D minus. Talking with fellow students, I found others who had performed just as poorly. Friends who had already taken the class warned that the teacher gave good grades only to those students who could "spit" back class readings word for word. I did not believe them.

When the second test came, I studied and felt proficient. My grade minutely improved to a D. By this time, many students had dropped the class completely. I elected to remain, primarily because I honestly enjoyed the class—although my grades still did not reflect it.

My tutor made it clear: "Nelson, go *memorize* the teacher's handouts, as if you were in a play. Let's face it, independent thinkers will not make it through this class. After all, the test is all that matters." I was confused. If the study of poetry is mostly interpretation, how could a teacher expect students to interpret major writers like Shakespeare, Milton, and Dante in only one way? This was not education, but indoctrination.

I began to ask myself why I had come to college in the first place. Was it to receive an education or to receive good grades? It was hard, but I decided that retaining my dignity as a thinking person was more important than living up to some arbitrary academic standard. I could not bring myself to memorize the lectures for the sake of soothing the ear of the instructor, compromising my own interpretive ability in the process. As a result, I earned a D plus on the final exam and a D for the semester.

In French class, I failed both academically and personally because I refused to learn. In poetry class, I received a failing grade but succeeded as a person. "To be or not to be, that is the question," wrote Shakespeare. In order "to be," we must have the courage to fail with our heads held high, knowing we have done our best.

Urban youth should learn the importance of retaining their dignity in situations where they may fail. Too many young people destroy themselves over their shortcomings in life. The urban youth intellectual will realize that self-denigration following a failure is far worse than the failure itself.

Refusing to be miseducated. Miseducation—the covert misrepresentation of certain historical truths for the benefit of one particular culture or political group—is a tragic reality in urban America. Dr. Carter Godwin Woodson, in his 1933 classic *The Miseducation of the Negro,* states a thesis directly relevant to the urban predicament: "When you control a man's thinking you do not have to worry about his actions."[26]

Woodson drew a distinction between uneducated and educated African Americans. Critically analyzing the differences between these two groups, he concluded that uneducated African Americans have been the most responsible for the advancement of their race. His reasons were simple: the more educated African Americans became within the American system, the more they were intellectually miseducated against their own cultural group. The books they read and the lectures they were taught pointed them against themselves. If the subject was Geography, Africa was portrayed as the land of savages, not civilizations. If studying art, European works were considered masterpieces while others were primitive. World history consisted of that of Europe and America only.[27] Everywhere the "highly educated" turned they were forced to see themselves as inferior, and surreptitiously set at odds with their own culture. American higher education was to blame.

Woodson wanted educated African Americans to lead their culture. He was not against education, but miseducation.

> If the "highly educated" Negro would forget most of the untried theories taught him in school, if he could see through the propaganda which has been instilled into his mind under the pretext of education, if he would fall in love with his own people and begin to sacrifice for their uplift—if the "highly educated" Negro would do these things, he could solve some of the problems now confronting the race.[28]

Although there have been innumerable educational developments since his book was written, Woodson's thesis cannot be denied. Various minority youths tell me again and again that the lessons they learn in school either treat their histories as if they do not exist or refer to them only in a negative or derogatory fashion.

Urban youth workers are responsible for reappropriating their teens' education. Essentially, urban teens must receive *two* educations: one given by society, the other by themselves. Intelligent teens will refuse to learn improper information about who they are. Here are some immediate ideas you can give to your youths to help them reject miseducation in the school system.

- Always be prepared to ask the teacher, "Do you know if there are any significant persons of my ethnicity in the field we are studying?" If enough people ask this question, it will expand the teacher's awareness that the class wants more.
- Ask if you can make a special presentation during class to re-educate others about an issue they may be miseducated about.
- When given a class reading assignment, ask if you can read a cultural classic.
- Always ask for extra credit on an issue important to reeducation.
- Always carry a book to school that can help you reeducate yourself. Read it on the bus or at lunch.
- Give teachers ideas that can assist in the reeducation process, such as book lists, people who can come speak to the class, and events going on in the community.

Pursuing higher education. Every urban teenager can obtain higher education. We underestimate the ability of these youths when we construct programs that expect them not to attend college. What amazes me about the urban youth ministry profession is what it fails to say to teenagers. A host of educational programs seek to educate urban youth, yet do not do what is necessary to push them to higher intellectual heights. Somehow, many have convinced themselves that urban youths are to be educationally subservient, and while we may not voice this opinion overtly, our *programs* speak louder than words. Do you see your educational ministry as simply teaching illiterates and dropouts to read and get a GED? Or can you bring yourself to imagine your teens receiving higher degrees, even doctorates?

I once met a beautiful young lady who happened to be handicapped. She did not let her disability deter her from entering college, in spite of others' low opinions of her ability. Before the first semester was completed, she had spellbound her classmates. Watching her palsied body as she would struggle to walk, one would tend to pity her and overlook her mental ability. At times, students would wonder if she could adequately handle the pressures of college. Once all was said and done, however, she achieved in spite of others' initial doubts. Any teen that wants to succeed, can.

According to a 1988 survey report published by the Center for Education Statistics, minority groups have made noticeable increases in college enrollment since 1976. Hispanic enrollment broke the 600,000 mark in 1986 and continues to increase in the 1990s. Asian and Pacific Islander enrollment more than doubled. African American enrollment has been steady at about 1.1 million since 1976. Enrollment of women has steadily increased in all races, now constituting fifty-three percent of the entire enrollment body.[29] Less than one percent of those enrolled in college in 1982 received their Bachelor's degree within four years, indicating that, while many drop out, others have chosen to stretch their education out over longer periods of time.[30]

Urban minority youth have clearly found greater success in their own cultural colleges and universities than in general universities. Latino, Native American, African American, and predominately Asian colleges, most of which are accredited, strive to teach students how to enter mainstream America without feeling alienated or miseducated. Controlled by their particular ethnic group, these colleges foster a warm, distinctive cultural atmosphere. Not exclusive, they specialize in affirming cultural contribution and are open to any person, race, or creed that seeks learning.

The statistical successes of these colleges demand our attention. For example, a system of over twenty-eight Native American tribal colleges has been in place since the early 1980s, which in 1991 enrolled almost twelve thousand Native Americans nationwide.[31] According to the Native American community, these colleges are necessary to boost cultural self-esteem and bring educational hope back to the tribe. Incredibly, ninety percent of reservation Native Americans who enter four-year colleges drop out, while those who attend tribal colleges first, then transfer, have forty times the chance to succeed.[32]

According to Jeff Hooker, a science teacher at Little Big Horn College in Crow Agency, Montana, between 1900 and 1985 there were only two Crow Tribe scientists. In just the four years beginning in 1986, however, Little Big Horn College "graduated eleven students in science and sent them on to four-year schools."[33] Crow Chief Plenty Coups summarizes the real importance of these schools: "Education is your most powerful weapon. With education, you are the white man's equal; without education, you are his victim."[34] See Appendix 3 for a listing of the twenty-eight Native American tribal colleges.

There are 117 African American colleges and universities, found predominately in the southern and lower midwestern states. Their histories are rooted in the reconstruction era, when they were founded as part of an attempt to fully educate freed slaves. Enrollment between 1986 and 1991 rose seventeen percent, compared with an eleven percent national average increase.[35] Morehouse College in Atlanta reported a sixteen percent increase, Xavier University in New Orleans was up eighteen percent, Virginia Union University in Richmond posted a thirty-seven percent hike, and Cheyney and Lincoln Universities (both in Pennsylvania) rose thirty and twenty-two percent respectively.[36]

Interestingly, one report states that while close to eighty percent of all African American students attend European American colleges, only twenty-five percent of their degrees are received there. In other words, seventy-five percent of African American degrees are granted by African American universities. One newspaper report held that these universities are responsible for "fifty percent of black business leaders and elected officials, seventy-five percent of black military officers, eighty percent of black federal judges and eighty-five percent of black doctors."[37] These colleges and universities account for "fourteen percent of the institutions granting B.A.'s in biology to blacks in

1980–1981, [and] forty percent of the biology degrees awarded to blacks."38

The National Association for Equal Opportunity in Higher Education (NAFEO), publishes a list of historically and predominately African-American colleges and universities, which is reprinted in full in Appendix 3. I am the executive director of the Christian Education Coalition for African American Leadership (CECAAL), which plans highly academic college tours for churches, schools, and other groups interested in exposing their teens to the cultural beauty of the abovementioned schools. These trips have a fourfold purpose: leadership training, education, exposure to culture, and religious development. CECAAL not only proclaims the Christian message, but provides opportunities for urban youth to inherit Christian skills. The motivation is sevenfold:

- To recognize higher education as an obtainable goal.
- To recognize education as a tool of leadership and social empowerment.
- To provide teens with the opportunity to meet young African American role models from varied social circumstances.
- To give teens the chance sit in on classes and talk with professors privately about educational and leadership options.
- To challenge teens to ask questions about vocations and what they must do *now* to begin pursuing them.
- To challenge teens on Christian stewardship: using their talents and time for Jesus.
- To teach teens how to do their part to contribute to cultural uplift.39

Numerous Spanish colleges have helped educate non-English-speaking Latinos in both their cultural significance and American ideals. These schools have been growing significantly. Hispanic enrollment in college has grown from 384,000 in 1976 to 680,000 in 1988.40 In the 1986–87 school year, Latinos received 26,255 bachelors degrees, 6,661 masters, and 721 doctorates.41 See Appendix 3 for a list of a few notable predominately Latino colleges.

Asians have no colleges of their own in America. However, Asian American college students form on-campus networks that facilitate cultural unity, self-esteem, and togetherness. These ethnic networks form generally along national lines. The Asian population of all minority groups has educationally been very successful. In 1976, 198,000 Asian Americans were enrolled in American colleges. This number more than doubled to 497,000 in 1988.[42] In 1987, 31,771 Asian students received bachelors degrees, 8,108 got their masters, and 1,057 received doctorates.[43] A list of colleges with strong Christian Asian networks appears in Appendix 3.

Having said all this, it is important to point out that pursuing higher education does not necessarily mean obtaining a college or high school degree. What I am advocating is that urban young people never sell their cognitive ability short. By achieving intellectually, they can become qualified to remedy some of the ills of their existence. Ask city teens how far they want to go educationally. Many have never been asked that question. For many urban adolescents, college seems an impossible dream—it is not. Learning is a never-ending process. If a person's brain is fully operational, expect thinking from it. Here are nine ways to pursue higher education and keep the mind at top level beyond high school:

- Pre-college credit courses. Many colleges offer courses to high school students during the summer months and at night that can be transferred to their college transcripts.
- Attend a two- or four-year institution. Here the teen can work on a specialized bachelor's degree and, if desired, can more easily pursue a master's or doctorate degree.
- Attend a mechanical or technical school. These schools teach specific skills that can be immediately used by businesses or can lead to entrepreneurial ventures.
- Attend a community college. These schools give good degrees; never underestimate them. They offer classes for teens who need to strengthen themselves in basic subjects before transferring to a major university.

- Work and learn. Some teens who have family responsibilities can take evening courses while they work. Also, some jobs will pay for training.
- Attend significant conferences and seminars. If college is not an option, keep a pulse on the seminars, workshops, and conferences offered by churches and colleges.
- Surround yourself with people who will challenge you intellectually. The mind must be sharpened by interaction with others. College may not be a possibility, but discussing and debating issues can still challenge the mind.
- Teach yourself. One's situation may not allow any of the above options. Find an interesting subject and study it thoroughly. Become an expert at independent study—there are many such people in urban America.
- Keep abreast of all major issues and develop opinions. Higher education requires a person to know the issues of the day and have thought-through opinions on them.

Being a role model. Training urban teens to become Christian role models is part of bringing the Kingdom of God into any community. The intellectual teen realizes that changing individuals is not an impossibility, because part of the change already exists in them. Role models lead the pack, examples of what others should become. They are disciplined individuals who charge through the obstacles others have set before them, as a testimony that progress can and will be made. When someone asks, "Can anyone make it in this dog-eat-dog urban environment and retain their love for Jesus?" the urban youth intellectual answers, "Yes! Look at me!" Positive role models are, in many communities, the first fruits of an indispensable generation. Role models do not just happen—they must be prayed for and made to happen.

The Apostle Paul, encouraging Timothy in his pastoral position, writes, "Don't let anyone look down on you because you are young, but set an example for the believers in speech, in life, in love, in faith, in purity"[44] (1 TIM. 4:12). Paul, realizing the obstacles Timothy will

have to overcome, impresses upon him that the most important discipline one must follow is to "train oneself toward Godliness" (I TIM.
4:7–8). Theologian George Eldon Ladd would consider this as training to become the "presence of the future."[45]

My mother makes wonderful cakes. If I am in the kitchen when
she is baking, I will taste some of the batter without a second
thought. By sampling the batter, I gain present foreknowledge of the
tasty richness of the future cake, thereby becoming fully aware of its
succulent and mouth-watering quality before the cake is completed.
The urban youth role model is likewise an ingredient in the Godly
batter of the present, yet coming, Kingdom Cake.

"Godliness has value for all things, holding the promise for both
the present life and the life to come" (I TIM. 4:8). Whatever godly role
models accomplish with their lives will hold promise and strength for
others. The discipline they apply to their lives via their commitment
to Christ will be noticed in their actions. The Christian youth intellectual who attempts to be a useful role model is:

- Committed to keeping families together.
- Responsible for his or her finances.
- Free of substance abuse.
- Sexually responsible.
- Environmentally responsible.
- One who helps others (especially younger peers).
- One who chooses non-violent means to ends.
- An example for his or her peers to emulate.

A role mode has the potential to be an example to the whole community. The hope is best expressed by the children's song "I am a
Promise."

> I am a promise, I am a possibility.
> I am a promise, with a capital P.
> I am a great big bundle of *Potentiality.*

Having religious integrity. Having intelligence but no relationship with Jesus is like being at the door of a gold vault inheritance without the combination. Everything I have described in this chapter collapses to naught if Jesus is not in control of our thinking processes. To think is to think Jesus. He has given all of us the ability to worship him with our thoughts. Urban youths must learn and know that God is deeply concerned about their minds. Why? Because Satan is too.

We cannot control our minds with our own strength. We must depend on God to protect our thoughts from every adversary, in order to "take every thought captive for Christ" (2 COR. 10:5). The worst form of miseducation is not cultural or political—it is spiritual, because the result is the loss of one's soul (MATT. 16:26). Urban youth intellectuals must become students of God's word, which will guide them as thinkers on a path pleasing to Christ (2 TIM. 2:15, PS. 119:105, MATT. 4:1–11).

Lead youth to realize that there is a spiritual struggle going on "in high places," a struggle for their minds which they will not win without Jesus' help (EPH. 6:12). They must search for God not only with all their heart and soul, but with their intellectual ability as well (MATT. 22:37).[46] Those who keep their thoughts on the Lord will be kept in perfect peace (ISA. 26:3), and their minds will be renewed in Christ (ROM. 12:2). Religious integrity is the willingness to make Jesus Lord of our thoughts.

Being a visionary. The ability to dream is the highest gift given to the intellectual. It is not enough for urban adolescents to desire a better community. They must also have the ability to visualize it. Have your youth write down specific hopes and ideas they have for their life. Dreams need to be described in detail in order to be carried out. "A person without a dream is like a bird without wings—let's see how far they'll fly."[47]

An intelligent youth visionary has three distinct qualities beyond a specified dream: the knack to see potentiality in people, the mental fortitude to inspire others, and the creativity to begin moving toward beneficial progress.

The ability to see other peoples' potential begins with seeing one's own. God has created each young person with great potential to achieve and succeed in life. Visionaries nurture others to become what God has created them to be. They never see a useless person. Educationally, intellectual teens see hope for others and push themselves to be challenging examples of educational excellence.

Visionaries also have the mental fortitude to inspire others. It has often been said, "a single dream can change the world forever, but the dreamer has limited time." In order for a dream to continue, others must be inspired to carry it on and make it their own. The urban youth visionary will rouse others to do bigger and better things than he or she alone is capable of. People without vision perish (PROV. 29:18). The highways and byways of urban adolescence are littered with the wreckage of those who had no dream, no hope, no *vision*. Inspiration must be shared in order to effectively infect others with the love of learning and the love of God.

Finally, visionaries have the creativity to begin moving toward beneficial educational progress. The road to educational excellence is difficult for an urban person. High school can be dangerous and college costs money. But the visionary never gives up.

It is a monumental task for urban youth and youth workers to inspire the young people of this nation to become the best they can be when they have been systematically convinced they will not be able to succeed. The secret is to encourage those who have the vision to lead, to make them realize they have our backing. In the words of an old African Proverb, "Find a good tree to climb and we will lift you up." God is faithful to those adolescents who dare to struggle to be their educational best and will not forsake them.

Do you not know? Have you not heard? The Lord is the everlasting God, the Creator of the ends of the earth. He will not grow tired or weary and his understanding no one can fathom. He gives strength to the weary and increases the power of the weak. Even youths grow tired and weary, and young men stumble and fall; *but those who hope in the Lord will renew their strength.* They will soar on wings like eagles; they will run and not grow weary, they will walk and not be faint.

Isaiah 40:28–31

producing a practical work ethic in urban youth

7

TEACHING IMPOVERISHED URBAN YOUTH THE VALUE OF WORK CAN BE strenuous. By the year 2000, "a stunning 57% of all labor-force growth will be black, Hispanic, [female] or other minorities."[1] As the work force darkens, teenagers (many of whom belong to ethnic minorities) will have to be trained in the basic skills needed to enter this force with adequate salary and position. In 1965, car mechanics had to know an estimated five thousand pages of manuals; today that figure is well over 465,000.[2] Be clear on this issue: urban teens *will* be a part of the lower strata of America's future work force unless youth workers create practical plans to forestall this coming atrocity.

Many youths do not want to work simply because they see adults existing off the welfare system with no concern for getting a job. In many instances, low-cost housing authorities are constructed in such a way that parents who find jobs will automatically have their rent elevated. This system poses one problem: if the family desires to move to a better place, the elevation in rent extinguishes the elevation in income, leaving very little money to "save up" to move. There are many progressive families who thereby become doomed to pay more rent for less services. They soon realize that they are trapped in a state of social stagnation.

Teenagers and children, observing this situation, figure out early that the housing and welfare system is set up not for their benefit but for their progressive destruction. Some conclude, like their parents, that "If the system won't help me, then I will make it captive to me as I am captive to it, continually nursing from its breast beyond what I am entitled to." Inspiring a person with this mentality to get a job is tough.

A teenager's attitude toward work is closely related to his or her societal self-development. The inclination to work is an inner attribute. It must come from the inside out. Sparking it in urban youth requires much of the youth worker: time, effort, discipline, and the unwavering message, "Work is your attitude toward it!"

Teens assume work means earning money. Simply bringing home a paycheck is not work, however—it is hire. To be hired is to be paid for work effort; work itself is a positive attitude toward the job one does, regardless of the pay. For example, if I volunteer to help twice a week in a homeless relief program, I will not be paid. If I'm not being paid, should I really put forth the effort to work? Or should I just do what I want, as often as I want? After all, they ought be thankful I'm giving them an extra hand, right? Wrong!

There are some forms of work teenagers should be inspired to do for nothing at all. Once pay has become the inspiration for work, we lose the possibility of inspiring teens without pay. Urban teenagers must learn that while payment for one's services is necessary for survival in this society, it should never be the motive for performing the service.

Volunteer service is a worthy undertaking for a teenager. The results will be priceless. Not only will people be helped, but the teenager will gain valuable experience that may otherwise be unobtainable without a degree. My goal is to make youth employable. Many times, job skills must be gained by volunteering. Then, when teens walk into a job interview, they are not seeking skills, but offering experience.

Urban youth need to gain a positive attitude toward work that is not necessarily hire. To work is to enjoy the satisfaction of your handiwork. When God created the universe, seven full days were required. Can we fully pay God for making us, the heavens, and the earth? Of course not. So why did God work so hard? Simple: "God saw all that was made and it was *very good.*"[3] The value of doing work for the goodness of one's own craftsmanship is a lesson the world must hear. If urban youth workers can inspire youth to live by this basic principle, perhaps we can solve a few problems confronting youth employment.

The world is generally concerned about money and making plenty of it. For those living in capitalistic countries, there are two forms of institutional work ethics crucial to the psychological development of teenagers today. The first comes from Adam Smith; the second, John Calvin.

ADAM SMITH'S "INVISIBLE HAND" OF COMPETITION

Adam Smith, in his 1776 magnum opus *The Wealth of Nations,* provided for capitalism what fuel does for fire. He believed that the free enterprise system is directed by an "invisible hand" which ensures that the greatest good in society is obtained.[4] If profit were pursued according to the interests of each individual or corporation, then good would take place. The goal is not necessarily to act morally or with a sense of social responsibility, but to maximize profit. The only rules are those of supply and demand, and restrictions of national law.[5] Competition becomes the medium through which the system operates.

Unfortunately, urban youth live by this philosophy. Teenagers observe that unless you are strong, you will not survive. "Obtain or be obtained." "Live and let die." Competition is the supreme directive for "making it" in this society. I raise this question: are these principles Christian ones, ones upon which an adolescent follower of Christ should operate in the world of work? My experience says no. The ethic of Adam Smith, so prevalent within urban youth culture, can be reduced to three ideologies: egocentric individualism, conspicuous consumption, and competitive attitude.

Egocentric individualism. I encounter teenagers who care for nothing but themselves. They don't need you, me, or Jesus. Their goal in life is to make a heap of money for themselves and no one else. They can survive alone. My warning begins when youth being influenced by the economic ethos conclude, "I do not need anyone. I can pull myself up by my own bootstraps." In essence, they make themselves the answers to all their problems. They become egocentric in the first degree.

Breaking through this unhealthy mentality involves being patient and providing opportunities to give. I will occasionally give a dollar's worth of dimes to little children and later ask for twenty cents. "No!" is the normal response, the reason being that it is *their* money and they want to keep it. I continue by asking, "For what?" "I don't know yet" is the response. Finally, when I ask a day or so later what the money was used for, "candy" is the typical reply.

Monetary egocentric individualism must be combatted by the youth pastor of Christian influence. Urban adolescents must come to understand that wealth is not for them to use solely on themselves— it must be discreetly utilized according to the needs of others. The goal is to give youths the opportunity to combat the monetary problems that face them. Teenagers should learn early in life that *they* are the solutions to the problems of their communities. I try to impress this thought process upon teens:

- I have some money.
- I have a need.
- Supply my need.
- Someone else has need.
- I have extra.
- Give the extra, to meet their need. (One should be sure a need is being met. For example, if a homeless man wants some coffee, don't just give him the money. Go buy the coffee and give it to him, thus insuring the proper use of your funds.)
- The community has progressed.

Economic selfishness has no place in the Christian mind. Urban teens must come to a biblical understanding of wealth in regard to personal need. Members of the early church, many of whom were extremely disadvantaged, provided for one another by attempting to unselfishly meet the needs of others.

> All the believers were one in heart and mind. No one claimed that any of his possessions were his own, but they shared everything they had. . . . There were no needy persons among them. For from time to time those who owned lands or houses sold them, brought the money from the sales and put it at the apostles' feet, and it was distributed to anyone as he had need.[6]

The word *need* must be emphasized. A need is something critical to biological, mental, social, or spiritual life. All else is want. It is my hope that we can help the teens of urban America see that they cannot progress as a neighborhood, family, youth group, or individual, by supplying wants. A Christian supplies needs.

Conspicuous consumption. Teaching youth the value of monetary temperance is tough. People buy things because they want them. Our society is based on supplying wants. When I was a child, I would sit in front of the television for hours during the Christmas season, waiting for commercials to present the toys I must have to be satisfied. I would write all of them down, reduce my list to fifteen items and give it to my parents, to give to Santa. My father would give the list back to me and say, "Santa wants you to reduce this list to the best five." This was tough, because the television told me they would all satisfy me indefinitely. It would often take two or more days to reduce my list.

When Christmas arrived, I would receive these toys. They were the greatest thing in the world for about seven hours, becoming markedly less enjoyable after that. Somehow, my toys didn't seem as fun as the ones on television. I became another victim of greed.

Conspicuous consumption is the want for things that do not satisfy. Simply put, it is to be greedy for nothing. Teenagers constantly fall prey to this syndrome. Disadvantaged youth may not have much, but as long as they have a television or radio in their home, they want the same things advantaged teens want.

Urban youth ministers must enlighten teens about the reality of greed—it does not satisfy. Furthermore, we must give them a satisfactory intellectual understanding of why this is so, the crux of which should include the following insights:

- Greed makes us want what we do not need.
- Greed makes us spend what we should save.
- Greed makes us think we are incomplete without certain things, only to discover that those things do not satisfy.
- Greed makes us consume resources that could be used to help others.
- Greed's end is the destruction of individuals and society. (World hunger, energy shortages, contaminated lakes and streams, poverty).

Extra money can be used either for good or for evil. Teach your youths to be intentional both when they save and when they give. It is not enough to save money; money must be saved *toward* something. The same is true for giving. The "Teaching of the Twelve" (Didache) puts it well: "Let your alms sweat in your hands until you know to whom to give."[7]

Competitive attitude. Competition is the mark of a capitalistic economy. The purpose of freedom within the system is to gain profit, whatever the means. The rich are the best competitors, and often achieve acclaim by climbing over and standing upon the carcasses of other people. Under the influence of Smithian philosophy, we take those who have reached the top and make them into gods of capitalistic victory, calling them "philanthropists" instead of "robber barons."[8] Their ends may include giving, but their means did not.

The competitive attitude is prevalent in urban life. In a dog-eat-dog environment, competition is necessary. I am foolish enough to believe, however, that the Christian follows an ethic above that of competitiveness—one that seeks to encourage people toward good ends through good means. To defend youth against the dangers of a competitive attitude, impress these guidelines upon them:

- Competition breeds distrust.
- Competition breeds unnecessary secrecy.
- Competition means one will win and another will lose.
- Christian harmony seeks an attitude wherein both win.
- Live your life in such a way that the good means are more important than the end result.
- Live your life in such a way that you consider people more important than money.

To implant this philosophy within the context of urban ministry is contrary to the ideals of city life. Life is not for money, and neither is money for life. Both must maintain a relationship pleasing to God, following the "invisible hand" of Jesus rather than that of Adam Smith.

JOHN CALVIN AND THE PROTESTANT ETHIC

John Calvin, one of the fathers of the Reformed Christian tradition, performed an experiment in the city of Geneva, Switzerland between 1541 and 1564. It became one of the first attempts to promote protestant beliefs as a basis for the operations of the state. The city was democratic in nature and became a haven for Calvinistic protestants (often refugees) seeking an environment where their ideals were glorified. Calvin's central idea was a "vision of a city in every way dedicated to the glorification of God."[9]

Geneva's history put its ideals in close contact with capitalism, wealth, and prosperity. The marriage of these influences created a "protestant ethic" which has influenced most of today's capitalistic societies, and which indelibly affects the orientation of urban youth toward the world of work and their place in society. We will examine the pros and cons of two concepts derived from the protestant ethic: the "calling" of vocation, and the attitude of labor.

The "calling" of vocation. The leaders of the Reformation deeply believed that all Christians were "called" to be the priests of Jesus Christ by fervently serving the Lord in all activity. If a tradesman, trade honestly to the glory of God. If a shoemaker, make shoes that result from love for Christ. Both the priest and peasant have an equal role in spreading the message of God through daily service.

A job was not viewed as a place to "goof off." It was an instrument with which individuals pleased both God and themselves. Too many city teens goof off, rationalizing, "Now that I have a job, I'll just let the money roll on in." They often forget that they must work first. It is one thing for non-Christian youths to have this attitude, but Christian teenagers should have a new perspective fully opposed to their old one.

Youth groups around the country are beginning to extend their role to that of a job training center. We are beginning to focus on training youth in the basic life skills needed to survive as adults. Computer literacy, mechanic training, business etiquette and communication skills can all be taught within the framework of youth outreach.

Impress upon teenagers a sense of "calling" to do God's work. Inspire them to follow the Christian message that their *attitude* towards work is an extension of their relationship with Christ, which must work itself out in the context of each individual's occupational decisions. The youth worker's manifesto to urban teens should be, "If you are called to be a street sweeper, sweep streets as Michelangelo painted or Beethoven composed music, or Shakespeare wrote poetry. You should sweep streets so well that all the hosts of heaven and earth will pause to say, 'here lived a great street sweeper who did the job well.' "[10]

The attitude of labor. There is a difficult aspect of the protestant ethic that need not be presented to urban teens any longer: the assertion that spirituality can be measured economically. Sociologist Max Weber, in *The Protestant Ethic and the Spirit of Capitalism,* describes our society's tacit marriage to Calvinistic principles.[11] Disadvantaged people in our society, who have few jobs and may be receiving some form of public service, are considered unspiritual. Monetary gain is considered proof of God's blessing.

Teenagers, who have just been told by the youth worker that they are "called" by God to serve in whatever occupation they choose, will hear the conflicting message, "Getting rich is the sign of God's presence." This is untrue. The rich have often discovered that money is not the prerequisite for happiness.

The purpose of money is to be a means of common exchange in a society of trade. It can only buy tangible things. Happiness, love, and self-esteem cannot be purchased, although many believe otherwise. Seeking God's Spirit has nothing to do with money. As a matter of fact, an economically deprived family in Harlem can be even wealthier than a rich family in Beverly Hills, because God's means of exchange is not the dollar, mark, yen, ruble, or pound—faithfulness to Jesus is the only means of exchange God accepts.

I am advocating a tough-minded attempt by all urban youth pastors to consider the economic message you send to disadvantaged youth. If you are asking teens to gain money to get rich, you sin. The message is simple: future progress for the underclass depends upon economics, and getting a job is the first step in that direction. But remember, money is not the end of earning; neither is it an end in itself. It should be used as a tool to improve both others and yourself, "for what does it profit someone if they gain the whole world, but lose their soul?"[12]

A Practical Work Ethic for Urban Youth

A systematic work ethic is desperately needed for city youth and youth workers. Teenagers will often ask me for help finding a job, particularly during the summer months. I give them the right phone numbers to call and a few pointers on how to go about an interview. Many still do not get jobs. Initially, I could not understand why, particularly when having a job was something these youths desired. Was it discrimination? Were the youth inadequately prepared? Did the high unemployment rate affect their search? Or was it because they did not have the inner tools necessary to gain and maintain work? While all these explanations fell true, those teens strong in this last area almost never had a problem seeking and finding work in spite of everything else.

I became determined to find a method that concentrated on helping teens strengthen their inner tools for the betterment of their
lives—a work ethic. I suggest that urban youth workers take the following fourfold approach to implanting a solid work ethic in their
adolescents: establishing values toward self-improvement, maintaining enthusiasm, developing talents, and training youth to be entre-
preneurs.[13]

Values toward self-improvement. The appreciation for moral and
ethical values crumbles daily among city adolescents. Few teenagers
overtly call for an unwavering standard in their lives that demands
moral decision-making. With the increase in juvenile crime, America
has come to realize that even the value of human life is no longer
sacred among teenagers.

The value structure of urban teenagers has changed tremendously
in the last few years. As I interact with teenagers, I've noticed a grad-
ual hardening of their hearts toward any hope for tomorrow.
Ultimately, we will end up with teenagers who have no interest in
improving themselves, because they believe life itself has no worth.
Once youth have no care for their own lives, they will never care
about yours. This tragedy must be fought every step of the way.

The University of Michigan did a survey ranking the major influences on children in both 1950 and 1980. Listed in decreasing order
of importance, these influences were:

1950	1980
1. home	1. home
2. school	2. peers
3. church	3. television
4. peers	4. school
5. television	5. church[14]

I often joke that if this study were carried out today, the priorities
would be: peers, television, school (for mischief, not education),
home, and church. This may not be far from the truth. Values of self-
improvement must be believed by the youth worker first. You cannot
expect teenagers to want to improve themselves through work unless

they first believe that they are employable. Work is important, especially among older teens. Going too long without a job can cause teens to think of themselves as unemployable—an attitude which must be changed. The following are ten values I have observed in urban youths who have a sound personal work ethic, which I encourage all teens to follow.

- Know that the basis of finding a job is not to actually get one, but to *believe* you are qualified for employment.
- Know your uncompromising limits, the things you will not do out of respect for yourself on or for the job.
- Have an ultimate employment goal and know what you must do now to reach that goal.
- Never remain in a position that becomes immoral, oppressive, or not true to Jesus' "calling" in your life.
- There is no job that is below you, nor is there one too high for you to obtain.
- People are more important than money.
- Gain an expert understanding of your career and study it.
- Be generally cordial to others and angry at injustice.
- When unemployed, never give up seeking a job.
- Make good use of your time—always be productive.

Teenagers having these ideals a priori are often the exceptions. Most of the time it takes training, discipleship, or a job program governed by stable Christian principles to produce such young people. Use these principles to your advantage and encourage your youth group members to be concerned with their societal and economic improvement.

Maintaining enthusiasm. Youths growing up in our television-geared society expect to be entertained constantly, and will lose interest quickly if they are not. If a problem is presented, it has thirty minutes to resolve itself (as in most sitcoms) or they will lose interest in finding a solution. Such impatience will often negatively influence job finding, as jobs often take days, weeks, or months to find, and there are no quick solutions for getting them. The teenager with this quick-results mentality will often give up prematurely in a job hunt—not because there is no employment, but because the process just takes too much time.

Time and enthusiasm are directly related for urban teens in this "television society." If problems cannot be solved quickly, it is assumed they cannot be solved at all. As we all know, finding employment can take much longer than an hour. How can enthusiasm be maintained? Two important ingredients are self-entertainment and affirmation from others.

Self-entertainment, or the ability to motivate oneself out of boredom, is of primary importance. Boredom cannot be an excuse for urban youth to avoid a job search. Teach them the lesson that boredom is an inner attitude, not an external condition.

I was once in a play by Lorraine Hansberry called *A Raisin in the Sun.* During one rehearsal, the young boy actor who played my character's son had to sit out a scene for about an hour. After a little while he looked to his Godfather, who was taking custody of him, and said, "I'm bored!" His Godfather replied, "And what am I supposed to do—entertain you?" The boy responded, "OK." The Godfather, whose eyes prefixed that this would be his final statement on the matter, uttered, "You are responsible for your own entertainment and motivation. If you are bored, it is because you have decided to be boring. Don't blame anyone but yourself."

This message is appropriate for the many urban youth who fail to seek work solely because of lack of motivation. Let teens know upfront that the boredom they feel comes from within, and that they must overcome it and inspire themselves with enthusiasm for work.

Affirmation from others is also necessary to maintain enthusiasm. It is unreasonable to expect a teenager to weather a brutal job hunt without some inspiration from others. The youth worker must constantly pray for and with those young people searching for jobs. They must know that someone is behind them who will rejoice with them once a job is found. We tend to pray only for the sick and shut-ins in our youth groups; we ought also to pray for the jobless.

Throwing an "I found a job party!" is a fun thing to do during your youth group for a person who has been searching for a while and has finally found success. It's like a birthday party, complete with streamers and plenty of decorations, except the cake says, "Happy Job Day!" Such an event can be a significant encouragement and should be held for any type of job. A teen who receives such a gala for a minimum wage job will be much inspired to proceed further vocationally.

Developing talents. It is important for young people to develop their abilities into skills—the fundamental basis of any job. By focusing on skills, we make adolescents employable. Employers want experienced workers, people who do not need to be trained but who come as their own already well-developed "package."

Developing the talents of urban teenagers involves, at the minimum, the following three aspects:

UNDERSTANDING PERSONAL STRENGTHS. It is not enough to see giftedness in youths—they must also see it in themselves. Becoming good at something starts with recognizing that it is worth spending time on. The initial quest is introspective. Teenagers need to search out their own gifts. Some might have difficulty recognizing their strengths; help them by pointing out what you have noticed about their interests. If nothing else, go over the school subject they most enjoy, which will tend to be the one they most enjoy as adults.

Next, they should be challenged to harmonize these perceived strengths with their goals. For example, a youth weak in mathematical skills may want to be an engineer, not realizing that engineering is an extremely mathematical occupation. Help teens align what they see as their strengths with the talents they need for their occupational interests. This process will provide a good basis for discovering the vocations presently compatible with them. Lastly, help them name three jobs they would want to pursue.

ACCESSIBILITY TO OCCUPATIONS OF INTEREST. It is tantamount that teenagers have some access to the jobs they are interested in. Researching occupations in the library is not too far-fetched, as it will give better insight into what is involved in particular jobs, and may help teens to narrow their choices to one or two interests.

The best option is to actually visit with people working in an occupation of interest. Such experience will allow a young person to realize the hours involved in the job and the sweat and toil it might entail. Youth interested in a particular occupation need insights from those actually working in that field. I have seen many who, once they realized what was involved in a job, decided to look elsewhere. Better that they make this decision at a young age, when they are better able to explore other directions. Setting up a job visit is generally easy, requiring a few phone calls from the youth director, and transportation.

I once worked with a thirteen-year-old boy named Andrew, who, when asked about his interests, consistently said he had none. When asked what subjects he liked in school, he was never sure of anything. After some time all I could determine was that he liked food. Since this was my only lead, I questioned him further about the types of food he liked. He kept answering, "Everything." Eventually tiring of trying to guess a food he did not like, and desperate to pin him down on something, I asked, "How do you like your food prepared?" Things took off from there. Andrew went on for at least seven minutes about how he believes people "mess up" food by not preparing it correctly. I was amazed at his culinary vocabulary.

With this information, my deduction was simple. Andrew should consider entering the restaurant business or becoming a chef. I suggested the idea and got him to agree that it was one he at least liked a little.

The next day I called the Hershey Hotel, which has one of the finest restaurants in town, and arranged a kitchen visit with the head chef. When we arrived, the chef, fully arrayed in his apron and hat, took us on an extensive tour of the restaurant. For two hours, we went into freezers, looked in ovens, talked about safety regulations, cut up onions for a salad, talked to busboys, hostesses, and servers. Before we left, the chef took us into his office and told Andrew everything he needed to know about the food industry. They conversed for about twenty minutes. The chef explained the long, lonely hours involved and the training needed for every position imaginable. When all was finished, we received complementary chef hats and were on our way.

This experience changed Andrew's life tremendously. The next school year, he rearranged his junior high schedule to include home economics. He fell in love with food preparation. Job visits such as this one are crucial, as they can prevent teenagers from becoming stuck in occupations they do not like, or cement their zeal to continue doing what they love.

THE OPPORTUNITY TO VOLUNTEER. The power of volunteerism must be harnessed for the purpose of making urban youth employable. Many teens will not find work because they are either too young or lack necessary skills. Working at a fast food restaurant is acceptable. If a teenager's interest is in the medical profession, however, the skills gained there may be irrelevant at best.

Skills are acquired through work experience, and volunteerism is one way to gain that experience. Many professional organizations will not hire a fourteen-year-old to do any significant work, but they have nothing to lose by taking on a volunteer. Volunteers are free. If matters concerning teenager volunteer employment are set up well in advance, employers rarely say no. It is exciting to realize that your teens can help out (usually part-time) in a medical, law, or real estate office. The sky is the limit.

The Stephenson County Farm Bureau in Freeport, Illinois, for example, takes advantage of both youthful and elderly volunteers. With an office staff of one full-time and one part-time employee, many of the 4,700 mailings needed each year could otherwise not be done adequately and on time. This office intentionally makes use of volunteers because of the economic realities it faces.[15]

If his or her work is impressive, many large employers will often hire a teenager volunteer for a menial job. Such work is an excellent way both to teach youth basic skills and allow them to see the inner workings of their future occupations. Set up your teenagers as volunteers in their fields of interest. It will keep them off the streets, and provide them with skills and insights targeted toward their future occupational goals.

TRAINING YOUTH TO BE ENTREPRENEURS

Entrepreneurial knowledge is one of the greatest gifts that can be given to urban youth. It leads young people to consider the possibilities a positive work ethic can offer in their future. The skills they acquire will last a lifetime. Best of all, whatever success or satisfaction adolescents gain from their entrepreneurial ventures will derive solely from their own effort.

When I was twelve years old, my junior high offered a weekly workshop on aviation. Flying had always been a passion of mine, although I had never yet been off the ground. On the first day of class, the teacher announced that when the workshops ended we would go to a small airpark outside of Baltimore and put what we had learned into practice, by actually serving as copilot on a flight. The cost was ten dollars, which to me seemed more like one hundred.

I knew that my mother, who was struggling to make ends meet at the time, did not have it. My options, then, were limited—either don't go, or figure out some way to make the money. After some thought, I decided I would go around my community and raise money for the United Way Charities. My plan was to attempt to raise thirty dollars, twenty of which I would give to the United Way, and the remaining ten as pay to myself for the trip. After two weeks of knocking on doors, going almost a mile from my home, I had raised $32.67. I immediately took out my ten dollars and sent the rest to the United Way.

When the plane took off down the runway, with my hands on the controls, I knew I had done more than just raise a few dollars—I had taught myself how to survive. A few weeks later the United Way sent me a letter expressing their gratitude for my efforts. I was proud of myself and decided to go back around the community one more time, this time giving everything I raised to charity. This is basic entrepreneurship.

Principles of entrepreneurial success. My concern for entrepreneurial programs in the city is deep. Speaking with teenagers, who desperately want work but cannot find any, makes me doubly convinced that such ventures are essential for expanding their opportunities. To become an entrepreneur is to mingle with the economic system proactively—not necessarily searching for a job, but creating one.

Our economic fate often depends upon the unemployment rate. When unemployment is high, fewer jobs are available for teenagers. Entrepreneurship, on the other hand, is not deterred by high national employment, as it is concerned with creating a job for oneself out of nothing. When I wanted to fly an airplane as a youth, I was too young to be legally employed; my options were limited. Entrepreneurial options never are. I created a job for myself that employed me for the time needed to raise what was needed.

We must drive urban teenagers not only to seek employment, but to see themselves as the self-employers and employers of the future. This mentality is the heart of any entrepreneurial program. Too often, urban youth workers attempt to teach their youth the skills needed to work for someone else. Instead, we should teach them how to begin their own businesses, pharmacies, and hospitals. Entrepreneurship teaches not how to learn to fish by watching someone else; it teaches how to fish for oneself by making the rod, hook, and sinker. Then, the next person who arrives at the pond without a rod can purchase it from you. We must take full advantage of the resources available to us and assume the risk of starting basic enterprises.[16] The four basic techniques involved in teaching Christian youth entrepreneurial programs are:

Choose a product. The first step in building a business is to choose a product or service. For example, a cookie company, weekend car wash facility, T-shirt factory, card company, pizza company or bike repair shop are all doable enterprises for urban teenagers. Be sure your product will be "sellable" in the community you are working in. There is nothing worse than producing a product that no one will buy. In choosing a successful business product:

- Find out what the public wants, then produce the best of its kind.

- Advertise the product so that everyone will know it is available.
- Distribute it everywhere so that everyone can get it.
- Keep making the product better so that more people will like it.[17]

Have the young people thoroughly scrutinize their product choice before deciding to produce it. It must be tenable, given the human and economic resources available.

Teach business over trade. A graduate of Haverford College and Eastern College's MBA Program in Christian Economic Development, Mr. Frank R. Kennedy, Jr. has gained an immense amount of experience directing entrepreneurial youth programs with the National Foundation for Teaching Entrepreneurship and World Impact. Mr. Kennedy stresses the importance of teaching business over teaching a trade. In his opinion, merely teaching youths a skill is not enough—they must learn the entire business process, including production and sales.

Teaching a trade involves training youths in one particular skill, in order to produce a product that someone else will sell. Teaching business trains in both production and sales, involving teenagers in the entire process. Thus they gain not only the knowledge of how to make the product, but are forced to learn business savvy in order to sell it. Their income directly results from whatever amount can be sold above the cost of production.

Teaching a trade supplies the youth with experience in a particular field, good basic job skills, and an income.[18] This is an extremely production-oriented approach, however—one in which youths work solely in the labor segment. While production should be an important part of any entrepreneurial program, true entrepreneurship must also involve learning sales.

In the name of "getting kids off the streets," many urban entrepreneurial programs operate not as entrepreneurships, but as plantations. That is, the youth are involved only in producing the product, not selling it or making "powerful" strategic decisions concerning it. A teen has not gained the knowledge of an entrepreneur until he or she can explain every aspect of the business.

Teaching business is a much more worthy approach. It involves teenagers in both sales and production, providing the skills that will lead them into full ownership and control of the operation. In addition, learning to run a business supplies the youth with job skills applicable to any business structure, the ability to hire and fire if necessary, business literacy, knowledge and experience in trade, and an income.[19] With good training by the youth director, the teens will be able to run the program fully on their own. By doing so, teenagers are employing themselves, and have the power to employ others and influence the public with a good product.

Savings and future projection. A more difficult task for the youth director is to help teenagers make wise spending decisions. Disadvantaged youths are extremely "present-oriented" when it comes to spending their income. They live their lives for *today,* never considering whether money earned should be saved for any noble purpose. To them, money is meant to be spent immediately. In the not too out-of-the-ordinary event that an urban family wins a thousand dollars in a lottery, the entire amount will be spent within a week on items that have nothing to do with the family's social progression. We must guide city adolescents to both spend for needs and save for needs, striving to give them a "future orientation."

Edward C. Banfield has noted that the further one can realistically project oneself into the future, the more one is willing to make present sacrifices to reach future goals. Inner-city teenagers live very much in the present—they must, after all, as urbanization and poverty are extremely immediate realities. Banfield has insightfully noticed that the more present-oriented one is, the more one will use money to comfort instant demands. The future-oriented person uses monetary resources only in relation to prospective goals.[20]

Teaching economic entrepreneurship involves challenging youth toward a more future-oriented outlook. This is crucial. Teenagers will not save for college if they cannot see that far in the future. Banfield finds present-mindedness especially prevalent within the urban lower class.

The lower-class individual lives from moment to moment. If he has any awareness of a future, it is of something fixed, fated, beyond his control: things happen to him, he does not make them happen. Impulse governs his behavior, either because he cannot discipline himself to sacrifice a present for a future satisfaction or because he has no sense of the future. He is therefore radically improvident: whatever he cannot use immediately he considers valueless.[21]

Urban teens think saving money is "stupid." Initially convincing them that saving is wise can be as fun as pulling hair. I offer three suggestions for helping teenagers save money.

First, take each teen to a bank easily accessible to them and have them open a savings account. Work on a savings budget with them so they can see how much they can save over a period of time. Saving for saving's sake won't work in this context—the teen must be saving *for* something, such as a camping trip, college, Christmas presents, or a watch. Once the goal is reached, teens will see the practicality of saving, and may try it again.

Second, some teens want to learn how to save, but realize they cannot control their spending. If they agree, work out an amount that will automatically be taken from their pay, and save it for them.

Third, make saving a fun challenge. Offer to add thirty dollars to the accounts of those who successfully learn saving skills. This incentive will attract their interest. Have each youth privately tell the youth pastor the amount he or she wants to save over a six-month period and the purpose for which the money is being saved. Next, help them open an account at the local bank. After the account is opened, they are responsible for placing part of their paycheck in the bank periodically. When the six months are completed, those who have saved correctly will receive the extra monetary reward.

Keep it Christian. Christian principles must govern an entrepreneurial program. Things can quickly degenerate into a greedy enterprise in which the youth become more concerned with their profit than with producing a good product. When this attitude develops, it must be confronted immediately before it infects the group. Fair wage, charity, honesty to the customer, the use of company time, integrity of service, good bookkeeping, working together, and cleanliness of the workplace must be guiding ethics, so that the business can be a witness for Jesus Christ in the community.

TWO ENTREPRENEURIAL EXAMPLES

Steve Mariotti, the former financial analyst for Ford Motor Company and business teacher in the Bronx who is now President and founder of the National Foundation for Teaching Entrepreneurship to Handicapped and Disadvantaged Youth (NFTE) in New York City, was once mugged by a group of teenagers for a trivial amount of money. Afterward, he pondered, "Why would a group of kids go up to someone and demand five or ten dollars when that same group of kids, if they were working as a team in business, theoretically could make a lot more."[22] Thus began his quest to form NFTE.

NFTE is a large non-profit organization that specializes in teaching entrepreneurial skills to 1,300 disadvantaged or handicapped children and youth. Mariotti has set up extensive courses and curriculum that train teens in business skills. He believes that "each child has enough knowledge to begin his or her own small business."[23] "Take the business sense that inner-city kids develop on the streets or in financially stressed homes and turn it into a legal way out of poverty. 'Almost all of those that go to jail go for entrepreneurial activity that society has defined as illegal.... If you take all that energy and ability and street smarts and put them in other businesses, they could begin to accumulate capital.'"[24]

Although NFTE is not specifically a Christian organization, it is a gem of an example of what the effort of large organizations can do. NFTE tells teenagers that "it's a major error to assume that business ownership is just for white males.... It is definitely for blacks and hispanics and women and all other minorities as well."[25] This principle must be kept in mind for all youth ministry organizations or we will fail miserably.

The second entrepreneurial example is a very small cookie company in Minneapolis led by Sister Jean Thuerauf. For nine years, in a community presented with single-parent families, gangs, and drugs, Sister Jean invited children into her home to bake cookies so that they could find solace, constructive recreation and "have something to be proud of." This group of kids eventually organized into a club and decided to sell cookies to the community. The idea was a success.

According to Sister Jean, the group made over $4,000 in the first two years. In good faith, she promised that if they could reach $5,000 they would begin a cookie company. When that goal was reached, "So excited!" were the words used to describe the youngsters' jubilation. These young people, through their own will to produce a business in their community reflective of their potential, mustered the cohesive economic savvy needed for such an enterprise to take place.

At this point Sister Jean had to come through on her promise. Through prayer, word-of-mouth and five thousand dollars, she managed to acquire ten thousand dollars of baking equipment and a good building in which to maintain the business, with eight hundred dollars to spare. The Sister gleefully indicates that all this came not of her effort, but of the determination of the children involved and the hand of God. "Sister Jean's Cookies" was born. The young people took ownership in their enterprise and soon renamed it to "Our Cookie Cart."

Those near thirteen years of age are involved in production (making the cookies), while the younger kids, beginning with age seven, are involved in sales (selling the cookies). Those who wish to earn money will ask if there are positions available for the day. Each child is given four bags and receives more once they are sold. On their hour-and-a-half shifts, they receive twenty-five percent of every bag they sell, allowing them to hire others if needed. Those who work in the kitchen receive a salary for their time. Every person is expected to present themselves with discipline or be suspended.

These kids are popular in their community. Sister Jean does not call what the kids do a job, but "training." She sees the cookie company enabling young people to gain professional skills that will help them in the future. As a result, there are restaurants, delis and stores that are hiring members from this respected enterprise. "The Cookie Cart" has given this Minneapolis community more than edible morsels. It has given the neighborhood both *respect for* and *hope in* the potential of its young people.[26]

responding to
teen profanity

8

THIS CHAPTER, WHICH ADDRESSES THE TOPIC OF URBAN TEEN PROFANITY head-on, will disturb some readers. While some believe this issue is irrelevant to urban ministry, I disagree. An effective, holistic ministry in the city must ram every bastion of urban teen life it encounters with the message of Christ. Urban youth workers need a consistent opinion on profanity. Let's face it, teenagers curse like there is no tomorrow. We must challenge them to use a vocabulary worthy of the Kingdom of God. This chapter not only describes why cursing exists, but provides biblical lessons meant to lead youth in a different direction.

With respect to the reader, the harsh swearwords mentioned in this chapter will be comfortably cloaked as, for example, the B-word, the MF-word, A—hole, and the like. It is time Christian youth workers stop being embarrassed by this issue. We must grapple with profanity aggressively, so that we may save some of our teens from its influence. Until we can honestly and openly talk about this topic as a *problem,* seek solutions for the average urban youth director, and say, "This is why . . . ," we have no business asking a teen to stop cursing.

Profanity is not a new phenomenon. Its use has spanned the history of humanity and has been a vibrant part of almost every cultural group. Profanity can be both verbal and non-verbal. "The finger," for example, is often unaccompanied by words, but most people know what the gesture means. In ancient Rome, Emperor Caligula would extend his arm in obscene gestures toward those who opposed him. Even the Egyptians would carve profanities into their hieroglyphics.[1]

Curse words rotate in and out of cultural acceptance, depending on changing opinions about what is profane and what is not. During the Victorian era, *limb* and *lower extremity* were used in place of *leg*, which was considered too strong to use in public.[2] Clark Gable, in the 1939 cinema classic *Gone With the Wind*, shocked the nation with "Frankly, my dear, I don't give a d—," which was allowed "only after months of arguing, payment of a $5,000 fine by the producer, and shooting of the scene with the alternate line, 'Frankly, my dear, I don't care.'"[3] The use of profanity has expanded to such an extent, however, that in my opinion obscenity has come of age.

In some circles it is chic to curse. To business men, throwing in a "good" curse word or two during a high-powered meeting can gain respect. To lawyers, how better to sway a jury than by repeatedly making a point with a profanity? Presidents declare their patriotism with, "This is one hell of a country." Sports wouldn't be the same if the coach didn't exhort, "Now let's get out there and kick some a—."

My ultimate concern is not with the usage of these words, but with the way they are used toward others, especially when taken out of context. I have recently noticed veterinarians and farmers seeking alternate words to describe their animals' sex, because traditional ones have lost their meaning. A female dog is often described by veterinarians as a lady dog, she dog, girl dog, or mother dog, because the B-word now carries different connotations.

While taking a group of urban teenagers on a tour of an Ohio farm, the farmer began to describe the animals around us, saying, "Look, you are surrounded by animals. To your right are mules, to the left are lambs. In front of you are steers, and behind you are heifers." The group, in one voice, said "Ooooooh!" and began to laugh. One of the teens said, "He cussed!" It took four minutes for the farmer and me to explain that *heifer* is the proper English name for a female cow.

Profanity is displayed everywhere in urban America, apparently acceptable for all, and feeding off of two basic techniques: using a word out of its original context and using the thwarted meaning to dehumanize others. Walking down the street, one sees shirts for sale that say, "S— happens," "Life's a b— and then you die," or "Same s—, different day." It is no wonder, then, that a Kindergartner I once tutored would say, "Shut the f— up."

How should the Christian youth worker respond to this situation in the context of ministry? Must we simply accept cursing as a part of teenagers' daily lives? This cannot be our perspective, because if the task of the urban youth minister is to call teenagers to a personal relationship with Christ, that relationship must also extend to their mouths. Before considering responses toward profanity as it presents itself to us today, we will examine the extent of the task before us by isolating some causes and discussing specific words.

Five Causes of Urban Teen Profanity

Profanity among urban teens is a *social reality*. If you have never heard curse words, you will learn them quickly in a city. Teenagers, particularly those from lower economic circumstances, live in an environment where cursing is a normal form of expression. There is no escape from the insults and profanities thrown back and forth. The only option is to live with it and perhaps learn to swear yourself.

Eloquence in profanity will gain acclaim for teens in some groups. Street gangs are not looking to recruit spelling bee champions; they want someone who can "hold their own" in the streets. Mastering profanity is one quick way to gain a reputation, because it specializes in put-downs and "makes [teenagers] feel accepted, . . . draws attention, . . . [and] makes them seem 'tough.' "[4]

A good number of teenagers look for what I call "cuss-groups." These are small (diffuse gang structure) groups which become a type of "secret society" that gets together for the purpose of learning the practice of cursing; members simply hang out together and bat profane insults off one another. Some of these teenagers, when not with the group, may never curse at all.

Social scientists have noted that one's economic situation may be a determinant upon the frequency and manner in which one uses curse words; I see this hypothesis confirmed all the time in my travels. Both the enfranchised and disenfranchised curse. In a wealthy group of individuals, however, cursing is viewed as a sort of game. It is usually never directed at a particular person, but used only as an idle expletive to keep the conversation sparky. In an inner-city, low-cost housing development, cursing is normally directed at a specific target or the expletives are used as adjectives. Interestingly, the richer one is, the less one needs to curse. One report contends that "an improvement in the American economy and a decrease in social tensions may result in an effort to clean up the language."[5]

Cursing may often be an expression of *anger* among urban teenagers. When I ask teens why they curse, anger is the usual reason. This emotion has a way of changing a person's disposition toward another in such a way that it will result in a verbal profanity. In 1982, clinical psychologist Chaytor Mason of the University of Southern California and Harvard psychiatry lecturer Thomas Cottle noted, respectively, "Swearing is an overt action, and when under strain it releases tension." "We are frightened by things that are real and angry about things that are very, very real."[6]

Anger is a genuine emotion that arises when one feels wrongly threatened or frustrated. Clearly, one cannot deny that anger against injustice is justified in order to preserve personal dignity. However, profanity cannot be utilized as a tool of anger. In essence, part of our task involves helping teens learn how to directly face their anger without cursing. Dr. Gary Collins, author of *Christian Counseling*, describes four ways in which people react to anger:[7]

- *Withdrawal*—occurs when people do not express their true feelings and avoid a hurtful situation, ultimately gaining little improvement in their well-being. The anger remains, but is suppressed.

- *Turning inward*—results when individuals hold on to their anger for too long, and it begins to effect them either psychologically or physiologically.
- *Attacking a substitute*—the talons of anger lash out at an innocent person or object that takes the place of the actual offender.
- *Facing the sources of anger*—to accept the hurt, but to take steps to rightly rid oneself of the anger without the use of profanity. This response can be the beginning of liberation from anger.

Another reason city adolescents curse is *addiction*. A friend in California has a brother who is addicted to cursing. Whenever I visit and have a conversation, every other word is an expletive. An object cannot simply be described by the addicted person. To say "I see a cat" is not enough; the sentence must include an expletive. "I see a f—ing cat." This goes on and on, and is far from healthy.

Something about cursing allows one to become used to it. The first few times one may curse with hesitation, but if the pattern continues one will become used to the word and no longer hear its vulgarity. This is the law of diminishing returns: the more something is done, the less effective it becomes. An addiction to cursing convinces the addict that nothing is wrong—after all, they're only words. Words can have both an evil and angelic nature (JAMES 3:9–12). If we consistently say evil things, those things will become internalized into our character, making it difficult to stop (PS. 109:17–19). Cursing can become an addictive sickness and can affect many people.

The Maryland Senate Budget and Taxation Committee recognized the addictive and repulsive nature of cursing when they enacted an unofficial "cussin' tax" known as the Undeleted Expletive Revenue Enhancement Act of 1982. Delegates caught cursing during meetings had to pay a fine ranging from twenty-five cents to a dollar. Likewise, a group in Cambridge, Massachusetts decided to fight addictive cursing by founding Curseaholics Anonymous, but threw in the towel within a month because of all the "foul-mouths" on the 24-hour hotline.[8] If your youth group has teens who curse profusely, seek help for them, as their problem may involve more than just words.

A fourth observation on cursing is that it is *cultural.* Words considered unacceptable in the American context are fully normative in some other countries.[9] The F-word and the S-word are not taboo in many countries and are used much more freely. If a teenager is new to this country their normative social language, therefore, may clash as an expletive.

As an example, in England a *fag* is a cigarette, while in the United States it is a slander for a male who is gay. The American term *fanny* is highly offensive to women in New Zealand as an allusion to their "private parts." What is considered obscene, then, is in fact determined by cultural standards. What is the international youth worker to do? Are there any universal principles concerning cursing? Yes.

This chapter is most relevant to the American linguistic cultural context, as the words discussed are drawn from that frame of reference. However, there is a universal principal with which we can evaluate curse words in any culture: simply put, all language which flows from the mouth of Christians must *build up* individuals, not put them down. We have a mandate from Christ to see him in others, and respect others' self-worth in everything we say and do. Matthew 25:40 states, "I tell you the truth, whatever you did for one of the least of these my brothers of mine, you did for me." The language we use with others must be seasoned as if we were speaking to Christ himself. If we can keep close to this principle, we will have a consistent guideline against expletives for every city in the world.

The last reason for the use of profanity is a *lack of distinction between the sacred and profane.* For many teenagers, cursing has no restrictive bounds. Profanity and social vocabulary become one, neither good nor bad, and the individual no longer makes a distinction between appropriate and inappropriate language. I have taken teenagers with me on preaching or speaking engagements on many occasions, only to be forced to remind them in the midst of the service to stop cursing.

One's awareness of profanity's unacceptability begins with an awareness of God. A person without such an awareness has no genuine understanding of right and wrong. Sociologist Emile Durkheim, in his book *The Elemental Forms of the Religious Life,* observed that even the most "elemental" religious societies distinguish between the sacred and the profane.[10] I have seen many adolescents change their "bad mouth" habits simply because they were made aware that profanity is not a Godly trait.

Nasty Words

Caliban, a slave in the Shakespearian play *The Tempest,* utters "You taught me language, and my profit on't is, I know how to curse."[11] Adolescence is a time to explore the intricacies of language, a time when teenagers not only learn the language of love and friendship, but may master nasty language with meanings unfamiliar to the youth worker. The following definitions of the ten expletives heard most often from the mouths of urban teenagers are subdivided into two categories: religious profanities and four-letter words.

Religious profanities. This variety of profanity consists of those words that profane the name of God. "You shall not misuse the name of the Lord your God, for the Lord will not hold anyone guiltless who misuses his name." Exodus 20:7 states this biblical truth. Many have become desensitized to the use of God's name as a profanity. The biblical canon states quite clearly that there are spiritual consequences for failing to uphold the purity and sanctity of God's precious name.

GOD D—!

> *Base meaning:* This expression alludes to the action of God condemning another to Hell. Biblically, God the Father will administer damnation to those who do not believe in his Son, Jesus.[12]
>
> *Street meaning:* I have noted this word used in three contexts. The first is surprise. As the teen enters the room for his surprise birthday party, for example, after the shock he says, "God d—, you didn't have to do this for me." Everyone laughs. The second is disgust. A dog is brutally hit by a car, and a girl says,

"That's a god d— shame!" The third is condemnation, normally expressed as "God d— you!"

JESUS CHRIST!

Base meaning: Jesus Christ, the Son of God, Yahweh. The one of whom Isaiah spoke in chapter 9:1–7, and whom disciple Peter confessed in Mark 8:27–30. Jesus served as a propitiation for our sin, and has imputed righteousness to all who believe in him. Only through him can one receive Heaven.

Street meaning: Of two common usages, the first involves saying something angrily, "with weight behind it."[13] At a business meeting, every time an opposing viewpoint arises the meeting director yells this expletive so that others will know he has made up his mind. Secondly, the expression is used almost as a simple prayer, to calm the nerves in a shocking situation.

    Once, during a large meeting, I had to inform a young teen to call the hospital immediately, as her mother had taken ill. She looked at the ceiling and muttered wearily, "Jesus Christ!" I list this variation because it can be taken to extremes. In some Catholic and Protestant backgrounds a one or two word "quick prayer" is acceptable. However, speaking Jesus' name with no reverence or belief in his ability to fix the situation is blasphemy.

GO TO H—!

Base meaning: A command expressing the hope that one be condemned to Hell forever. Human beings can make this demand, but only God can implement it.[14]

Street meaning: This phrase often accompanies emotions of disgust, anger, and frustration. It is almost always uttered as a command, rarely a question. After I broke up a fight between two guys, they simultaneously told me to "Go to h—!," frustrated that had I stopped them. If stated as a forceful question, the expletive would be rendered as, "Would you please do me a favor and go to h—?"

The four-letter words. The following words, expletives of the highest degree in American urban youth culture, are listed in no particular order of severity. These words need to be critically observed, and the ways in which adolescents use them must be understood. I believe that profanity is an evil that defiles a teenager's inner purity. The Latin term for profanity is *profanum,* made up of *pro,* meaning "before" or "outside," and *fanum,* "temple."[15] Cursing, therefore, is an obscenity that should be kept outside the inner temple of the soul.[16]

A—HOLE

> *Base meaning:* The sphincter muscle, which controls digested intestinal bowel flows. *Ass* properly refers to a family of long-eared mammals, of which the donkey is one member. Also used profanely to signify buttocks.
>
> *Street meaning:* This word is usually used on the streets to describe a person. I've heard too many disagreements end with, "You're an a—hole!" This put-down implies that the target is nothing more than a body part that casts forth dung, and almost always causes that individual to respond in kind.

THE F-WORD

> *Base meaning:* To copulate, make love, have sexual intercourse. The F-word has been introduced into our language as a profanity, and has no neutral base meaning. The proper terms to describe the sexual act are listed above.
>
> *Street meaning:* This word is used most fluently on the streets. It is expressed in a sexual, emphatic or derogatory fashion. Driving a van full of teenagers to a sporting event, I overheard two young ladies comment on a muscle-bound man we had just passed. One said, "Yeah, baby! I want to f— him." Her comrade replied, "Me too." I immediately hollered, "What did I hear you say?" I never received a response. They got my point. I was shocked, primarily because these were two young ladies with such a vocabulary. This poem by an unknown author, "An Ode to Those Four-Letter Words," comments:

Though a lady repels your advance, she'll be kind
Just as long as you imitate what's on your mind.
You may tell her you're *hungry,* you need to be *swung,*
You may ask her *to see how your etchings are hung.*
You may mention the *ashes that need to be hauled;*
Put the lid on her sauce-pan, but don't be too bold;
For the moment you're forthright, get ready to duck—
The woman's not born yet who welcomes "Let's f—."[17]

This author obviously did not have the latter half of the twentieth century in mind.

Among young males, the F-word is used inadvertently to describe a girl as an object, in such phrases as, "She's a good f—," or "You f— them and leave them." This type of thinking is damaging because it significantly decreases the possibility of acknowledging women as anything more than sexual objects. Second, this expletive may be used for emphasis. A car dealer once told me, "Now that car over there is f—ing cheap." The third use is to abruptly end a conversation with a put-down, as in "F— you."

THE B-WORD

Base meaning: A female canine. Or, occasionally, a female canine in heat.

Street meaning: Some teenagers use this word simply to refer to any woman. Whether speaking of a girlfriend, mother, aunt, or teacher, the mental deduction is *female = b—.* It is also used for a female who is known to have sex often. Third, it is used by males only to refer to a woman who is loved "in an affectionate and admiring way."[18] A married gentleman once expressed, "Well, it's time for me to get home to my loving b—." A fourth use is as a comment on a bad predicament, as in, "Now ain't this a b—," and "Life's a b—." Lastly, if used singularly, the B-word is a pronouncement of disgust.

THE D-WORD

Base meaning: The penis. This word, which is believed to have originated as a personal name, is not proper English unless it is being used as such.[19] Even then, some audiences will consider it a "naughty word." As I was visiting a Kindergarten classroom, I noticed two boys giggling softly as the teacher began to read a Dick and Jane story book. When I asked them to pay attention, one of the two ridden with laughter commented, "She said a nasty word." These kids had somewhere heard the D-word in its profane context and associated it with the proper name.

Street meaning: Used pervertedly to represent the penis, as in the common phrase, "Suck my d—." Secondly, it is a label for someone who is "uncool." For example, "You're a d—head" or "Don't be a d—."

THE P-WORD

Base meaning: Historically referring to a female feline, this word has gained an expletive meaning synonymous with *vagina*.[20]

Street meaning: First, if used strictly, the sexual definition applies. Two pre-teens standing on a bus corner were overheard singing, to the tune of "Frère Jacque:"

> We want p—,
> We want p—,
> Yes, we do.
> Yes, we do.
> In and out and then some,
> In and out and then some,
> The baby's not mine.
> The baby's not mine.

The secondary usage is as an insult to a male friend or enemy which implies that he is feminine, as in "You're a p—." Finally, this word is used to describe a gay male.

The MF-word

> *Base Meaning:* Someone who commits incest with his or her mother. This type of act violates the incest taboo present in almost all societies, which strictly prohibits sexual relations within the nuclear family unit.[21] The term first appeared in *print* in the 1960s, but seems to have originated in the African-American community around 1930.[22] It is hardly ever taken literally.
>
> *Street Meaning:* One use arises as part of an angry question. "Who is the MF-er who spilled my drink?" Second, the word is used as a description for close and sincere friends. A street gang member once said, "These MF-ers have been with me through thick and thin." A third way to use the MF-word is as a singular exclamation, to denote surprise or a demand.

The S-word

> *Base Meaning:* Excrement, defecation, dung. This word has existed in various forms since before 1000 A.D.[23] In the American context, it is not proper English.
>
> *Street meaning:* First, it can be uttered as an exclamation. Second, it can indicate active disgust in a present circumstance, most often expressed as, "I'm sick of this s——." Lastly, this word can be used by an individual to describe his or her feelings. "I feel like s——" is a popular phrase. I once received a letter that read, "...the majority of the time I feel shut up in a box and s—— upon."[24]

How is the Youth Worker to Respond?

Contemporary urban youth workers must be equipped to respond to the use of profanity. This task should not be taken lightly—if our campaign is to turn teenagers' minds "on" for Jesus, the same must be done with their mouths. Three types of responses will be considered: personal, policy, and biblical.

Personal responses. The conduct of some Christian youth workers concerning profanity is atrocious. On one hand are youth workers who curse as much as the teens they are attempting to correct; on the other are those who pretend they do not hear vulgarity. Both are equally hypocritical, and both must be corrected.

For many adolescents, profanity is a social activity. Offenders do not always know they are offending you—they may actually think you are entertained by profanity. Many people must get the message from the way you react to them verbally and non-verbally. Four different personal responses are appropriate.[25]

- *Awkward delayed response.* Some teens will get the message that cursing is not welcomed in your presence simply by a delayed response. Social conversations are based on dialogue; that is, each person involved must build upon what has already been said. If your conversational partner uses a four-letter word, breaking the rhythm of the conversation by remaining silent for a few seconds can express your thoughts most effectively.
- *Body language.* Visibly wincing can cause a young person to realize that you do not accept their language. You may choose to shake your head, frown, make a noise, or look away. Others may immediately end the conversation. A family member of mine will make an audible "Uhh!" when someone uses displeasing language near her. I cannot recount the number of apologies she has received.
- *Satire.* A humorous approach may be easier for some teenagers to swallow. The purpose is to not embarrass them, but to put them in their place gently. One woman, responding to another's repeatedly profane choice of words, chided, "Now I know what I'm going to get you for Christmas—a thesaurus, so you won't have to use that word anymore."[26] A light touch can work wonders.
- *Speaking up.* This most direct method leaves nothing to the other's imagination. For youth, I find this to be the best approach. They know exactly where you are coming from and

where you stand. A simple phrase like, "I would appreciate it if you would not curse around me," can do the trick. If their behavior persists, you will need to be more forceful. I have a friend who says, "Curse again and I'll walk away." He has done so on many occasions.

Policy responses. The youth group should be a "sacred" place. Some adolescents have difficulty distinguishing between the street and the youth group. It should be clear that these two environments have completely different standards of behavior. A sign hung on the meeting place door, such as NO CURSING BEYOND THIS POINT, sends an explicit message to all who enter. Draw up a policy with your youth. We need not only be concerned with preventing physical fights, but verbal ones as well. Here are three fun suggestions:

ACTIVITY ONE: THE CUSS POLICY. If you are serious about taking a stand against profanity, implement a policy the whole group agrees upon. Be up-front with your teens, and present this as a very serious issue. Let them know that cursing is not a Christian trait, and that it therefore has no place in the youth meeting.

Next, break them into small groups (ideally four to a group, and never more than six). Give each group a sheet of paper and writing utensil. Their task is to come up with a "Cursing Constitution," which will include three sections:

- Definition of cursing—which words constitute curse words. For example, one group decided that *hell* and *damn* were not curse words.
- The consequences for cursing—a systematic plan for punishing first-time and multiple offenders.
- Redemption from cursing—the conditions to be met in order for a person to return to the group.

Discussion should last twenty-five minutes. Once finished, have each group report their decisions and write them down on poster board. Begin a discussion that will pull together similarities the whole group can agree upon. Once a general consensus has been reached, have a vote and accept this new constitution. Don't worry if it isn't as conservative as you wish. As the year progresses, you may come back to it and amend it. This is a wonderful, non-imposed model that will give you something to fall back upon.

One evening after senior high youth group, I was driving a van-load of teenagers back to their neighborhood when I heard one of the guys use the F-word. Knowing that these teens knew the rules on profanity, I confronted him promptly. "Brahim, please do not curse. There will be no profanity in or out of this van." He then said to me, "F— you, b—."

My response was calm but firm: "Who do you think you are? You will not curse in this van and remain in this van." Brahim was very angry by now, primarily because I was correcting him in front of his friends. He retorted, "F— you, MF-er! I don't need this s—!" I gently pulled the van off the road and said loudly, "Then you do not need this van. Get out!"

Brahim lambasted me with every expletive he knew for the next minute. Not taking me seriously, he remained in the van. I turned off the van and pronounced, "Anyone who chooses to curse tonight may walk home with Brahim. This van is not moving until he at least has removed his body." I then pretended to rest my eyes, knowing that the power of peer pressure would soon resolve this situation. Before long, other teens needing to get home asked him to leave. After about five minutes Brahim and two others finally left, swearing all the way.

As we pulled off, I drove up next to the boys and called Brahim to the van. When he came to my window I said, "You know the rules. Cursing pleases neither Jesus nor me. When you calm down and can give me ten reasons why I should not allow cursing, give me a call." The following day Brahim called me with seventeen reasons.

ACTIVITY TWO: THE CUSS SESSION. There are some teenagers who use curse words without knowing anything about their actual meanings. Some youths, if asked what the B-word means, would genuinely believe that it is slang for a female. This activity enhances teens' understanding of what various expletives really mean and the correct context for their use.

During an hour-long session, go over every one of the words dealt with in this chapter, adding more if necessary. Be bold. In this context, use the expletive as you are explaining its correct usage and how it should not be used. Trust me, you will gain everyone's attention simply by using these words.

With the knowledge of their correct usage, encourage youths never to use these words out of original context and to use them skillfully in context. It is time for the urban youth worker to fight profanity face-to-face, in order to save teens from misguided misusage.

ACTIVITY THREE: THE CUSS TRANSFER. This game must follow a discussion of profanity, which should include mention of how anger causes many of us to say words that harm. Tell your teens that the following activity will be an attempt to come up with new words, so that our anger can be transferred without cursing. Now the fun begins.

This activity works best with groups of seven. Make flash cards with all the expletives, but with missing letters. For example: S _ _ _, F _ _ _, _ O T H _ R F _ _ _ E _. The group which can create the most non-curse words in six minutes from the cards given is the winner. To make it a real challenge, offer an exciting prize. Repeat the process if necessary. Finally, close this activity by stating that it takes tough thought to correct cursing habits. But it can be done with the help of others.

Biblical responses. More than anything else, we must understand the Bible's response to profanity. God's word is to be "a lamp for our feet and a light for our path" (PS. 119:105). Six biblical passages that have been helpful in my ministry are provided for your use, along with my notations.

BLASPHEMING GOD'S NAME

Now the son of an Israelite mother and an Egyptian father went out among the Israelites, and a fight broke out in the camp between him and an Israelite. The son of the Israelite woman blasphemed the Name with a curse; so they brought him to Moses. (His mother's name was Shelomith, the daughter of Dibri the Danite.) They put him in custody until the will of the Lord should be made clear to them.

Then the Lord said to Moses: "Take the blasphemer outside the camp. All those who heard him are to lay their hands on his head, and the entire assembly is to stone him. Say to the Israelites: *'If anyone curses his God, he will be held responsible;* anyone who blasphemes the name of the Lord must be put to death. The entire assembly must stone him. Whether an alien or native-born, when he blasphemes the Name, he must be put to death.'"

Leviticus 24:10–16

There are six lessons to be learned from this passage. First, the sin committed was using God's name blasphemously. To use God's name out of a holy context is sinful. Modern examples are God d—, Jesus Christ! and the like.

Second, notice that the blasphemer was not a full Israelite—he was half Egyptian. There will be teens in our youth groups who are not full members. That is, in many inner-city youth groups some teens will come because they enjoy the fellowship of the group, but will not fully accept the rules of the group.

Third, this fight broke out when God's name was taken in vain, and one of the Israelites took offense at having God's name slandered. Every teen in the group should likewise be willing to confront anyone who does the same.

Fourth, Moses could not initially deliver a verdict on this situation because there was no immediate rule available for someone not fully Israelite.[27] Let this be a lesson to the youth worker: never be caught without a rule. The most difficult situations to resolve are those for which an applicable rule does not already exist.

Fifth, all those who heard the young man blaspheme had to bear testimony by laying hands on him. Similarly, teenagers are to be encouraged to report the use of profanity by others. This is easier said than done, but if your group is to take this problem seriously, every youth must be a part of the process. The youth worker ought never be the Grand Inquisitor, always looking for wrong; everyone is a marshal of the rules.

Last, the penalty was stoning, and was applicable to both Israelites and non-Israelites. Profanity is so negative that the rules we establish for it must apply to both members and visitors.

PROFANITY AS A CONSEQUENCE OF THOUGHTLESS OATHS

> ...if a person *thoughtlessly* takes an oath to do anything, whether good or evil—in any matter one might carelessly swear about—even though he is unaware of it, in any case when he learns of it he will be guilty.
>
> Leviticus 5:4-5

There are many decisions we must make in life. The ones that cause us the most grief are those we make thoughtlessly. This scripture suggests that bad decisions can cause one to "carelessly swear." We have an obligation, therefore, to think through decisions thoroughly in order to give full respect to the issue at hand.

Secondly, notice the words "good or evil." Even if the decision is a good one, "guilty" remains the verdict for not having given the issue thought. Teens often make split-second decisions that can land them in *big trouble*. Whether or not a decision comes back to haunt us, our sin is that of omission.

Sin is committed in three fashions: "where intentionality cannot possibly be involved;...where intentionality may or may not be involved; and...where intentionality must be involved."[28] Although we may never utter an expletive, the rash and hasteful decisions we make condemn us as if we had.

PROFANITY INTERNALIZED

> He loved to pronounce a curse—
> may it come on him;

he found no pleasure in blessing—
    may it be far from him.
He wore cursing as his garment;
    it entered into his body like water,
    into his bones like oil.
May it be like a cloak wrapped about him,
    like a belt tied forever around him.

Psalm 109:17–19

Three messages are presented here. First, this is a description of people who allow cursing to become their lifestyle, wearing it as a garment. They deliberately cloak themselves with cursing and injure others verbally, which ultimately works to their own destruction.

Second, profanity soaks the souls and characters of people, entering into them and rendering them addicted and in need of detoxification. Urban youth need to notice this truth: cursing can and will affect the individual using it, either by uncomfortableness (in the virgin profanity user), or by immunity (in the veteran).

Third, the clothing of cursing is extremely difficult to remove once donned; it gets heavier with every profane word. Therefore, it takes the help of others to remove it.

BEING DISTURBED BY PROFANITY

Whoso is *partner* with a thief hateth his own soul:
    he heareth cursing, and bewrayeth it not.

Proverbs 29:24 (KJV)[29]

I intentionally avoid reading into this passage more than is here. There is one simple message I derive from it: we must be disturbed by the profanity of others and discover tactics to confront it. If cursing is heard, we must reject it unequivocally.

TAMING THE TONGUE

Likewise the tongue is a small part of the body, but it makes great boasts. Consider what a great forest is set on fire by a small spark. The tongue also is a fire, a world of evil among the parts of the body. *It corrupts the whole person,* sets the whole course of his life on fire, and is itself set on fire by hell.

All kinds of animals, birds, reptiles and creatures of the sea are being tamed and have been tamed by man, but no man can tame the tongue. It is a restless evil, full of deadly poison.

With the tongue we praise our Lord and Father, and with it we curse men, *who have been made in God's likeness.* Out of the same mouth comes praise and cursing. My brothers, this should not be.

James 3:5–10

Three messages are pertinent: first, to tame the tongue is to control a fire that can consume the entire person. What we say to people can destroy them; worse, it destroys us. Controlling the profane tongue can be more of a task than the user bargained for.

Second, the tongue has the ability to both bless and curse. It can promote the Kingdom of God or disgrace it. Teens must be challenged to realize that the words they speak must be selectively chosen for the blessing of others.

Lastly, to profane others is to disrespect those "who have been made in God's likeness." God has created every person, including those who anger and disgust us. To use bad language is to dehumanize people and consider them objects, rather than precious pottery made by the hand of God.

REMAINING PURE AROUND PROFANITY

What goes into a man's mouth does not make him "unclean," but what comes out of his mouth, that is what makes him "unclean."

Don't you see that whatever enters the mouth goes into the stomach and then out of the body? *But the things that come out of the mouth come from the heart,* and these make a man "unclean." For out of the heart come evil thoughts, murder, adultery, sexual immorality, theft, false testimony, slander. These are what make a man "unclean."

Matthew 15:11, 17–20a

Urban teens live in an environment inundated with profanity. It is inescapable, but it by itself does not make these young people "unclean." Some Christian teenagers live in highly expletive households, where *not* using bad language is abnormal. On many occasions I have been confronted by this problem, and this scripture is my solution. With Jesus Christ guiding one's life, an environment seething with profanity can be digested without harm to the individual. Evil words simply pass through.

Second, the source of "uncleanliness" is the heart. All inner expressions come not from our thoughts, but from the emotions generated deep within our hearts. It is thought which puts the brakes on negative emotion toward others before it reaches our mouths. Ultimately, if one's heart is pure, language will follow suit.

May this chapter be a blessing to all who read it, and make a significant contribution to a topic that has taken a back burner for entirely too long. Get over the embarrassment quickly, and learn to openly discuss the moral, social, psychological, and spiritual dangers of expletives with urban youth. Have courage and faint not.

helping adolescents
confront cultic religions

9

THE CITY OFFERS A PLETHORA OF RELIGIOUS INFLUENCES. WHEN I HEAR
others proclaim that the urban metropolis is devoid of religion, I
often ask, "What planet are you thinking of?" In truth, there are
many religious groups competing for the souls of urban teens in
every major city in this nation: the Nation of Islam, Jehovah's
Witnesses, Orthodox Islam, Mormons, and the New Age movement
are just a few. Although such influences are abundant, urban youth
ministry must come to grips with the painful truth that the Christian
presence in the city is often anemic.

Religious counseling of adolescents has become difficult; you
spend half your time sorting through thwarted religious beliefs and
the other half redefining religious language. Simply asking, "Do you
believe in God?" can bring to mind an impersonal Karma, a fleshly
being, a ghost, a state of oneness with the universe—a whole host of
possibilities. Urban teenagers' minds have become intensely polluted
with false religious constructions having little or nothing to do with
the Christian message. We discover that even the name of Jesus has
become soiled as we search for definitions free from cultic tampering.

A large senior high group I once led became an unbelievable pro-
gramming challenge because its members fell into five belief categories: Christian, Black Muslim, Mormon, Jehovah's Witness, and
agnostic. When pressed, all of them believed in a God—they just

didn't know which One to follow. I would often ask these youths, "Why do you come to this Christian youth group?" They would consistently answer, "Because Jesus is my Savior too."

In urban America, Christ is proclaimed in many forms. To the Muslim he is a great prophet. To the Mormon he is a Son of God. To the Jehovah's Witness he is God's first begotten. The agnostics tend to believe in Jesus as a historical figure. Simply stating the name "Jesus" is not enough in the urban context, as there are too many conflicting definitions. To reach urban teens effectively, I have had to specifically define what that name means, become overtly evangelical in my message, and proclaim that Jesus must become *Lord* of their lives.[1]

Urban youth ministers need to equip their teenagers to filter through the many cultic religious groups active in the city. Until we do so, we risk losing our teens to non-Christian religious assemblies merely cloaked in the garments of Christianity. We must not be ignorant about the cultic groups that target our youths, but must strive to identify, understand, and respond to them, training our youth groups to fight a deceiving Satan appealingly disguised in religious form.

INDICATORS OF A CULTIC GROUP

A cult is any religious or political sect that perpetuates a religious message opposed to the inerrant teachings of the Biblical canon, and which denies the *triune* nature of God and the *deity* of Jesus the Christ. Some urban Christian youths who stumble into opposing religious groups do not recognize them as such until they are too far involved. Most interestingly, a great number of popular cults have specialized in cloaking themselves as forms of Christianity, making it difficult for even the most perceptive to determine whether or not a particular religious sect is cultic.

Urban adolescents need pragmatic criteria for accurately judging and dismantling a cult's biblical and theological belief system. In their exceptional booklet *Why Mormonism is a Cult,* former Mormon Robert A. McKay and the founder of Utah Missions John L. Smith provide thirteen thorough criteria with which to identify and disarm cults.[2]

FAULTY INTERPRETATION OF BIBLICAL MATERIAL. Cults specialize in misinterpreting scripture, and city teens untrained in theology may have difficulty discerning whether or not a particular group is a cult. Historically, there has been polemic discussion among Christians about proper biblical hermeneutics (methodological principles of interpretation). Martin Luther's *sola scriptura* ("scripture only") proclaimed for Protestants the right to go directly to the scriptures and allow the Holy Spirit to direct in understanding God's word. Experience has taught, however, that independent contemplation on the scriptures can be dangerous for a teenager who does not understand how to weigh theological viewpoints against established orthodoxy.

For many Roman Catholic congregations, scriptural interpretation focuses more upon the Church's traditional, historical views on biblical material, as a precaution against those who may choose to mislead others with false interpretations. When dealing with cultic interpretation of the Scriptures, this method may prove extremely helpful.

QUESTIONING BIBLICAL AUTHORITY. Whenever the authoritative nature of the Bible as a guide for the Christian faith is called into question, the questioner must be questioned in turn. Opposing religions tend to view scriptural material as old-fashioned or incomplete. The Bible is true in all it teaches and is inerrant as a tool for perfecting and instructing the children of God. Jesus himself defended the authority of the scriptures, stating that not even the smallest letter or least stroke of a pen is insignificant (MATT. 5:18). The Holy Bible "is God-breathed and is useful for teaching, rebuking, correcting and training in righteousness, so that the children of God may be thoroughly equipped for every good work" (2 TIM. 3:17). The Bible alone is worthy of superior authority.

ADDING EXTRA-BIBLICAL SCRIPTURE. Not only do cults claim that the Bible is insufficient to direct the affairs of faith, they offer supplementary texts that supercede the Biblical canon, along with one of several possible justifications:

- The Bible is outdated, and should be discarded entirely.
- The Bible is a holy book but is incomplete without additional texts.
- The Bible is holy but is subservient to greater cultic works.

The Christian faith has consistently held the Bible to be the sole basis of instruction, and any group that insists otherwise is not Christian. No other text is needed or wanted.

THEIR GOD IS NOT THE GOD OF THE BIBLE. Instruct your youth group that any God spoken of in a cult is not Yahweh (the God of the Bible), but is a false God that does not inhabit salvation. The God of Christianity is triune (Father, Son, and Holy Ghost), meaning God *in* three persons, not God *as* three persons. Omnipotence, omniscience and omnipresence are his attributes. Love and justice are his primary concerns, and goodness and mercy fill his character.

THEIR JESUS IS CONTRARY TO SCRIPTURE. Jesus is the Son of God, who shares his essence in God and is God. His death on the cross propitiated for the sins of those who believe on him. "For God so loved the world that he gave us his only son Jesus Christ, that whoever believes in him will not perish but have everlasting life. He has come not to condemn the world, but that the world through him might be saved" (JOHN 3:16–17). Jesus Christ did not remain in his grave, but was resurrected with all authority.

The Jesus described by many cult groups is anything but the Christ. Opposing religious groups do not accept Christ's divinity. To some, Jesus is considered a mere mortal man, while others portray him as the first of all God-types. Beware of such sects which trade the lordship of Christ for the lordship of mankind (MATT. 24:24, 2 COR. 11:4).

THEOLOGICAL CONTRADICTIONS. Orthodoxy is a great thing. It allows us to digest the theological worthiness of religious ideas while spitting out the bones of contradictions. Youth ministry is obligated to become keenly aware of its own biblical theology, so that impostors can be quickly exposed and dismantled (GAL. 1:6–10). Familiarize your youth group members with the following procedure for when they are unsure if a particular religious group is cultic.

- Do not accept membership instantly, even if pressured. Tell the recruiters you will get back to them if you decide to join.
- Gather as much paraphernalia as possible. Get any brochures that are available. Get the address and phone number of the primary meeting place and determine the city and state of the group's headquarters.
- Ask questions like these and note the responses:
  —Is the Christian Holy Bible all that is needed to come to God?
  —Is the trinity real? Explain.
  —Describe the purpose and nature of Jesus Christ.
  —Where is Jesus now?
  —What does your group say will happen to me when I die?
  —Do God or his angels have names?
  —Name any great prophets since Jesus whom your religious group considers great men or women.
- Take the information you have gathered to a qualified person to verify the theological validity of the group and determine whether or not it is a cult. A parent, youth pastor or qualified adult should do this for the teen and give a researched response.

THE HEAD OF THE ORGANIZATION IS THE MEDIATOR TO GOD. One sure giveaway of a cultic religion is the requirement of total devotion to a mother organization, committee, or charismatic leader in order to be blessed by God. There is no human enterprise capable of representing us before God. However, we do not stand alone, "for there is one God and one mediator between God and men, the man Christ Jesus, who gave himself as a ransom for all men" (I TIM. 2:5–6).

CLAIMING TO ANSWER ALL RELIGIOUS QUESTIONS. Christians realize that all the questions of life cannot be fully answered, but serve a God who knows those answers. There is a definite ambiguity that goes with the religious life, and a great number of cults will thrive on that religious insecurity by claiming to answer all the questions of life. Some dispel the need to know what God is like by describing him as a bodily, fleshy person, while others assure that if people are in harmony with themselves they can control their inner and outer universes. These beliefs may offer temporary peace from anxiety, but ultimately will provide only a band-aid for spiritual sterility.

ATTACKING CHRISTIANITY. Although this trait is obvious, it must be stated. Any religious group that assaults Christianity does not see it as commendable of worship and must be blatantly rejected. Be cautious, however, as some opposing religious associations will claim to be Christian, but will declare the Church useless. To attack the Church is to attack Christianity. When Christ returns, he is coming for his Church—the body of Christ. It is one thing to seek to incite the Christian body into living up to what Jesus wants of it; it is another to abandon it as a hopeless case for spiritual resuscitation.

SAYING ONE THING IN PUBLIC AND ANOTHER IN PRIVATE. Whenever cultists attempt to recruit someone, they present their group's message in terms even your grandmother would find reasonable. One tends to believe this wonderful story, and thereby become disarmed of any damaging questions. The goal of the Christian teen is to avoid taking what is being said at face value, and to force recruiters to reveal the inner workings of their cult. Recruiters attempt to define a "common ground," in the hope that you will ask questions pertaining only to what they have described. To get to the heart of any recruitment attempt, never ask questions concerning the public traits of the religious organization. Your concern is with its private nature. (See the previous page for starter questions).

DOCTRINES ARE SUBJECT TO CHANGE. Religious cults are constantly in doctrinal flux, as their dogmas are both created and rehashed over time. Doctrines inerrantly true one day are subject to "new revelation" on another. Many doctrinal changes may not even be known to the followers, unless they are particularly perceptive in their understanding of their religious group.

FALSE PROPHESYING. Some cultic groups crucify themselves by offering false prophesy concerning the future; we can recognize them as cults from this characteristic (DEUT. 18:20–22, MATT. 7:15–20). As only a healthy tree can bear nourishing fruit, an infirm tree will bring

forth substandard fruit. Watch out for those groups that sensational-
ize apocalyptic material and claim to be able to predict the end of
times. The Bible is clear that the end will not be revealed to anyone
before it happens, but will come as a thief in the night. So we must
live a life that is watchful, but not predictive, preparing ourselves and
others for the unknown coming-time of Christ (MATT. 24:36–51).

CLAIMING EXCLUSIVE ACCESS TO GOD. Many cultic associations
believe that the essence of God can only be found or recognized
within their group, and that, therefore, no one can know God without them. Although Christians hold this same line, we do not and
cannot limit God's actions. God is sovereign and can reveal himself
to anyone—whenever and wherever he wills, even if outside the
boundaries of the Christian faith.

REACHING OUT TO CULTIC TEENS

Reverend Lester Porter of the Church Without Walls Ministry of
Philadelphia has worked hard to provide a method of sensitive outreach toward urban non-Christian religions which is bathed in the
activity of the Holy Spirit. This ministry hopes to reach out to those
outside the "normal walls" of Christendom and extend a biblical
method to those who would not normally consider Christianity. As
Porter explains, compassionate evangelism with adolescents in opposing religious groups entails:

SEEING THE TEEN FIRST AS A PERSON. When evangelizing, be aware
that you are ministering to a real person. Do not talk to youths as a
salesperson would a potential client. Jesus is not a product to be
bought and sold—he is a Savior who wants to be experienced. A
good sales job might get someone interested, but it will not save their
soul.

MEETING FOR BETTER UNDERSTANDING. The first step is to establish a
friendship with the adolescent, so that you both may understand
each other's religious position. A common understanding allows both
adolescent and youth worker to become sensitive to the other's perspective. The youth worker will then genuinely care about the

religious growth of his or her teens and rejoice with them if they decide to convert.

COMMUNICATING CHRIST'S DEITY. Jesus is not only the Son of God, he *is* God. Many cultic groups train their converts to reject Christianity as a religion that deifies a mere man. They also explain Christ as a god which all good people can become. Neither of these representations are the biblical Christ. Jesus was neither created nor promoted to God—he has always been and will always remain God. The divinity of Jesus Christ is both incomprehensible and immutable.

RECOGNIZING THE MINISTRY OF THE HOLY SPIRIT. Conversion is not a human act, but comes by way of the Holy Spirit's movement upon the hearts of those whom he has readied to his infilling. Do not rush a conversion. If it is to happen, it will happen when God is ready. It is a spiritual injustice to force someone to accept Christ. In God's providence, he orchestrates how those whom he has prepared will come to know him. Youth ministers are an instrument of this process. Some plant the seeds of the gospel message, others water it so that it may begin to germinate in a teen's heart—but it is God who does the converting.[3]

PUTTING THE CONVERT INTO IMMEDIATE SERVICE. Satan will seek to destroy the commitment of teenagers who have given their lives to Jesus Christ (particularly those coming out of cultic backgrounds). Every new convert must have an adequate avenue through which to encourage others to Christ, as they were. The Jehovah's Witnesses and Mormons have long recognized that the best person to convert is a convert. Get freshly-converted teens involved in a youth group or Christian activity that will put them on the front lines. A real commitment means real action.[4]

THE URBAN "BIG FOUR"

There are too many cults and opposing sectarian religious groups contending for the souls of urban teens than could possibly be accounted for in one chapter. The following four, however, are the most prevalent and pose the greatest difficulty to the Christian urban youth worker in this nation and throughout the world.

Orthodox Islam. The Islamic faith, with over 850 million members, is the second-largest religion in the world. Two out of every eleven people in the world are constituents of Islam. Europe alone boasts six million Muslims in western Europe and one million in Britain.[5] The Islamic population in the United States has grown to six million members,[6] with an estimated additional 77,000 Muslim foreign students in this country.[7] Islam is ubiquitous in America—particularly in urban areas, where growth has been phenomenal. In 1989, there were 536 mosques around the nation, with New York, Los Angeles, Chicago, Detroit, and Toledo, Ohio being the greatest strongholds. In 1953, New York State had only three mosques; by 1989 there were 112.[8]

Interestingly, the American Muslim population is one-sixth African-American.[9] As youth workers face the city, it is a given that they will come in frequent contact with African-American teenagers who profess Islam. Youths who embrace orthodox Islam rarely do so by choice; more often, they are indoctrinated by a unified family effort. Therefore, they will tend to completely reject anything that has do with a Christian youth group because of parental influence. Teens who will be swayed will more than likely be older adolescents.

HISTORICAL BIOGRAPHY. The word *Islam* means "submission" in Arabic, and a *Muslim* is one who submits to God's will.[10] To comprehend this concept is to understand the nucleus of all Islamic nature. Submission to personal wants and desires in order to please God is the goal of every true Muslim. In fact, Islam recognizes only two types of people: those who have submitted, *Dar ul-Islam,* and those who resist, *Dar ul-harb.*[11]

Ubu'l-Kassim, who became known as Muhammad ("the praised one"), is believed to have been born in the year 570 A. D.[12] His father, Abdullah, died before he was born, and his mother, Amina, passed when he was six. His grandfather, whom he had grown to love, died when he was eight. By this time, he had learned much about surviving the transitory nature of life. Shortly thereafter, he fell under the care of his uncle Abu Talib, where he matured and became a trader and camel rider in a caravan. Travelling with his uncle, he had many opportunities to converse with Jews and Christians and sought to understand their beliefs.

In 595 A. D., at age twenty-five, Muhammad married a rich widow named Khadijah, who was initially his employer. She was fifteen years his elder. The marriage proved to be a happy and fruitful one, producing six children. The pivotal event for Muhammad came in the year 610, when he reportedly received, at the age of forty, his first revelation in a cave on Mount Hira from the angel he identified as Gabriel. His experience is recorded in Surah (chapter) 96 of the Qur'an.[13] "Read [or proclaim] in the name of your Lord who created . . . man from a clot [of blood]," were the first words Muhammad heard.[14] Frightened, he obeyed these words and record-ed most of what he heard in the Qur'an, which means "recitation."[15]

The twenty-two years which remained of his life were spent build-ing the foundation of Islam for Allah. His message gained vast support throughout Mecca, although persecution drove him to Medina. After three major *jihad* ("holy war") battles, he was finally allowed a peace-ful truce which granted him safe return to Mecca. By Muhammad's death in 632 A. D., Islam had become the foremost religious force on the Arabian peninsula, challenging both Christianity and Judaism.[16]

MAJOR CULTIC DOCTRINES. Christians and Muslims have one com-monality—Abraham. We both look to him as the father of our covenants with God. God's covenant with Abraham was that he would be the father of a great nation that would bless all the peoples of the earth, a nation no one could number.[17] The account in Genesis 16 and 17 tells us Abraham fathered two sons, Ishmael and Isaac. As Abraham and Sarah were advanced in age, the couple ques-tioned whether they would succeed in bringing forth a child as God had promised. Sarah then encouraged Abraham to fulfill this promise with their Egyptian maidservant Hagar; she had a son named Ishmael. When Sarah was ninety and her husband ninety-nine, God announced that Sarah would have a child, Isaac, and that he would be the one through which God's covenant would be fulfilled.

This is the point where Muslims and Christians differ. Muslims believe that God established his covenant through Ishmael, and that it was him Abraham placed on the altar at Mt. Moriah, not Isaac.[18] The biblical account affirms that Abraham also hoped for Ishmael's seed to be increased (GEN. 17:19–22). God promised to greatly increase Ishmael's numbers but determined that Ishmael would be "a wild donkey of a man; his hand will be against everyone and everyone's hand against him, and he will live in hostility toward all his brothers" (GEN. 16:11–12).[19] In other words, the descendant of Ishmael (Islam) is a wayward *brother* who needs guidance back to the God of his salvation.

Every urban youth pastor should be familiar with the "five pillars" of Islamic faith, the second major doctrine to which every true Muslim must subscribe.

- All believing members are required to recite the declaration of *As-Shahada*, "there is no God but Allah and Muhammad is his prophet," in front of a judge or two members in order to become a member of the Islamic faith.

- The *Salat* is a prayer toward Mecca which is mandated five times a day: morning, noon, late afternoon, sunset, and bedtime. The prayer is often preceded by the ritual washing of hands, performed methodically with the head pressed to the ground. With time, a noticeable dark spot *(sudjda)* can form on the forehead from the continual pressing of the head to the ground.[20]

- The *Zakat* or tithe for the welfare of the poor is to be one-fortieth of one's income.

- Fasting *(Swam)* during the month of Ramadan is required, commemorating the month Gabriel reportedly came to Muhammad. Ramadan is the ninth month of the Islamic calendar. All those who are able-bodied must not eat or drink from sunrise until sunset. This practice demands a great deal of discipline, which is the overall goal.

- The *Hajj,* or pilgrimage to Mecca, is the journey every capable Muslim must attempt to make once in his or her lifetime. Tradition says every step taken toward Mecca will wipe out a sin. Believers are to come to the *Ka'ba,* which is a building housing a black stone (probably a meteorite) that every person who can get close enough must kiss. It is believed that this stone was white when Gabriel carried it to earth during Adam's time, but because of sin it has become black.[21]

Finally, the theological Islamic doctrines of God, the Christian Bible, Christ, and the trinity must all be understood to adequately indict Islam as a religion opposing the Christian faith. The Arabic word for God is Allah—a neutral term which Muslims use to express their belief in God. To Islam, Allah represents pure justice which must be strictly submitted to. His attributes can never be directly experienced in the human heart. "For God so loved the world, that he gave his only son . . ." (JOHN 3:16) is a foreign concept to the Muslim, for whom God is completely unapproachable in his holiness. The Muslim is never sure of forgiveness. Reaching heaven is an *act* of complete submission for those who love God, instead of the extended *grace* of a loving God concerned about humanity.[22]

The Christian Bible is respected among Muslims, but is considered incomplete without the Qur'an, which is God's final revelation given to Muhammad. Some Muslims will refer to the Bible as corrupt, arguing that it has textual errors and has been tampered with. The Qur'an itself condemns them by declaring Allah responsible for giving the Christians and the Jews their holy book, which no man can alter (SURAH 5:47, 6:34, 45, 92, 10:65, 32:24).[23]

To the Islamic faith, Jesus Christ was a great prophet but is not the Son of God. For anyone to claim equality with God is blasphemy. Although Christ is mentioned in the Qur'an as the Messiah, the Word of God, the Apostle of God, and his Spirit, he is never *deified.*[24] It is also believed that Christ was not crucified, but was taken up into heaven by Allah before the events of the cross. Jesus, as a mere man, could not possibly die for the sins of the entire world. As a prophet of God's word, Allah did not permit him to die directly; instead, a "likeness" of Jesus was executed on the cross. Surah 4:57, 158 explains:

> And their saying: Surely we have killed the Messiah, Isa [Jesus] son of Marium [Mary], the apostle of Allah [God]; and they did not kill him nor did they crucify him, but it appeared to them so [like Isa] and most surely those who differ therein are only in a doubt about it; they have no knowledge respecting it, but only follow a conjecture, and they killed him not for sure. Nay! Allah took him up to Himself; and Allah is Mighty, Wise.[25]

The Christian doctrine of the trinity is flatly rejected as a logical impossibility. God cannot be Father, Son, and Spirit at the same time; Allah is Allah alone. Muslims are specifically instructed to use non-trinitarian language (SURAH 4:169), because the essence of Allah is complete unity, with no other representations in his essence but himself.

PRINCIPLES OF CONSTRUCTIVE OUTREACH WITH MUSLIM YOUTH. *Respect the Bible.* I was sitting in a small circle with a former Muslim who noticed that I had placed my Bible on the floor. He immediately came over to me, picked up my Bible and said, "Don't you know you should never place a holy book beneath you?" I gently thanked him and kept the Bible in my lap. Muslims rightly recognize the Biblical text and their Qur'an as sacred books which should be treated gently and with respect. When reaching out to orthodox Islamic youth, treat the Bible and the Qur'an with respect.

Dietary rules. Many Muslims do not eat pork and generally eat healthily. A young person offered such an item may find it repulsive. It is best to politely ask if a certain food you are serving is appropriate and make changes if necessary.

Jesus as the Word of God. When working with a Muslim youth, initially refer to Jesus as the Word of God (as stated in the Qur'an) instead of the Son of God, until the teenager is sure of your intent to help him or her understand Christianity.

Be genuine. Do not present yourself as a know-it-all. Have a bona fide concern in teens' spiritual growth. Ask them how they came to be Muslims through dialogue, and share how you came to choose Christ. Encourage them to visit the youth group and look it over. This process may take time, but do not end the relationship unless they choose to do so. It is important that they feel comfortable with you. Include other adolescents in the process of helping teens understand what Christian fellowship is. Muslims appreciate honest fellowship.

Redefine Muslim. If *Muslim* means one who submits to God's will and *Islam* means submission, then the Christian is a Muslim to the will of Christ. Explain how submission (which is the object of every true Muslim) is also the struggle of being Christian. Reverend Carl Ellis explains:

> "I know I'm a Muslim," . . . .
>
> As a disciple of Jesus Christ, I am in submission to the will of God. This makes me a true Muslim or a practitioner of true Islam. At this point, I usually share Romans 10:1–4. Although this passage refers to non-believing Jews who have "a zeal of God, but not according to knowledge" (ROM. 10:2), it could also apply to Muslims.
>
> A Muslim, like a first-century Jew, lives under a law of discipline. According to the Bible, however, true Islam is submission to God's way of putting people right, and that way is Jesus Christ. Just as I am a true son of Abraham by the power of Jesus Christ, I can also be considered a true Muslim by the same power.[26]

The Nation of Islam. Otherwise known as Black Muslims, The Nation of Islam is an African-American nationalistic religious society with well over 100,000 constituents. A caricature of Islam whose influence can be easily felt throughout the northern states, the Nation is especially prevalent in urban America. Men of fame such as Cassius Clay, Lew Alcindor, and Malcolm Little, known respectively as Muhammad Ali, Kareem Abdul-Jabar, and Malcolm X, have all been involved in the Nation of Islam. Public Enemy, N.W.A. (Niggers With an Attitude), and 2 Live Crew produce rap lyrics tinged with nuances of the Nation's beliefs.

Although following many of its traditions, The Nation of Islam is quite different from orthodox Islam. It would be fair to say that the Nation has its roots not as a religion, but as a "social entity" founded to counteract African-American racism in America. Louis Farrakhan, the leader of the movement, has successfully preached a message appealing to underclass teens across this nation—a gospel of justice and retribution against European racism as it has manifested itself in the American context. Hearing Farrakhan in person has made me aware that while the Nation of Islam accurately portrays the history of Black oppression, it falsely incites young people to *completely* blame the "white man."

HISTORICAL BIOGRAPHY. Timothy Drew moved from North Carolina to Newark, New Jersey to found the Moorish-American Science Temple in 1913. He became known as the Noble Drew Ali and proposed an ideology asserting that Africans were of Moroccan origin, and that Jesus was a black man who was killed by the white Roman empire.[27] After serving in jail under suspicion of murdering a police lieutenant, Ali himself was assassinated.[28]

Shortly thereafter, Wallace Fard, a silk salesman in Detroit, professed that he was the reincarnation of Drew Ali, who had originally come from Mecca to abolish the "Caucasian devil." Fard is believed to be an incarnation of Allah, created half-black and half-white to be better able to intermingle in America—"to be accepted by the black people in America...while at the same time...move undiscovered among the white people, so that he could understand and judge the enemy of the blacks."[29] He, with his spokesman Elijah Muhammad (born Robert Poole), founded the Nation of Islam.

Fard is reported to have mysteriously disappeared in 1935. Muhammad thus became the messenger of Allah (Fard) and successfully recruited many black prisoners to the Nation of Islam while in prison for conscientiously objecting to World War II.[30] His central idea was that the white race was created as an evil race (see Yacob's history below) and that the Nation of Islam was the true "black man's religion." Members abjured "their faith in the ultimate solution of the race problem in the United States, rejected all names that might

imply a connection with white America, and sought complete separation from the white community."[31] Elijah Muhammad declared the
Qur'an to be the group's holy book, along with his rules of dietary
law.

Malcolm X was undoubtedly the greatest evangelist for the
Nation under Muhammad. Galvanizing young people to eradicate
oppression caused by the "blue-eyed devil," the Nation of Islam grew
tremendously. When Malcolm's image began to overshadow that of
Muhammad's, and internal power struggles sought to diminish
Malcolm's influence, he publicly denounced the Nation. The following period proved to be one of ideological reconstruction for
Malcolm X, who moved from a position of racial separatism to one
advocating the dignity of human rights. He was assassinated February
21, 1965 by one of Muhammad's rivals.[32]

When Muhammad passed, his son Wallace Muhammad took
over. Influenced by Malcolm X's latter thoughts, he redirected the
Nation away from separation toward orthodox Islam. His leadership
caused a break which resulted in an orthodox black Muslim sect (the
Bilalians) and the traditional Nation of Islam presently headed by
Louis Farrakhan.

MAJOR CULTIC DOCTRINES. The Nation of Islam's doctrine that all
white people were bred to be "devils" is rooted in Elijah
Muhammad's history of Yacob, which is a mythological explanation
of the origins of the black and white races. When the moon separated
from the earth, the first humans were created as a black people who
founded Mecca. Of those, thirty percent were dissatisfied. A Mr.
Yacob was born into this group, who was "to create trouble, break the
peace, and to kill," and whose head was very large.

Because of his rebellious behavior, Yacob was exiled to the island of
Patmos along with 59,999 followers. Angry with Allah, he began an
experiment which scientifically grafted the dormant gene of the blacks
and progressively bred an evil race, a "bleached-out" white race.

This white race eventually returned to the mainland to wreak
havoc on the black race, but was marched across the Arabian desert
to Europe to live in caves. Moses was sent to them by Allah to bring

them out of the caves and civilize them, whereupon they would rule the world for six thousand years. When this time was completed, Africans were to be sent as slaves to America, where Allah as Wallace D. Fard would begin the process of eradicating the "white devil" and reclaim his lost black Nation of Islam.[33]

"Christianity is the white man's religion" is another prevalent tenet of Black Muslims, an animosity historically founded in slavery. The Nation believes that Christianity was used by European-American society to neutralize rebellion and encourage slaves to hope for "pie in the sky when they die" rather than to radically challenge the injustice of enslavement. The Nation of Islam, therefore, "totally repudiate[s] Christianity as an ideology that perpetuated Black exclusion."[34] In its place, Black Muslims adhere to the belief that Islam is the Black man's religion. Presently, that view has been challenged by Molefi Kete Asante and others, who propose that the Islamic faith is no more qualified than Christianity because neither has definite roots in Africa.[35]

The need to change one's name is another notable message of Black Muslims. Blacks, robbed of their African lineage by the loss of their original tribal names, have been cut off from any definite understanding of who their real ancestors are. The purpose of name changing is *kujichagulia* ("self-determination"), or defining oneself independent of one's oppressor. Malcolm Little initially chose an "X" to symbolize that he was forever ignorant of his actual last name, and later went by the name El-Hajj Malik El Shabazz.

The most prevalent purpose of the Nation of Islam is the centralization and unification of the African-American community's economic power into a successful base for political empowerment. The Nation is completely confident that the difficulties of the black community must be confronted through the united leadership and monetary support of its own people. In the urban arena, the Black Muslim has successfully sent a message of self-help that has built a respected economic base in such cities as Detroit, Chicago, Washington, and New York.

The Nation has purchased a great deal of farmland in order to train and hire unemployed artisans, industrialize, and make it productive. Economic and cultural stamina is the goal. Black Muslims have begun businesses such as bakeries, supermarkets, and restaurants, and have helped nurture and develop entrepreneurial ability. Their influence has convincingly rehabilitated prisoners and drug addicts, and their campaigns against drugs are waged with their own bodies. In 1988, twenty-four hour patrols against drugs were created in the Bedford Stuyvesant section of Brooklyn and in Washington, D. C.[36] By presenting alternatives for urban empowerment, the Nation of Islam has in many instances forged ahead of the church in giving practical hope to the underclass.

PRINCIPLES OF CONSTRUCTIVE OUTREACH WITH NATION OF ISLAM YOUTH. *Beware of impostors.* The Nation of Islam's message is accepted only cognitively by many teenagers, who will tell you they are members of the Nation but whose actions contradict them. If they continually talk harmfully about their culture, have sexual relations before they are in a committed relationship, smoke, drink alcohol, or eat unhealthily, they have merely given lip service to the Nation of Islam. They are as hypocritical as the Christians they condemn as the same. Gently bring this to their attention.

Do not downplay the cultural aspects of the Nation of Islam. When attempting to convert Black Muslim teens, do not make the common mistake of failing to acknowledge the validity of teenagers seeking knowledge about their cultural beauty. This is a good thing; to discourage it can set you up for being called a "perpetuator of the white man's philosophy" and can rob teens of the knowledge of a past often foreign to them. I believe that the Nation of Islam is wanting in its cultural teachings because it fails to endorse cultural reciprocity (see Chapter 2).

Use Malcolm X's final conclusions as an example of how a noble African-American Muslim is to think. Malcolm X is a highly respected role model among urban African-American adolescents, for all the wrong reasons. Statements like "All white people are blue-eyed devils" and encouragement to seek change "by any means necessary" are what most teens believe Malcolm believed. A product of racial hatred and urban poverty, his predicament brought him to this conclusion while serving time in jail. He perpetuated this message during his entire tenure with the Nation of Islam.

Urban adolescents rarely know that during the last year of his life he denounced such rhetoric. Spellbound by the cultural unity he witnessed on his pilgrimage *(Hajj)* to Mecca, he returned to America a changed man. Tragically, he was assassinated before he could reveal his reconstructed view of African-American unity.

The first thing Malcolm concluded in Mecca was that there is a brotherhood that exists between all people who trust one another. In a letter to his wife Betty, he wrote:

> Never have I witnessed such sincere hospitality and the overwhelming spirit of true brotherhood as is practiced by people of all colors and races here in the Ancient Holy land. . . . For the past week, I have been utterly speechless and spellbound by the graciousness I see displayed all around me by people of *all colors.* [Everyone] from blue-eyed blondes to black-skinned Africans [was] displaying a spirit of unity and brotherhood that my experiences in America had led me to believe never could exist. . . .
>
> This pilgrimage . . . has forced me to *re-arrange* much of my thought-patterns previously held, and to *toss aside* some of my previous conclusions. We were *truly* all the same (brothers)—because their belief in one God had removed the "white" from their *minds,* the "white" from their *behavior,* and the "white" from their *attitude.*[37]

Malcolm X's second conclusion was that the "white man" was not necessarily a devil, but that evil exists in institutional racism that affects people's attitudes and behaviors. Individuals must be judged by the caliber of their character and not the color of their skin. Upon arriving back in America, he commented to an audience in Chicago:

> In the past, I have permitted myself to be used to make sweeping indictments of all white people, and these generalizations have caused injuries to some white people who did not deserve them. . . . I

no longer subscribe to sweeping indictments of one race.... In the future, I intend to be careful not to sentence anyone who has not been proven guilty. I am not a racist and do not subscribe to any of the tenets of racism. In all honesty and sincerity it can be stated that I wish nothing but freedom, justice and equality: life, liberty and the pursuit of happiness—for all people.[38]

His final deduction was that the African American must never stop the struggle for liberation, because vying for Black rights is an equal part of the total struggle for human rights. It therefore became easy for him to say, "No man has believed perfectly until he wishes for his brother what he wishes for himself."[39]

Jehovah's Witnesses. Without a doubt, the Jehovah's Witness religion has become a dominating presence in the urban underclass. Most know its members as the people that knock on doors with *Watch Tower* magazines, who constantly talk about prophesy, Armageddon, and living forever in paradise on earth. Or, the group is known because of the musical Jackson family's membership. Witnesses have also become known for non-participation in military service, national and religious holidays, pledging national allegiance, voting, and receiving blood transfusions.

Their great appeal and success in the city has resulted from their faithfulness in door-to-door outreach to unchurched peoples. With a worldwide population above 4.1 million and 200,000 new members a year, some consider the Jehovah's Witness faith to be a denomination of Christianity.[40] It is not.

HISTORICAL BIOGRAPHY. Charles Taze Russell, a Bible study leader who denied the existence of hell as a reality, the deity of Christ, and the trinity, set out to teach his beliefs to the public in 1879. Having only a seventh-grade education, he co-published a magazine, *The Herald of the Morning,* that provided a way for others to hear his message. In 1884 it was renamed *The Watch Tower Announcing Jehovah's Kingdom,* and sold 6,000 copies in the first month. The Witnesses now produce 800,000 magazines a day.[41]

In order to systematize his teachings, he founded what is presently known as the Watch Tower Bible and Tract Society. Russell believed that his teachings were superior to those of the Bible and that all other religious groups, including the Christian church, were Satanic and should be avoided. His teachings were heavily apocalyptic, frequently forecasting the exact year the end would come. When these dates came and went, his theology was reconstructed to make it seem accurate. Apocalypticism remains key to understanding the Witnesses.

When Russell died on a train in Texas in 1916, a Missouri lawyer named Joseph Franklin Rutherford succeeded him. In 1931, Rutherford changed the name of the organization to Jehovah's Witnesses, his proof text being Isaiah 43:10. Witnesses believe that *Jehovah* is the only acceptable name for God. The learned Rutherford discarded a few of Russell's questionable teachings. Upon his death, Nathan Knorr snubbed Rutherford's contribution with the same authority. Frederick William Franz, the President of the Watch Tower Society through the early 1990s, thus follows the pattern with "papal power."[42]

The indomitable governing body of leadership at the Brooklyn, New York headquarters makes all doctrinal decisions, which are final. Complete loyalty is granted this body. Witnesses are baptized in the name of the "Father, Son, and the Spirit-directed organization."[43] Any questioning of a ruling by this group may result in disfellowship. Because of the apocalyptic nature of the Witnesses' beliefs, theological restructuring is usually carried out for prophesy that did not come true. Changes are seen not as a contradiction but as "new light." Russell himself, in the February 1881 edition of *Watch Tower,* said, "A new view of truth never can contradict a former truth. 'New Light' never extinguishes older 'light,' but adds to it."[44]

The Jehovah's Witness holy book is entitled *The New World Translation.* It uses much of the Christian Bible's form but is drafted with certain passage changes or omissions here and there so as not to contradict Witness theology. The book is said to be a superior translation of the biblical text, and to the untrained reader it can seem orthodox.

MAJOR CULTIC DOCTRINES. The doctrine of heaven first denies the existence of hell. Hell is not an after-life reality; it is the grave. Jehovah's Witnesses believe there is no "conscious existence" after death. The body and soul are one, so when death occurs both the body and soul die. All faithful Witnesses will one day be "recreated" by Jehovah's memory to live forever on a heavenly earth.

Heaven is divided into two realms: the earthly realm and the heavenly realm. Earth is the lesser of the two and will become paradise for all those Jehovah recreates after Armageddon. Heaven itself is reserved only for the spiritual elect, the 144,000 mentioned in Revelation 7:4 and 14:1–5. This group was finalized by Jehovah in 1914. Therefore, all converts to Jehovah's truth henceforth will inhabit the earth and be ruled in goodness by the 144,000. This is the hope of all contemporary Jehovah's Witnesses.[45]

Next, we must understand the pivotal dates of prophesy upon which all Witness theology stands. The years 1799, 1874, 1878, 1914, 1915, 1918, 1925, 1941, and 1975 are referred to in Witness theology, with 1914 being the *vital* year upon which all present doctrine stands. The prophesy surrounding almost all of the above dates has been given "new light."

The year 1799 was to be the beginning of the end, and 1874 to be Christ's return as a "presence in the upper air." Both these events are now believed to have happened in 1914. Both Armageddon and the conclusion of the world system were to occur in 1914, but these are now prophesied to occur before the death of those who faithfully witnessed 1914.[46] Interestingly, members of the 1914 converted generation have either passed away or are in their nineties. In short, time has run out for this theory—although it is still adhered to.

Moreover, 1925 was expected to bring the resurrection of Abraham, Isaac, Jacob and others. To honor their arrival, an extravagant villa called Beth Saim was built for them in San Diego. Needless to say, when the year had passed Rutherford decided to move in and the villa was later sold.[47] The years 1941, 1975, and a few dates given in the late eighties have all folded as signposts for Armageddon. Yet do not be alarmed, as the Watch Tower Society's halls are littered with such dates of false prophesy. An alert youth minister will then recognize all future dates that are given as part of an attempt to shed "new light" on the 1914 doctrine.

A third doctrine of the Jehovah's Witnesses involves the assurance of salvation. Witnesses are never fully sure if Jehovah will recreate them after Armageddon; therefore they must *do* acts that will earn them favor. They are to attend Kingdom Hall services five times a week for training and fellowship. Door-to-door work is a requirement that must be reported, including the amount of literature sold.[48] The mother Society continually requires such acts, reinforcing the idea that it is not enough to be *assured* of heaven. It is not uncommon for the anxiety this causes to bring about psychological problems for members.

The final important doctrine concerns the Witnesses' view of Jesus Christ. Jesus is considered the first example of what can become of one who follows Jehovah's law perfectly. Because Jehovah's Witnesses reject the Christian doctrine of the trinity, Jesus cannot be equal with God. He is to be revered as God's first spiritual masterpiece of perfection—a super-angel, not an incarnation.

Jesus was not resurrected physically; his body disintegrated in the Tomb. Thereafter, he went to heaven as the archangel Michael, where he is presently preparing to bring about the culmination of the end time in the battle of Armageddon, that he may eternally and justly regulate the affairs of heaven for Jehovah.[49]

PRINCIPLES OF CONSTRUCTIVE OUTREACH WITH JEHOVAH'S WITNESS YOUTH. *The Jehovah-God of the Witnesses is not the God of Christianity.* It must be made clear at the outset of a relationship with a Witness teen that the *character* of the God of authentic Christianity is not compatible with the God worshiped by the Jehovah's Witness. The name Jehovah is used by Christians in a very different way. This pronouncement should not be threatening, but should set the stage for positive outreach. Over the years, I have known teenagers who have grown up Jehovah's Witnesses and who were convinced "their Jehovah" was one and the same with the Christian God. We must expose these young people to the authentic Jehovah who sent his *only* son Jesus Christ.

Prepare the teen for the consequences of disfellowship. The sensitive youth worker should be aware that one consequence of his or her outreach may be disfellowship for youths or their families. This possibility can be overlooked until too late and cause great grief. If trouble arises because of Christian evangelistic efforts, the youth worker must be prepared to respect the family unit and have the best interest of the adolescent in mind.

Teach them their religious history. Much of the above information on the false dates of prophesy given by the Watch Tower Society is unknown to the faithful convert. The entire history of the Jehovah's Witnesses, false dates and all, is shrouded from general believers, who believe the governing leadership has instituted correct information. Time has proven otherwise. Mention also the futile nature of predicting God's actions—as Matthew 24:36–51 informs us, God alone knows when the end will come.

Christ assures us salvation by his grace. The greatest revelation Witnesses can come to realize is that by accepting the authentic Jesus Christ into their lives, their sins are pardoned by his grace. Through Jesus we become beneficiaries of forgiveness. *Works* of righteousness therefore cannot gain us the courtesy of God; our sin predicament is too deep. It is Christ who imputes his righteousness to us by *grace* through faith—as a gift from God, not a reward for works carried out (EPH. 2:8–9).

Go to these teens directly. Do not be afraid to take the initiative. Since Witnesses are taught to stay away from Christian church functions, this may be the only way. For the committed Jehovah's Witness teen, adolescence is a time to abstain from all vital social behavior. Doing intense evangelism with Witnesses takes good preparation, because the Watch Tower Society sees to it that members are heavily indoctrinated in Witness apologetics. I offer one suggestion in my book *Great Games for City Kids,* called "Jehovah's Witness Visits."

Recommended for grades eight through twelve, the purpose of this activity is to give urban youth the opportunity to evangelize with the intent to spread the Gospel to Witnesses. This activity involves five weeks of preparation, one week of evangelism, and two weeks debriefing. This whole cycle is required, as underpreparation can be detrimental—even dangerous.

There are two facets to this project: adult leader training and youth preparation. Adult leaders should learn as much as they can about Jehovah's Witnesses and invite in an outside resource who can help in planning and strategy. Be sure this aspect is thoroughly planned before proceeding.

Once adult leaders have orchestrated their intentions, youth preparation and debriefing can take place. The following study plan has worked best in the past:

Week 1: Why do Christians evangelize?

Week 2: What Jehovah's Witnesses believe and what they think of Christians. (An outside resource is best.)

Week 3: Where Christians believe Jehovah's Witnesses stray and why Christianity is right. (The purpose is strictly apologetic.)

Week 4: How should we go about our evangelism? During this session, compile a list of homes of known Jehovah's witnesses that your group would like to evangelize. It can simply include family members, friends, a Kingdom Hall, or places to distribute pamphlets.

Week 5: Review, plan specifics, and pray.

Week 6: EVANGELIZE.

Week 7: What have we learned and why is evangelism important to the advancement of the Gospel?

Week 8: The mission is not over—where should we go from here? (You can use this opportunity to introduce another religion).[50]

The Church of Jesus Christ of Latter-Day Saints. The Church of Jesus Christ of Latter-Day Saints (whose members are known as Mormons), is the largest American cultic religion and the newest participant in urban religious outreach. Mormons tended to stay out of the cities until around 1978, when the Presidential Body decided African-Americans and other people of color could hold priesthood positions. This decision automatically led to greater involvement in the city. Since their arrival they have recruited heavily among the urban underclass, with the message that Mormonism builds strong families.

In 1988, Mormons numbered 6.7 million members worldwide, with a missionary force of 36,000[51] who produced over 200,000 new recruits a year.[52] Much of this force consists of young adults, who are required to give two years in missionary service if capable. Salt Lake City, Utah is the hub of the Latter-Day Saint movement. In 1988, Temple Square in Salt Lake City ranked fourth among the most visited places in America with 4.1 million visitors, beating out the Grand Canyon's 3.8 million.[53]

The Mormons begin construction on two new buildings every day. They own and operate the largest private American university (Brigham Young), over fourteen radio and television stations, and over 750 farms, ranches, dairies, food processing plants, canneries, hotels, newspapers, and shopping centers, with an aggregate total income to the Mormon church exceeding four million dollars a day and five billion in assets.[54]

Without a doubt, Mormons can be some of the warmest personalities you could ever meet. They definitely believe in what they say. The Mormon church, however, has slightly succeeded in its deceptive aim to gain a reputation as a Christian denomination. I have met youth workers and pastors who were ignorant of Mormonism's unorthodoxy and was even saddened at the conversion of a fellow urban youth worker. Nonetheless, closer study reveals that the deeper one's immersion in the religion becomes, the greater the secrecy involved—especially concerning the details of the temple practice. The original temple ceremony, which is no longer held, began by pretending to slit the throat (symbolizing a former consequence of non-secrecy) and continued with a Christian preacher and the devil collaborating against Adam to convince him God is a spirit instead of a man.[55]

One is never aware of such beliefs until fully involved in the religion. Outwardly, Mormonism seems perfectly Christian. The first

Article of Faith reads, "We believe in God the Father, and in His Son, Jesus Christ, and in the Holy Ghost."[56] To this most Christians would say "Amen," before realizing that the Mormons are speaking not of the trinity but of three separate entities. Latter-day Saint theologian Bruce R. McConkie expresses what he hopes all people will believe: "Mormonism is Christianity; Christianity is Mormonism; they are one and the same, and they are not to be distinguished from each other..."[57] Lip-service to Christianity, however, will not negate the history, theology, and actions of this opposing religion, which blatantly categorize it as a cult.

HISTORICAL BIOGRAPHY. Joseph Smith, Jr. was born December 23, 1805 in Sharon, Vermont, to parents reputed to be occult treasure seekers. By age fifteen the Smiths had moved to Palmyra, New York, where the young Smith reported receiving a vision of God and Jesus while praying in the woods. Three years later, he was visited by Moroni, the son of Mormon, who directed him to the underground hiding-place of a book made of gold plates which contained "the fullness of the everlasting Gospel." Using a pair of special glasses buried with the plates, Smith translated what would become the *Book of Mormon.* Upon completion of the translation in 1830, the plates where replaced where they were found.[58]

On April 6, 1830 Smith and four others formed the Church of Jesus Christ, known today as the Church of Jesus Christ of Latter-Day Saints. Cast out of many areas because of their polygamy— Smith had twenty-seven wives—they migrated to Ohio, then Missouri, and finally to Nauvoo, Illinois, where they industriously created a productive city with Smith as mayor.[59]

In 1844, seven men dissatisfied with Smith printed the tabloid *Nauvoo Expositor* to expose certain activities of the mayor and his council. Smith closed the press down after one edition, which intensely incited the non-Mormon constituents of the community. The atmosphere was so threatening that Smith enacted martial law. The governor subsequently arrested the mayor for abuse of power and ordered him to take himself to the jail in Carthage to await trial.

Although he considered escaping to Iowa, his wife convinced him to obey the governor's orders. While travelling to the Carthage jail, however, it had already become obvious that there was a plan to assassinate him. Some friends brought him a gun and remained for support, but to no avail. On June 27, a mad mob stormed the prison, and his single gun could not withhold the crowd of one hundred men. Smith was murdered.[60]

Soon thereafter, the group split into one faction led by Joseph Smith's son (which appears to be what Smith wanted), and another led by Brigham Young. The former restructured its theology, resettled in Independence, Missouri and chose the name Reorganized Church of Jesus Christ of Latter-Day Saints. The other Mormon body sojourned westward. Upon reaching the Salt Lake Valley, Young declared, "This is the place." The contemporary tradition extends from this group of Latter-Day Saints, although the other still exists.[61]

The Salt Lake Mormons soon began placing an emphasis on an organized presidential body led by "living prophets" who "stand as mediators between God and mortals."[62] All theological decisions are finalized by the First President and council, sometimes entailing intense doctrinal battles. What they choose as correct will then be considered a "revelation" and opposing doctrines will be rewritten or apologetically smoothed over.[63]

For example, dark-skinned people were denied both priesthood and entrance into the Mormon temples because they were considered descendants of Cain's curse and participants with the devil in the beginning. In 1978, First President Spencer Kimball proclaimed a "revelation" recanting this belief, which almost immediately sparked a crusade into the inner city.

The holy books of the Latter-Day Saints are the *Book of Mormon, Doctrines and Covenants,* and *The Pearl of Great Price.* Together, these are considered revelation superior to the Bible for the only true Christian church—Mormonism. Each book progressively indoctrinates: the first tells the stories of two ancient peoples who lived in the Americas, the Jaredites and Nephites (archaeologists dispute their reality); the latter two instruct in major doctrinal beliefs.[64] In spite of their claim to scriptural superiority, these books have been altered many times to support contemporary beliefs. The *Book of Mormon,* which has had 3,913 modifications applied between 1830 and 1964, is a prime example.[65]

MAJOR CULTIC DOCTRINES. The doctrine of God as the trinity does not exist. The Father, Son, and Holy Spirit exist as gods distinct from one another. Since Mormons believe in the plurality of gods, every person has the potential to become like God. To them God is a physical being, with the likeness of a real man. As stated in *Journal of Discourses,* "God himself was once as we are now, and is an exalted Man, and sits enthroned in yonder heavens... if you were to see him to-day, you would see him like a man in form."[66]

Brigham Young believed that Jesus was born out of a sexual relationship of God the Father (alias Adam) with the Virgin Mary. Satan, born in the same manner, was Jesus' evil half-brother. Mormon theology promotes Christ as an elder brother who attained Godhood before us.[67] To some, he believed in polygamy and practiced it himself with Mary and Martha.[68] More disturbing, after the crucifixion sixteen cities were violently destroyed, and a voice taking credit for this slaughter enunciated, "I am Jesus Christ the Son of God."[69] Although much of the Adam-God doctrine has been recanted, it continues to exert influence.

Another doctrine concerns celestial marriage, which is the highest form of fellowship that can be attained between two persons. The only people to receive the highest degree of heaven are those who have had their marriages sealed spiritually in the temple. It is the hope of such couples that one day they will ascend to godhood and populate their own planets of people, as Adam (God the Father) and Eve have done on Earth. A very small minority practice this belief as polygamy.

Latter-Day Saint theology envisions three heavenly kingdoms: the telestial, terrestrial, and celestial. The first is the lowest, containing those people who lived evil, displeasing lives on earth. The second is reserved for "lukewarm" Mormons and those who did not accept the Mormon gospel but lived well-behaved lives. Third is the kingdom that only true Mormons can enter. It is further divided into three kingdoms, the highest of which being the one where godhood is attained and founder Joseph Smith resides. He is the only one who can approve admittance into high-heaven.[70] To reach any of the three celestial heavens is grace enough for the Mormon, for "it is by grace that we are saved, after all we can do" (2 NEPHI 25:23). By diligence in service to the Mormon faith, the desired degree of heaven can be obtained.

The final doctrinal belief concerns baptism for the dead. Since death is not the end of hope for salvation, Joseph Smith maintained, "The greatest responsibility in this world that God has laid upon us is to seek after our dead."[71] Based on an incorrect interpretation of 1 Corinthians 15:29, a proxy is baptized to rescue an ancestor who has passed on without hearing the Mormon message. The ancestor is thereby promoted to highest-heaven.

PRINCIPLES FOR CONSTRUCTIVE OUTREACH WITH MORMON YOUTH. *Mormonism is not Christianity.* Urban teens accepting Mormonism will most likely do so under the pretense that it is a denomination of the Christian faith. Honestly explain why you have chosen not to embrace Mormonism and give specific reasons. Give teens time to critique your thoughts, but make it clear that Mormonism's doctrine does not parallel the character of biblical Christianity—so it should not be called that. This suggestion should not be made in a threatening manner, but simply as an attempt to provoke a judgement given the facts.

Always refer to God as one, not many. Christianity is a monotheistic faith, while Mormonism is polytheistic. As such, do not speak ambiguously with a Mormon. Make clear and pointed statements concerning God's oneness. Instead of saying "Yes, I believe in God!," respond, "Yes, I believe in one God—no other gods exist but him!" The greatest frustration to Christians who work with Mormons is that their theology accepts all of our jargon. The phrase "You must be born again!" will gain the response "Amen!" Instead, proclaim, "You must believe deep in your soul *while you are living,* that if you do not accept Jesus as the *one and only* Son of God, your fate will *never be reconciled* in hell." This will cause the best Mormon to cry heresy.

Salvation is for the living. Grim as it may seem, the Christian faith understands death to be the end of hope for salvation for those who reject Christ. There is no chance in the afterlife to accept Jesus. There is neither purgatory nor three-layered heaven, and baptizing oneself for a dead relative does not change this fact. Jesus Christ must be accepted while we are alive. It is appointed to all of us to die once, for after death comes the judgement of God (HEB. 9:27). Even Mormons must accept the legitimate Christ while there is still breath in their nostrils.

Determine if the teenager's family is Mormon. If the adolescent's family is Mormon, the youth worker must be committed enough to the process of evangelistic discipleship to avoid looking for a quick convert. Instead, get to know the family, being cordial and overtly Christian. Neither hide nor cloak your intentions, as in this way you will find out quickly what you are up against. A family with contrary beliefs can slow or end a youth worker's attempts. Regardless of the result, do not be dismayed; if rejected, continue to pray, shake the dust off your feet, and continue in ministry.

MAKING KNOWN THE "UNKNOWN GOD"

As youth ministry continues, we must remain cognizant that the multitude of religious influences in the city go far beyond the previous four. There are transcendental, occult, individualistic and atheistic influences that equally invade the urban religious atmosphere. This is not a new phenomenon. The Apostle Paul, during his second missionary journey, was confronted with a similar situation in Athens, Greece. Athens was the intellectual center of the Hellenistic world, graced by the legacy of such great men as Socrates, Plato, Aristotle, Epicurus, and Zeno.[72] Athenian religious beliefs were polytheistic, as many gods existed side by side.

Interestingly enough, contemporary society has reintroduced the plurality of godliness. In other words, "all roads lead to heaven." If this is true, the sacrifice of Jesus Christ on the cross was a mockery. As our society thirsts for spiritual fulfillment in a desert of emptiness, every fountain will drain dry except those springing from the well of Christ, who is "Living Water."[73] We who are responsible for spiritually guiding the adolescent community must do so knowing that God will complete the task set forth since the beginning. Therefore, let us raise up a generation of teenagers capable of responding to the vast sea of religious ideology and who will point others boldly to the *One Holy God*, as did Paul of Tarsus in the meeting of the Areopagus in Athens:

> Men of Athens! I see that in every way you are very religious. For as I walked around and looked carefully at your objects of worship, I even found an altar with this inscription: TO AN UNKNOWN GOD. Now what you worship as something unknown I am going to proclaim to you.
>
> The God who made the World and everything in it is the Lord of heaven and earth and does not live in temples built by hands. And he is not served by human hands, as if he needed anything, because he himself gives all men life and breath and everything else. From one man he made every nation of men, that they should inhabit the whole earth; and he determined the times set for them and the exact places where they should live. God did this so that men would seek him and perhaps reach out for him and find him, though he is not far from each of us. "For in him we live and move and have our being." As some of your own poets have said, "We are his offspring."
>
> Therefore since we are God's offspring, we should not think that the divine being is like gold or silver or stone—an image made by man's design and skill. In the past God overlooked such ignorance, but now he commands all people everywhere to repent. For he has set a day when he will judge the world with justice by the man he has appointed [Jesus Christ]. He has given proof of this to all men by raising him from the dead.
>
> Acts 17:22–31

the heroic revolution

THERE IS A SILENT REVOLUTION GOING ON IN THE CITY. THE LEFT HAND'S pretentious "status quoism" is systematically relegating brilliant and capable urban adolescents to a world of political and intellectual genocide, unaware that the right hand's grass-roots struggle for justice is increasing in strength and youth workers and teens across this nation are rising up with one symphonic cry: "We *can* overcome!" This revolution is a call to activism and heroic involvement rooted in the grace of Christ's act on the cross.

> Your attitude should be the same as that of Christ Jesus: Who being in the very nature God, did not consider equality with God something to be grasped, but made himself nothing, taking the very nature of a servant, being made in human likeness. And being found in appearance as a man, he humbled himself and became obedient to death—even death on a cross! Therefore God exalted him to the highest place and gave him the name that is above every name, that at the name of Jesus every knee should bow, in heaven and on earth and under the earth, and every tongue confess that Jesus Christ is Lord, to the glory of God the Father.
>
> Philippians 2:5–11

This revolution is humble and nonviolent, yet not timid—it gently calls into question the effectiveness of the entire urban social

politic, in a movement that began near two thousand years ago and
that will reach its teleological summation at the return of Christ. It is
a heroic revolution, radically challenging the household of youth
ministry to turn out teenagers who see the evil structures that oppress
them *as they really are* and contest them vigorously with Jesus.
Christ's revolution is not satisfied with simply understanding the
world—it wants to redeem it.

THE ACTIVE REVOLUTION

On occasion, I hear the complaint that youth activism breeds discon-
tent with the status quo. If so, rejoice! If we do not allow urban adolescents to remedy their own social situations we will lose them to a
militancy that will reap evil repercussions. To act against the age-old
dehumanizing exploits of urban reality is to stand up for self-dignity
and declare, "I am somebody, in spite of my present circumstances!"
Christian social action is revolutionary because it involves adolescents
in the process of Christ's concern for their own liberation. Jesus has
come that they might enjoy life to the fullest (JOHN 10:10), and bring
his will *to earth* as it is in heaven (MATT. 6:10).

Let's face it—to become socially involved, by voting, protesting a
rip-off business, rejecting police brutality, or recycling trash, for
example, is to own stock in the nation and neighborhood you are
part of. More so, it is to be a part of the activity of Jesus Christ as he
reconciles the world to himself. Youth groups need to learn about the
sociopolitical issues that bear upon their community; in doing so,
they will form the building blocks of improvement.

EVANGELISTIC SOCIAL ACTION

Christian ministry is holistic. That is, it attempts not only to "save"
the souls of individuals through evangelism, but to improve their
society through social action. A number of Christians commonly
believe that evangelism and social action are opposites. On the contrary—they actually compliment each other. Both contexts exist for

the purpose of conversion and both rely on the motto: *Repent,* the Kingdom of heaven is at hand.[1]

Evangelism exists to call individuals to repentance for their sins and lead them toward a vibrant relationship with Jesus Christ. Social action does the same, but focuses on social structures. Unifying the two creates *evangelistic social action,* a heroic social-spiritual process that seeks to simultaneously direct individuals and the structures that oppress them toward a more godly outlook. It is as much an exercise in prayer and faith as in demonstration and protest.

Evangelistic social action takes place first and foremost *within* the youth group, later expanding outward into society as that which *comes out from* the youth group.[2] The Christian teen ought to care enough for those who are suffering spiritually and socially to realize, as Jonathan Edwards did, that "We are to look upon ourselves as related to all [humanity]..."[3] Whoever shuts his ears to the cry of the downtrodden and hurting will one day cry out and not be answered (cf. PROV. 21:13). Edwards further explains:

> It is the duty of the visible people of God, to give for the supply of the needy, *freely,* and without grudging.... This is a duty to which God's people are under very strict *obligations.* It is not merely a commendable thing for [us] to be kind and bountiful to the poor, but our bounden duty, as much a duty as it is to pray, or to attend public worship, or anything else whatever; and the neglect of it brings great guilt upon any person.[4]

Evangelistic social action at its finest bubbles from the bottom up and spills over into social matters. When teenagers get excited about personal or structural acts of social goodness, encourage them. Never stand accused of putting a lid on "youth idealism," for everything that exists in the world was once an idea bubbling in someone else's mind. Your job is to control the flow.

STRUCTURAL EVIL AND THE REVOLUTIONARY MIND-SET

Christian social ethicist Stephen Charles Mott points out that "world" in the New Testament is actually translated from the Greek *cosmos.* While we tend to think of a world as a physical place, a cosmos could be better described as an "order, that which is assembled together well."[5] *Cosmos* represented, to many New Testament writers, "the twisted values which threatened genuine human life."[6]

In other words, there is a highly organized Satanic conspiracy that seeks to destroy all human and environmental creation, manifesting itself in dysfunctional social institutions, sinister leadership, selfish economic systems, and misuse of power, to name a few possibilities. Urban dynamics accentuate such behavior and make it much more noticeable. We all participate with the structural evil present in the cosmos, either overtly or covertly. Without a relationship with the living Christ, it is inescapable.

"For our struggle is not against flesh and blood, but against the rulers, against the authorities, against the powers of this dark *world* and against the spiritual forces of evil in the heavenly realms" (EPH. 6:12). Therefore, "do not conform to the pattern of this *world,* but be transformed by the renewing of your mind" (ROM. 12:2). To live as a Christian is to be radically opposed to the conformity the world systematically attempts to impose upon us. Appalachian poet Wendell Berry describes beautifully the revolutionary mind-set the author suggests for healthy youth activism:

> Every day do something that won't compute.
> Love the Lord. Love the world. Work for nothing.
> Take all you have and be poor. . . .
> Love someone who does not deserve it. . . .
> Ask the questions that have no answers. . . .
> Laugh. Laughter is immeasurable. . . .
> [But] as soon as the generals and the politicos
>   can predict the motions of your mind, lose it.

> Leave it as a sign to mark the false trail,
>> the way you did not go.
> Be like the fox who makes more tracks than necessary,
>> some in the wrong direction.
> Practice resurrection.[7]

To build a relationship with Jesus is to become a "public enemy" to the corrupt, entrenched order of the world, to the system that asphyxiates justice and makes love a street walker. Early Church Father Arnobius of Sicca, in view of the many sufferings the early church courageously endured, concluded that Christians "wholly deserve the odium of being public enemies . . ."[8] If we are honest about the implications of the gospel message, our youths will become revolutionaries by deduction. As urban youths discover the deep relationship between the entrenchment of societal sin and their impoverishment in life, it will become the springboard upon which activism can be launched.

Mott's observations about the cosmos and social reality include three piercing observations that can help a youth pastor recognize the lasting nature of structural evil.[9]

SOCIAL REALITY HAS FORMAL ELEMENTS MUCH OLDER THAN THE INDIVIDUALS WHO CONSTITUTE IT. Racism, sexism, poverty, unjust laws, and injustice did not begin yesterday; all have extensive histories which impact contemporary life and are perpetuated anew each day by those who accept them as the norm. For the Christian they are not to be considered normal. Sociologist Emile Durkheim understood the elements of social reality to be *sui generis;* that is, they arise out of the collective ideals of general society, in which all individuals take part, and which eventually act back upon us. In short, not only are we affected by the world, but our collective beliefs make it what it is. We have all taken some part in participating in and perpetuating the world we live in. "For all have sinned and fall short of the glory of God" thus acquires a more profound meaning (ROM. 3:23).

If you are open to seeing the evil resident in social structures as well as people, you may conclude that the Church is a formidable weapon against it. The Church will not expire after fifty years of life—it will last forever. Therefore, what better entity to reconcile the political order back to Christ and ensure that "the nations of this world will become the nations of our God." The Church embodies the great dynamic of justice that extends from love. Some would disagree, saying that the church's reign is love alone while the state rules justice. Jonathan Edwards, however, believes such people "hide their eyes" by dismissing the web of social evil as individual lacks rather than a social mishap.[10]

SOCIAL REALITY HAS LITTLE DEPENDENCE ON CONSCIOUS INDIVIDUAL DECISION-MAKING OR RESPONSIBILITY. Certain elements of social reality impact urban youngsters regardless of their faith life or the amount of social activism they do. Society can on occasion act as an insatiable beast that devours whomever it wills. For example, young people living devoutly religious lives in communities known for violence will separate themselves from the drug wars going on in the streets, but this will not prevent the stray bullets of gang-related cross fire from taking their lives on the way to bible study. An individual decision to transfigure a certain aspect of personal behavior does not guarantee a noticeable change in society, but does make space for it to happen. The overall focus of your activism should not be in establishing lasting change, but in promoting lasting hope. Change is transient, but hope is rooted in the reality that *God* can make a better tomorrow. Without this belief it would be better if your teens did not act at all.

SOCIAL REALITY CONSISTS OF COMPLEX PROBLEMS FOR WHICH THERE SEEM TO BE NO SOLUTIONS. Every youth pastor who has chosen to advance justice primarily in the city faces this fact. The urban metropolis can be complicated at times, and can make what should be simple complex, what is mundane, critical—leading even the most perceptive and optimistic person to ask, "Is social action worth the effort?" "Is it worth having fed forty hungry persons today while millions remain that could not be fed?" "Should one boast of having taught youths to be peaceful, when violence increases before them daily?" At times, it seems as if injustice has an advantage over justice, and youth workers find themselves declaring in bewilderment, as the Ecclesiastical writer did, "When I surveyed all that my hands had done and what I had toiled to achieve everything was meaningless, a chasing after the wind; nothing was gained under the sun."[11] Yet even this pessimistic writer retained a glimmer of promise by concluding, "God will bring every deed into judgement, including every living thing, whether it is good or bad."[12] This reasoning points to the heart of Christian social activism. Admitting that human social efforts are at best incomplete allows whatever social progress that takes place to be attributed to God, while the agents of change—the youth groups—symbiotically surrender their will to the bidding of God's justice.

This process is powerful, because adolescents discover that as soon as they move to rectify the wrongs around them, they are no longer alone. Instead, there is "a God that strives within [their] striving, who kindles his flame in [their] intellect, sends the impact of his energy to make their will restless for righteousness, and always urges [them] on toward a higher combination of freedom and solidarity. [This *one* God will be] the source of their energies, the ground of their hopes."[13]

Three Simultaneous Revolutions

The word *revolution* frightens some people because it carries an image of dramatic, all-encompassing social change—an uncomfortable image, since the idea of an urban revolution most often suggests a situation similar to the Los Angeles insurrection of 1992. If it is our position to teach young people to become revolutionaries for Christ, then we must clearly define what it means to be a revolutionary. Prerequisite to positive social change is the recognition that present society is not yet in harmony with all of its members, but can be effectively improved. If the desire for civil advancement is left unchecked, it can manifest itself in either constructive or destructive revolutionary directions. Using the Los Angeles revolt as a metaphorical case study, we will review three ways in which revolution can take place in urban American society; the latter two are most relevant to youth workers.

Revolution by anarchy. "No justice, no peace" was the call to arms during the uprising of Los Angeles, California. The city would burn until the officers acquitted for beating Rodney King were served due justice. A great number of working-class poor concluded from the acquittal that, since there was clearly a double standard working against the disenfranchised and people of color in this country, it was necessary to take such unreliable justice back into the hands of each individual.

The energy and philosophy that incited many teenagers and young adults to revolt can best be understood in the context of Karl Marx's beliefs on class conflict. While few, if any, direct allusions to Marx were made during this crisis, the ideology propelling it was similar on many fronts. In his *Communist Manifesto,* Marx stated that "society as a whole is more and more splitting up into two great and hostile camps, into two great classes directly facing each other: *bourgeoisie* [upper class] and *proletariat* [working class]."[14] The powerful bourgeoisie, steeped in personal privilege, will rarely remedy the social inequities that face the working class and poor; it is therefore the proletariat's responsibility to completely overthrow the bourgeoisie and redistribute resources that should be shared equally by everyone.

The tremendous overtones of class conflict evident in the riots of 1992 were expressed by city teens throughout this nation. More than once they said, "None of this would have happened, no property would have been lost or fires started, if we hadn't been shut out of the American system." The violence and looting was justified to these adolescents because it redistributed the pain they were feeling to an entire nation. They felt that perhaps now their genuine needs would be attended to. Marx recognized such violence as the "birth pangs" of a new social order attempting to be born.

It was readily apparent that the Rodney King incident was merely an initiating impetus for a community which refused to remain silent about years of injustice. Large communities of people with dramatic needs had come to realize they were trapped at the bottom of the social ladder without the skills or resources needed to improve their lot. They had been transformed into welfare junkies and children of paternalism. Their sentiments continued to build until many concluded that "they had nothing to lose but their chains." When people become this desperate and their very existence hangs in the balance, many decide, like the mouse cornered by a cat, to "strike out against the persecutor anyhow," as there is only "a world to win."[15]

Urban youth workers must gird themselves against the negative urban associations (such as gangs, disgruntled pacts, religious and political extremists) that will encourage youths to endorse programs of anarchy. These may be *quick* fixes, but are they the *right* and most *Christian* ones? Do they fix anything at all? And if so, for whom? Admittedly, such approaches would be sufficient if there were no God—but there is!

Is there ever a time for anarchy? Perhaps. But the ground upon which Christian youth groups stand is always theologically moral. Therefore, we must search for higher moral ground from which adolescents can communicate their case, lest our attempts at justice are defeated at a lower level.

Revolution by covenant. Another way to bring about revolution is to mend the "broken covenant" of democracy.[16] The Los Angeles situation was more than an uprising of people in anarchy—it was a consequence of a tear in the fabric of democracy itself, one that could be mended only by positive litigation and social revolution. Many who had been blind to urban reality were forced to recognize that not only was the urban citizen in need of a revolution, the federal system itself needed one in order to be redirected toward its original purpose—equal democracy for *all* its citizens. Thomas Jefferson believed every generation ought " 'to begin the world over again,' and that 'Nothing is unchangeable but the inherent and unalienable rights of man,' and he felt it would be a good thing to have a revolution every twenty years."[17]

Did Jefferson mean a Marxist-type revolution? Certainly not. His revolution involved a continual reevaluation of the federal system put in place to distribute democracy. In like fashion, people such as representative Maxine Waters recognized that realistic, longer-lasting change is achieved not by *completely* overthrowing the federal social order, but by demanding the full allocation of rights and blessings guaranteed by the Constitution through legal and political means. "The word *federal* derives from the Latin *foedus,* which means covenant."[18] Every citizen of this nation or any other democracy is born into a covenantal relationship with it. The nation ensures every citizen the rights of freedom and self-determination; the citizen in turn will promote, even protect, the vitality of the nation's ideals.

This understanding has vanished from many urban communities. An entire culture of underclass minors believe there is no need to advocate any national patriotism or hope, because the dictates of the Constitution must have been meant for someone else's family— namely someone of European descent. Is this true? Or is there a blockage in the aqueduct of justice and democracy? Is Rodney King a citizen or "just another minority" complaining about his right to equal treatment under the law? If King were white would his treatment have been the same? Who is the law for anyway? These are the questions that arise out of mistrust throughout urban youth culture. They can only be answered by improving justice, which is the adhesive that binds public trust together.[19]

Instruct your youths that the great principles of democracy were not made to improve the nation; the nation was founded to improve democracy. The democratic concepts of freedom, justice, liberty, health, and equality are a part of God's plan, and until each nation unclogs for its citizens the promises therein, it is guilty of sin, and must reconcile itself to the citizens most affected by the breach in contract. Dr. Martin Luther King, Jr., expresses this thought well:

> When the architects of our republic wrote the magnificent words of the Constitution and Declaration of Independence, they were signing a promissory note to which every American was to fall heir. . . . It is obvious today that America has defaulted on this promissory note in so far as her citizens of color are concerned. Instead of honoring this sacred obligation, America has given the Negro people a bad check; a check which has come back marked

"insufficient funds." We refuse to believe that there are insufficient funds in the great vaults of opportunity of this nation. And so we've come to cash this check, a check that will give us upon demand the riches of freedom and the security of justice.[20]

The Constitution must be set free in its entirety across this land, not to benefit the few, but everyone—to benefit, as poet Maya Angelou wrote, "the Asian, the Hispanic, the Jew, the African, the Native American, the Sioux, the Catholic, the Muslim, the French, the Greek, the Irish, the Rabbi, the Priest, the Sheikh, the Gay, the Straight, the Preacher, the privileged, [and] the homeless . . ."—who by birth under this covenant have the right to be who they are or choose to be.[21] Citizens should never claim or complain about the benefits of their nation until they themselves are willing to stand up for the democratic rights due them. Teach this to city adolescents on the brink of anarchy. All is not lost. Let them see for themselves what the Declaration of Independence, the Constitution, and the Bill of Rights say (refer them to history textbooks or their local library). It is there that their case of social injustice may be given public ear. Improve their awareness of the covenant between government and citizenry, and allow them opportunities to seek out places within their own social reality where it has fractured. If the revolutionary task of mending the covenant of America is possible, it will require the analytical powers of us all, carried out though prayer and social action.

The bad news, however, is the fourfold dilemma surrounding any revolution by covenant. First, the litigation and group determination necessary for social progression may takes years, even generations, to blossom. "If so," some argue, "then why not riot? At least things move faster." Second, did the founders practice what they preached? It would seem not. Many of these same architects had slaves, deprived women of equality, killed multitudes of Native Americans, and ignored the covenants of other preexisting peoples. Third, assuming the covenant can be mended over time, how can we realistically expect anything achieved by human effort to fully redeem its promises, particularly since its ideals are ultimately beyond human control? Lastly, do not Christians ultimately have their covenant and citizenship made with a Kingdom not of this world? This quandary leads us toward a third type of revolution, needed for the Christian youth worker to be satisfied.

Revolution by heroic love. Christian adolescents who put their faith into action (not lip-service) practice heroic love—the pivot upon which Christian activism and social involvement rest. Heroic love is central to the cross because it drives the Christian youth group to do evangelistic acts of love and grace. These revolutionary acts are motivated not simply by external change, but by spiritual change.

Heroic love must be continually associated with toughness, durability, and confrontation, rooted in the unbending love of Christ for all persons and in the justice God demands as due to the oppressed. In short, heroic love does resist because God "is not a non-resistant God."[22] It "is action-oriented; it does not avoid conflict but seeks to confront and resolve it."[23] Heroic love is passive when it comes to taking life, and active in saving and defending life.[24]

Urban teenagers must become inspired to be the revolutionary instruments of Christ's heroism as he seeks to salvage joyously those who would come to him. Poetically speaking, this revolution is capable of turning a gun user into a love user, a violent teen toward self-esteem, a dope dealer into a hope dealer. It is evangelistic social action at its best—which does not seek the limelight, because it is a light unto itself.

During the Los Angeles multicultural insurrection, revolution by anarchy and covenant were equally attended to, yet a third, less popular revolution also took place, one that could best be detected with spiritual oculars and that was based on Christian love and civil service in defense of the soul of humanity. As we saw a white man named Reginald Denny being pulled from his truck, beaten heinously by gang members, and left for dead, what we didn't see were the African Americans who heroically drove him to the hospital and saved his life. We witnessed stores being emptied by looting bands of people, but did not see the droves of prayers that filled many disparaged souls. When young Hispanics and African Americans argued that their problems exist because white people are evil, they forgot that the world would never have known of Rodney King's beating had a white man not heroically used his personal video recorder to tape the incident. As we saw a hispanic gentleman bleeding profusely upon the ground, we forgot to see the preacher standing over him with his Bible drawn, pleading, "Lord, help this man!" Our vision honed in upon Korean merchants being vandalized and resorting to protection by the gun; what we did not witness were those non-Korean citizens that told their neighbors to "Leave that store alone!" While we saw gang members encouraging people to kill and to fight, society too quickly glanced over those heroic gang members who decided to form a peace patrol. Finally, as we watched the fatigues of Marshal Law patrolling a city gone awry, many overlooked God's Law, revealed as tough love from churches seeking strategic ways to serve as luminous lighthouses in deep darkness.

This type of revolutionary courage, faint as it may be, is the substance lasting social harmony is made of. When you encounter a teen rightfully angry at wrongdoing, always remember that "the best and worst in a society or an individual are often closely related. The *energy of creation* and the *energy of aggression* are often only a hair's breadth apart."[25] "The more the drive toward life is thwarted, the stronger is the drive toward destruction; the more life is realized, the less is the strength of destructiveness. Destructiveness is the outcome of unlived life."[26] Therefore, the discipline of becoming a hero is to transfer the destructive energy of hatred into the constructive energy of love.

Ernst Troeltsch, in *The Social Teaching of the Christian Churches,* contends that the "ethic of Jesus is heroic," and as such, does not "compromise with the claims of the life of the world."[27] Active heroism (evangelistic social action) helps make the world a better habitation by focusing on the quality of society's *soul* and on its impact on the individual.[28] Simplicity and intimacy are the basic foundations for a heroic social revolution.[29]

Our task as youth ministers is to provide adolescents the chance to become the heroes of their communities. A Christian hero always has one foot on reality (social) and the other on potentiality (spiritu-al). Teens will make sacrifices and take risks if they recognize them to serve the benefit of a better tomorrow.

How to Evaluate a Heroic Revolution

All heroic revolutionary actions performed by Christian youth groups can be evaluated by two basic criteria:

THE ACTION IS BIBLICALLY SOUND. Heroic social deeds are common in the Christian biblical tradition. The Bible itself, properly under-stood, encourages the greatest commandments: " 'Love the Lord your God with all your heart and with all your soul and with all your mind and with all your strength.' The second is this: 'Love your neighbor as yourself.' There is no commandment greater than these" (MARK 12:30–31). Commandments are never meant to be pondered as conditional guidelines; they must be enacted unconditionally toward those both in and outside the Christian faith.

Social activism is never a replacement for serving Christ—it is an extension of one's conversion experience. We love others because Christ first loved us (I JOHN 4:19). "As we have opportunity, let us do what is good to all people, but especially to the family of believers" (EPH. 6:10). Heroic acts of love and justice extend from one's love of God. Listen to 1 John 3:17–20a at this point:

> If anyone has material possessions and sees his brother in need but has no pity on him, how can the love of God be in him? Dear children, let us not love with words or tongue but with *actions* and in *truth*. This then is how we know that we belong to the truth, and how we set our hearts at rest in his presence whenever our hearts condemn us.

James goes further along these lines:

> Be doers of the word, and not hearers only deceiving your own selves.... What good is it, my brothers, if a man claims to have faith

but has no deeds? Can such faith save him? Suppose a brother or sister is without clothes and daily food. If one of you says to him, 'Go, I wish you well; keep warm and well fed,' but does nothing about his physical needs, what good is it? In the same way, faith by itself, if not accompanied by action is dead. But someone will say, 'You have faith; I have deeds.' Show me your faith without deeds, and I will show you my faith by what I do. As the body without the spirit is dead, so faith without works is dead.

James 1:22 (KJV), 2:14–19, 26 (NIV)

We are pilgrims in this strange land, yet are not loners—in the world, but not of it. As such, we must go beyond the comfortable confines of simply enacting the biblical text within our own church walls, which can create a pseudo-spiritualism in teens. Instead, let us become inspired by the social truths and mandates within the Bible, which at its core edifies the saints and brings sinners to personal and social repentance. Christ is our best example:

And so Jesus also suffered outside the city gate to make the people holy through his own blood. Let us, then, go to him *outside the camp,* bearing the disgrace he bore. For here we do not have an enduring city, but we are looking for the city that is to come.

Hebrews 13:12–14

THE ACTION IS EXECUTED WITH A NONVIOLENT ETHIC.[30] Heroic actions of love and justice are interested not simply in desirable ends, but in moral means. Morality and heroic nonviolence are complementary, because each improves the other. Although the philosophy of nonviolence subscribes to an understanding that all people *could* surrender to its practice, it does not negate the reality of sin but attempts to expand the base of social confidence in it. For this kind of social action to happen in your youth program, confidence must be built in two directions.

Moral revolution from the inside out. Nonviolent heros are constantly at war for their ideology. At its height, their battle is not about physical violence (although that may be one consequence), but about the power of God's truth and the strength of ideas. Victor Hugo once said, "An invasion of armies can be resisted; an invasion of ideas cannot." On another occasion, he wrote, "[No] army can withstand the strength of an idea whose time has come."[31] Nonviolent heroic action must be waged with truth as its vanguard.

In order for nonviolent resistance to be a useful urban premise, it must take on the characteristics of a "moral equivalent of war."[32] That is, it is not merely passive non-resistance to evil, but proactive truth. William James commented, "The war against war is going to be no holiday excursion or camping party."[33] It will take great moral stamina, with love at its core.

Your teens will need self-discipline to maintain a nonviolent approach, a change in consciousness which provides the worthiness to practice peace. Heroic nonviolence is both a *courageous* and *emotional* practice; self-discipline, therefore, must be strongest in these areas.

Courage improves character, yet it does not exist for its own benefit. It exists for the defense of truth. When courage defends itself instead of truth, it becomes an empty, easily-fractured shell. "Nonviolence requires the highest kind of moral courage and the strictest discipline."[34] Cowardice, then, is actually a greater profanity than violence. Courage imparts to an adolescent the ability to overcome cowardice.

Teenagers establish convictions through active courage. Convictions are the nonviolent hero's internalized truths, gained through the experiences of one's own lived-out philosophy. They are useless, however, if they do not challenge the nonviolent to challenge themselves. Heroic deeds have social and personal dimensions. The true patron must be willing to face both with an equal amount of courage.

Moral action also requires discipline in the expression of emotions. Heroic nonviolence is emotive in practice, because it shares in the joys and pains of others. Contrary to the beliefs of a great number of philosophers, *right* emotion is equally as important as *right* reason. Plato dismissed emotions as dangerous and irrelevant, Ignatius advised those who sought God's will to detach their emotions, and Kant defended stoic ideals, saying "the prudent man must at no time be in a state of emotion, not even that of sympathy with [a] best friend."[35] Their assumptions were: reasoning can be disengaged wholly from emotion; detached reasoning is trustworthy and unbiased; and, emotions only bias and cloud moral decisions.[36] Nonviolent heroism refutes this premise on the grounds that emotion is equally as important a strand of human personality as is reason. Humans cannot develop nonviolently without emotion, since love and the will to protest are not initially thought, but felt.

Emotions provide a sense of self.[37] As Sidney Callahan notes, "they provide us with our sense of reality and give vividness to the experience of being alive."[38] Emotion is not greater than reason—it is its partner in truth. Together, they expand the total reality of youths who choose to act heroically. These teenagers must discipline themselves toward empathetic thinking, which involves both a conceptual and perceptual element.

Moral revolution from the outside in. The social structure desperately needs a moral overhaul. Just as nonviolent heroism strives to build harmony between individuals, so must it include institutions. Social structures are rarely neutral—the "moral values imbedded in them" make them good or bad.[39] As mentioned earlier, they are human products that eventually act back upon their producers. They must be constantly held in check by society, lest they stray from their original purposes. Structural evil must be combatted with structural good.

Since teens must live as citizens in this society, subject to the government they are in covenant with, they ought to impact it with nonviolent resistance when injustice arises (see Appendices 1–2). Nonviolent resistance, whether Christian or secular, is humanitarian in nature and promotes the full moral development of humans and their institutions as peaceful agents in society. To be heroic citizens, your teenagers must be willing to live an anti-violent lifestyle that improves human relations, one which will galvanize others to social resistance when civil inhumanity fails to be reconciled.

A HEROIC CITIZEN WILL ENDORSE NONVIOLENT LAWS. Urban teens need to understand that the purpose of the law is to keep order. Laws should serve to protect the dignity of individuals from all forms of violence. This dignity is rooted in the reality that all persons are created by God and are thereby imbued with "certain unalienable rights."[40] Nonviolent laws should be publicly endorsed by the heroic citizen and happily followed, to demonstrate the laws' validity; violent laws must be challenged, for injustice is their nucleus.

Bad laws are not always blatant. They can seep their venom into urban culture by covertly paralyzing positive legislation. They can cause a compromised proposal to be enacted that is diluted of any real impact, and produce "a fantasy of liberation" when in reality there is no social progression at all.[41] Unjust laws are not laws but endorsements of disunity. They are, according to St. Thomas Aquinas, "acts of violence," no matter how well disguised.[42] Knowing this, the heroic youth leader courageously attempts (when possible) to search out and expose the potential violence hidden in legislation.

A HEROIC CITIZEN PERFORMS GOOD IN ORDER TO DO RIGHT. Heroic goodness has two distinct qualities: it is redemptive, and it defends the uniqueness of every human being.[43] The time to do good toward another is *now,* because goodness is not relative in nature but is a strand to be woven into all social relationships. Goodness is not an end unto itself, but is the best nonviolent Christian resource for doing what is *right.* Using good to do right lays its "emphasis upon *salvation from evil* rather than aspiration after the good."[44]

To save people spiritually or save them from social injustice is to do good to them, for this is right. Rightness is enhanced by doing good toward others. This cannot wait—putting it off would be criminal.[45] Because the universe is based upon order and not chaos, nonviolence is "good," and is grounded in the creation.[46] Violence has never received this honor. To kill or to resort to brutality (as in revolution by anarchy) reduces good to a mere redemptive option. It has been said that the dilemma of conscience is to choose whether "to use violence or to allow the wicked to do as [they] please; to use the sword or to be a coward."[47] This is a religious low road not founded in creation. The heroic high road of the nonviolent conscience recognizes goodness as the right force of resistance. "To do good or to do harm, that is to save or to kill."[48]

A HEROIC CITIZEN IS COMMITTED TO PEACEFUL RECONCILIATION. Establishing peaceful harmony is difficult in any society, because it is evaluated by the faithfulness of all its constituent forces. In other words, harmony begins with reciprocity. Beyond this, however, is an understanding that peace and harmony are actually religious concepts that have had their place with "all the people of antiquity."[49] The adolescent committed to heroic nonviolence will recognize that peaceful reconciliation requires much more than human effort. The acknowledgement of God is the beginning of peace, for there can be no lasting peace without faith in God.

WARNING: HEROIC LOVE MAY BE HAZARDOUS TO YOUR HEALTH

Violence is an incredible, everyday reality which may face every heroic person. In a number of our urban communities, violence has escalated to such proportions that it has forced many a youth program to ask a timely question: "How heroic are we to be?" Standing up to the evils that have drenched the city can endanger the lives of the adolescents involved. In every city, we find the graves of adolescents who took a stand against iniquity—and lost. Was it worth it? Is there ever a time when we must have the courage of our convictions in spite of the consequences? These are questions every urban youth program must answer for itself.

But if I may persuade you, the answer to this moral dilemma can be found by reviewing the biblical tradition and the lifestyle of Christ. Christian heros who give their allegiance to Christ must understand clearly that their revolutionary radicalism may lead to the same fate as that of the Christ they follow—death. This is never the goal, but because heroes are existential in nature, *theirs must be a lifestyle that is chosen,* not forced. Heroism is a courageous act of love that in its purest form will much prefer martyrdom over cowardice.

This is not to encourage one to desire death—that is counterproductive, not Christian, and near to heresy. But sincere urban heros will not let the fear of death overcome them, since they see an even greater spiritual agenda at stake. Few urban problems will improve until the Church itself (including its youth groups) overcomes its fear of death. Only then will existing and future generations have the possibility of enjoying a better life. It is often to our detriment that the children of darkness exhibit a greater propensity and courage to change the city for good than do the children of light.

Living out the full implications of the heroic life for Jesus will be dangerous in any context, but the few that will champion Christ's cause in love should resolve: It is more noble to serve God and lose than to close our eyes to injustice. Let us teach adolescents to confront violence by practicing the principles of heroic love:[50]

HEROIC LOVE CONFRONTS INJUSTICE BY:

- centering itself on the belief that the power of God's love can overtake all violent situations. The Church ought to be the most active example.
- never forcing individuals to live by it. Instead, they must be won over by their own belief in its validity.
- transforming the empty promises and jargonistic rhetoric so many urban communities are used to into organized action toward social and spiritual change.
- using a spectrum of active and passive nonviolent means.
- expanding the base of community justice, with the goal of restoring harmony to the city.
- recognizing that although heroic action may end in failure, suffering, or death, it is better to fail confronting injustice than to complacently accept it.
- respecting the God-likeness in every life.
- going directly to the source of hurt, recognizing that healing on all levels must begin by exposing truth directly in its purest possible form.

- channeling anger and hopelessness into empowering and constructive work.
- acknowledging that urban communities can at any time mobilize and declare war against violence, to increase peace, provide protection, and to ensure safety for all community members.
- promoting self-protection as that which deflects, restrains, and absorbs violence, but does not reflect it.
- overcoming the fear of those who intimidate urban communities with unbending, tough, unaffected love.
- championing economic justice as the most practical form of social liberation.
- bridging gaps between the peace community and the grassroots social justice community.

At this point, I wish it could be said that joining the heroic revolution for Christ will guarantee immediate victory. That is not the case. What is consistent with the Christian tradition is not that God will *always* save us when acting heroically in love, but that God will *always be with us* when we stand with proper conviction. In that vein, although we may fail, truth will prevail.

It is true that David stood courageously with only a slingshot and his faith in God and won against the giant Goliath;[51] but do not forget Stephen, who preached God's message directly to the Sanhedrin and was stoned.[52] Daniel receives high regard for surviving an all-night ordeal with lions whom God had given lockjaw;[53] yet John the Baptist, who was given the heroic privilege of announcing the coming of Christ, was beheaded.[54] The three Hebrew boys in Shadrach, Meshach, and Abednego were recovered unsinged after being cast into a fiery furnace;[55] but Jesus, the Son of God, had to die on a cross in order to heroically save us all.[56]

We must move toward the day when the youth programs of this nation tremble no more before the fear of death, for the task before us can only be accomplished by the gallant. When this happens, Christian heroism may prove itself as the best, most liberating tool for youth groups participating in the urban revolution of God. May your youth respond affirmatively when presented with the heroic question, "Whom shall I send, and who will go for us?" May they, like Isaiah, respond with great zeal, "Here am I Lord, send me!"[57] Either way, *some* will step forward—they will be all you need to begin—who do not fear to make a stand for Jesus, and who will muster the moral determination to say, "O drug user, O pimp, O pusher, O prostitute, O rip-off business, O wicked political represen-tative, O racist, O sexist, O apathetic church member, we will not allow you to do business as usual anymore without proactive resis-tance from the heroic people of God. We have come to say, with the three Hebrew boys and with Esther, 'Our God is able to save us from anything you do to us, but even if he does not, we want you to know we will never support what you do.'[58] *'If we perish, let us perish.'*"[59]

postscript:
put up or shut up

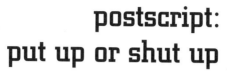

ONE OF THE ECHOS I HEAR REPEATEDLY IS THAT THERE ARE NOT ENOUGH *good* resources accessible to the urban youth worker. While this is true, it is not a final decree. The issue is not what urban ministry can do for the youth pastor, but what the youth pastor can do for urban ministry. If you work with city teens and you have self-tested curricula, plays, resources, games, songs, and ideas, compile and publish them. Your profession needs them.

The city is not a melting pot—it is a stir-fry. Our resources, therefore, must come from every segment of the multicultural, social urban reality. We need resources that can be accessed for and by Hispanics, Asians, African Americans, Native Americans, Polynesians, Arabs, and European descendants, to give breadth and depth to the urban Christian youth worker's program.

The complaining must stop, for the time has come for the youth workers of the city to take hold of this tremendous profession resourcefully for Jesus. There is no one in this occupation who cannot contribute. In short, put up or shut up! This field of study is fully capable of producing a bountiful harvest of effective programs. If you have any practical ideas or resources that you want to be considered, check around at your local library or bookstore for the publisher that will send your product to the audience you want to hit. Furthermore, feel free to write me personally at the Christian Education Coalition for African-American Leadership, P. O. Box 31804, Philadelphia, Pennsylvania, 19104. When all is said and done, let it not be said before the throne of God that we consigned our creative contributions to those who neither worked where we worked, nor had our own dynamic reality in mind.

appendix 1: six steps for nonviolent social change

THE SIX STEPS FOR NONVIOLENT SOCIAL CHANGE ARE BASED ON DR. King's nonviolent campaigns and teachings, which emphasize love in action. Dr. King's philosophy of nonviolence, as reviewed in the Six Principles of Nonviolence, guide these steps for social and interpersonal change.

ONE: INFORMATION GATHERING. In order to understand and articulate the issue, problem, or injustice facing the community, you must research, investigate, and gather all vital information that will increase your understanding of the problem. Know all sides of the issue, including the other party's position. This information can be gathered from many sources, including newspapers, television, various organizations, the library, and personal discussions, and is used to guide the development of campaign strategy.

TWO: EDUCATION. It is essential to inform others about your issue. This minimizes misunderstandings, and gains you support and sympathy. This can be accomplished through the same sources used for information gathering. Essential to this step is coalition building with groups or individuals, and meeting with the other party to keep lines of communication open.

THREE: PERSONAL COMMITMENT. Regularly check and affirm your faith in the philosophy and methods of nonviolence. Eliminate hidden motives and prepare yourself to accept suffering, if necessary, in your work for justice.

FOUR: NEGOTIATION. Using grace, humor, and intelligence, confront the other party with a list of injustices and a plan for addressing and resolving these injustices. Nonviolent communication does not seek to humiliate, but to call forth the good in an opponent. Negotiation is viewed as a growth and learning experience that can lead to a genuine meeting of the minds.

FIVE: DIRECT ACTION. Used to morally force the opponent to work with you in resolving the injustices, direct action imposes a "creative tension" into the conflict. There are over 250 different direct action tactics, including boycotts, marches, rallies, rent strikes, work slow-downs, letter-writing and petition campaigns, as well as various acts of civil disobedience. These are enhanced when they also illustrate or document the injustice.

SIX: RECONCILIATION. Nonviolence does not seek to defeat the opponent, but to seek his/her friendship and understanding. It is directed against evil systems, forces, policies and acts, not against persons. Reconciliation includes the opponent being able to "save face." Through reasoned compromise, both sides resolve the injustice with a plan of action. Each reconciliation is one step closer to the Beloved Community. Not only are individuals empowered, but so is the entire community. With that comes new struggles for justice and a new beginning.

Reprinted the with permission of The Martin Luther King, Jr. Center for Nonviolent Social Change, Inc. 449 Auburn Avenue NE, Atlanta, Georgia 30312.

appendix 2: six principles of nonviolence

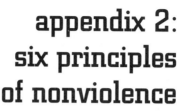

PRINCIPLE ONE: Nonviolence is a way of life for courageous people.
  It is active nonviolent resistance to evil.
  It is aggressive spiritually, mentally, and emotionally.
  It is always persuading the opponent of the righteousness of your cause.
  It is only passive in its non-aggression towards its enemy.

PRINCIPLE TWO: Nonviolence seeks to win friendship and understanding.
  The end result of nonviolence is redemption and reconciliation.
  The purpose of nonviolence is the creation of the Beloved Community.

PRINCIPLE THREE: Nonviolence seeks to defeat injustice not people.
  Nonviolence recognizes that evil doers are also victims.
  The nonviolent resister seeks to defeat evil not people.

PRINCIPLE FOUR: Nonviolence holds that suffering can educate and transform.
  Nonviolence accepts suffering without retaliation.
  Nonviolence accepts violence if necessary, but will never inflict it.
  Nonviolence willingly accepts the consequences of its acts.
  Unearned suffering is redemptive and has tremendous educational and
    transforming possibilities.
  Suffering has the power to convert the enemy when reason fails.

PRINCIPLE FIVE: Nonviolence chooses love instead of hate.
  Nonviolence resists violence of the spirit as well as the body.
  Nonviolent love is spontaneous, unmotivated, unselfish, and creative.
  Nonviolent love gives willingly knowing that the return might be hostility.
  Nonviolent love is active, not passive.
  Nonviolent love is unending in its ability to forgive in order to restore
    community.
  Nonviolent love does not sink to the level of the hater.
  Love for the enemy is how we demonstrate love for ourselves.
  Love restores community and resists injustice.
  Nonviolence recognizes the fact that all life is interrelated.

PRINCIPLE SIX: Nonviolence believes that the universe is on the side of justice.
  The nonviolent resister has deep faith that justice will eventually win.
  Nonviolence believes that God is a God if justice.

Derived from "Pilgrimage to Nonviolence" in Dr. King's *Stride Toward Freedom,* Harper
and Row, 1958. Reprinted the with permission of The Martin Luther King, Jr. Center for
Nonviolent Social Change, Inc. 449 Auburn Avenue NE, Atlanta, Georgia 30312.

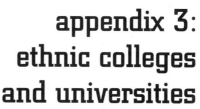

appendix 3:
ethnic colleges
and universities

AMERICAN INDIAN HIGHER EDUCATION CONSORTIUM

ARIZONA (1)
   Navajo Community College, Tsaile

CALIFORNIA (1)
   D-Q University, Davis

KANSAS (1)
   Haskell Indian Junior College, Lawrence

MICHIGAN (1)
   Bay Mills Community College, Brimley

MINNESOTA (1)
   Fond du Lac Community College, Cloquet

MONTANA (7)
   Blackfeet Community College, Browning
   Dull Knife Memorial College, Lame Deer
   Fort Belknap Community College, Harlem

Fort Peck Community College, Poplar
Little Big Horn College, Crow Agency
Salish Kootenai College, Pablo
Stone Child Community College, Box Elder

NEBRASKA (1)
Nebraska Indian Community College, Winnebago

NEW MEXICO (2)
Crownpoint Institute of Technology, Crownpoint
Southwest Indian Polytechnic Institute, Albuquerque

NORTH DAKOTA (5)
Fort Berthold Community College, New Town
Little Hoop Community College, Fort Totten
Standing Rock College, Fort Yates
Turtle Mountain Community College, Belcourt
United Tribes Technical College, Bismark

SASKATCHEWAN, Canada (1)
Saskatchewan Indian Federated College, Regina

SOUTH DAKOTA (4)
Cheyenne River Community College, Eagle Butte
Oglala Lakota College, Kyle
Sinte Gleska College, Rosebud
Sisseton Wahpeton Community College, Sisseton

WASHINGTON (1)
Northwest Indian College, Bellingham

WISCONSIN (1)
Lac Courte Oreilles Ojibwa Community College, Hayward

This list is endorsed and approved by the American Indian Higher Education Consortium (AIHEC), 1228 M Street NW, 3rd Floor, Washington, DC 20005. For a Christian-based college tour of any of these universities contact the Christian Education Coalition for African-American Leadership (CECAAL), c/o Leadership College Tours, P. O. Box 31804, Philadelphia, PA 19104.

HISTORICALLY AND PREDOMINATELY BLACK
COLLEGES AND UNIVERSITIES OF THE CECAAL

ALABAMA (14)
Alabama A & M University, Huntsville
Alabama State University, Montgomery
Bishop State Community College, Mobile
Carver State Technical College, Mobile
Concordia College, Selma
J.F. Drake State Technical College, Huntsville
Lawson State Community College, Birmingham
Miles College, Birmingham
Oakwood College, Huntsville
Selma University, Selma
Stillman College, Tuscaloosa
Talladega College, Talladega
Trenholm State Technical College, Montgomery
Tuskegee University, Tuskegee

ARKANSAS (4)
Arkansas Baptist College, Little Rock
Philander Smith College, Little Rock
Shorter College, N. Little Rock
University Of Arkansas, Pine Bluff

CALIFORNIA (2)
Charles R. Drew University of Medicine and Science, Los Angeles
Compton Community College, Compton

Delaware (1)
    Delaware State College, Dover

Florida (4)
    Bethune-Cookman College, Daytona Beach
    Edward Waters College, Jacksonville
    Florida A & M University, Tallahassee
    Florida Memorial College, Miami

Georgia (12)
    Albany State College, Albany
    Atlanta Metropolitan College, Atlanta
    Clark-Atlanta University, Atlanta
    Fort Valley State College, Fort Valley
    Interdenominational Theological Center, Atlanta
    Morehouse College, Atlanta
    Morehouse School of Medicine, Atlanta
    Morris Brown College, Atlanta
    Paine College, Augusta
    Savannah State College, Savannah
    Spelman College, Atlanta

Illinois (2)
    Chicago State University, Chicago
    Kennedy-King College, Chicago

Indiana (1)
    Martin University, Indianapolis

Kentucky (2)
    Kentucky State University, Frankfort
    Simmons University Bible College, Louisville

Louisiana (7)
    Dilliard University, New Orleans

Grambling State University, Grambling
Southern University System, Baton Rouge
Southern University at Baton Rouge
Southern University at New Orleans
Southern University at Shreveport
Xavier University, New Orleans

MARYLAND (5)
Bowie State University, Bowie
Coppin State College, Baltimore
Morgan State University, Baltimore
Sojourner-Douglass College, Baltimore
University of Maryland, Eastern Shore, Princess Anne

MASSACHUSETTS (1)
Roxbury Community College, Boston

MICHIGAN (3)
Highland Park Community College, Highland Park
Lewis College of Business, Detroit
Wayne County Community College, Detroit

MISSISSIPPI (12)
Alcorn State University, Lorman
Coahoma Community College, Clarksdale
Hinds Community College Utica Campus, Utica
Jackson State University, Jackson
Mary Holmes College, West Point
Mississippi Valley State University, Itta Bena
Natchez Junior College, Natchez
Prentiss Institute Junior College, Prentiss
Rust College, Holly Springs
Tougaloo College, Tougaloo
Utica Campus Hinds Junior College, Utica

MISSOURI (2)
   Harris-Stowe State College, St. Louis
   Lincoln University, Jefferson City
NEW YORK (3)
   Florello H. Laguardia Community College, Long Island City
   Medgar Evars College, Brooklyn
   New York City Technical College, Brooklyn

NORTH CAROLINA (11)
   Barber-Scotia College, Concord
   Bennett College, Greensboro
   Elizabeth City State University, Elizabeth City
   Fayetteville State University, Fayetteville
   Johnson C. Smith University, Charlotte
   Livingstone College, Salisbury
   North Carolina A & T State University, Greensboro
   North Carolina Central University, Durham
   Saint Augustine's College, Raleigh
   Shaw University, Raleigh
   Winston-Salem State University, Winston-Salem

OHIO (3)
   Central State University, Wilberforce
   Cuyahoga Community College, Cleveland
   Wilberforce University, Wilberforce

OKLAHOMA (1)
   Langston University, Langston

PENNSYLVANIA (2)
   Cheyney University, Cheyney
   Lincoln University, Lincoln

SOUTH CAROLINA (8)
   Allen University, Columbia

Benedict College, Columbia
Claflin College, Orangeburg
Clinton Jr. College, Rock Hill
Denmark Technical College, Denmark
Morris College, Sumter
South Carolina State College, Orangeburg
Voorhees College, Denmark

TENNESSEE (6)

Fisk University, Nashville
Knoxville College, Knoxville
Lane College, Jackson
Lemoyne Owen College, Memphis
Meharry Medical College, Nashville
Tennessee State University, Nashville

TEXAS (8)

Huston-Tillotson College, Austin
Jarvis Christian College, Hawkins
Paul Quinn College, Waco
Prairie View A & M University, Prairie View
Southwestern Christian College, Terrell
Texas College, Tyler
Texas Southern University, Houston
Wiley College, Marshall

VIRGIN ISLANDS (1)

University of the Virgin Islands, Saint Thomas

VIRGINIA (6)

Hampton University, Hampton
Norfolk State University, Norfolk
Saint Paul's College, Lawrenceville
The Virginia Seminary And College, Lynchburg
Virginia State University, Petersburg

Virginia Union University, Richmond

WASHINGTON, D.C. (2)
Howard University
University of the District Of Columbia

WEST VIRGINIA (2)
Bluefield State College, Bluefield
West Virginia State College, Institute

This list is a conglomeration of the colleges and universities endorsed and approved by the National Association for Equal Opportunity In Higher Education (NAFEO) and the United Negro College Fund (UNCF). For a Christian-based college tour of any of these universities contact the Christian Education Coalition For African-American Leadership, c/o Leadership College Tours, P.O. Box 31804, Philadelphia, PA 19104.

SELECTED LATINO COLLEGES AND UNIVERSITIES:

EAST COAST
Boricua College—Brooklyn, New York
Hostos Community College—Bronx, New York
Mercy College—Dobbs Ferry, New York
Spanish Eastern School of Theology—Swan Lake, New York

MIDWEST
Berean College—Springfield, Missouri
Seminario Biblico Hispano—Chicago, Illinois

WEST COAST
Bethany College—Santa Cruz, California
Latin American Bible Institute,San Antonio, Texas
Latin American Bible Institute of California—La Puente, California

Seminario Teologico Bautista Hispano—San Antonio, Texas

SELECTED UNIVERSITIES WITH STRONG CHRISTIAN ASIAN NETWORKS:

EAST COAST

Columbia University—New York
Cornell University—New York
Rutgers College—New Jersey
University of Maryland College Park—Maryland
University of Virginia Charlottesville—Virginia
Wellesley College—Massachusetts

MIDWEST

University of Illinois Champaign—Illinois
University of Michigan Ann Arbor—Michigan

WEST COAST

California Polytechnic in Pamona—California
University of California Berkeley—California
University of California Los Angeles—California
University of California Santa Barbara—California
University of Hawaii—Hawaii

notes

INTRODUCTION

1. See Matthew 13:24–30.
2. Cf. Manning Marable, *The Crisis of Color and Democracy: Essays on Race, Class and Power* (Monroe, Maine: Common Courage Press, 1992), p. 234.
3. Cf. Acts 9:1–19, 13:9. Saul was Paul the Apostle's name before he was converted.
4. Cf. Marable, p. 22.
5. "The Salvation Army Song," to the tune of "The Campbells are coming." See Tim Dowley, ed., *Eerdman's Handbook to the History of Christianity* (Grand Rapids: Eerdmans, 1977), p. 518.

CHAPTER 1: INTRODUCING THE NEW AGENDA

1. See David Martin, *Tongues of Fire: The Explosion of Protestantism in Latin America* (Oxford: Blackwell, 1990), p. 180.
2. Nathan A. Scott, Jr., *Mirrors of Man in Existentialism* (Nashville: Abingdon Press, 1978), p. 136.

3. "Rap: No More 'Easy Listening,'" *Boston Bulletin of Young Life Boston Urban,* June 1991, p. 1. Young Life Boston Urban is the present-day Boston Urban Youth Foundation.
4. See also James 2:14–26 and 1 John 4:20–21 for a supporting text.
5. Winthrop S. Hudson, *Walter Rauschenbusch: Selected Writings,* Sources of American Spirituality (New York: Paulist Press, 1984), p. 184.
6. From the Walter Rauschenbusch poem "The Little Gate to God," ibid. p. 48.
7. The poem "A Dream Deferred" by Langston Hughes opens the play *A Raisin in the Sun,* and can be found in Lorraine Hansberry, *A Raisin in the Sun,* twenty-fifth anniversary edition, revised script (New York: Samuel French, Inc., 1984), p. 3.

Chapter 2: Building Cultural Selfhood

1. Nelson E. Copeland, Jr., *Great Games for City Kids* (El Cajon, Calif.: Youth Specialties, 1991), pp. 174–175.
2. See Molefi Kete Asante, *Afrocentricity,* Second Edition (Trenton, N.J.: African World Press, 1989), p. 1.
3. See Paul Tillich, *The Courage to Be* (New Haven: Yale Press, 1952).
4. "If" is a poem by Ruyard Kipling that expresses the value of self-determination. To read it in its entirety, check your local library or see Burton Egbert Stevenson, *The Home Book of Verse: American and English* (New York: Henry Holt and Company, 1957), pp. 2952–53.
5. Tillich, p. 79.
6. See Asante, p. 31–43.
7. "Miseducated" is a term utilized by Carter Godwin Woodson to describe those who receive an education expressing the values of the larger society only. Any educational program must teach not only societal values but cultural values. See Carter G. Woodson,

The Miseducation of the Negro (Washington: The Associated Publishers, 1933).

8. Asante, p. x.

9. Langston Hughes, *The Ways of White Folks* (1934; reprint, New York: Vintage Books, 1971), pp. 49–53.

10. See also Deuteronomy 10:18–19.

11. Revelation 7:9. See also Matthew 25:32.

12. To view this text further see Jay P. Green, Sr., *The Interlinear Bible: Hebrew-Greek-English* (Peabody: Hendrickson Publishers, 1986), p. 955.

13. Robert H. Mounce, *The New International Commentary on the New Testament: The Book of Revelation* (Grand Rapids: William B. Eerdmans Publishing Company, 1977), p. 171.

14. See Alex Thio, *Sociology: An Introduction* (New York: Harper and Row, 1986), pp. 225, 226. This section gives three ways ethnic groups can live together in one society, explaining them mathematically as:

$$\text{CULTURAL ASSIMILATION: } A + B + C = A$$
$$\text{CULTURAL AMALGAMATION: } A + B + C = D$$
$$\text{CULTURAL PLURALITY: } A + B + C = A + B + C$$

15. Booker T. Washington, *Up From Slavery* (New York: Airmont Books, 1967), p. 136.

16. See Galatians 3:28. Those with an assimilationist or amalgamationist view of society will often use this text to argue against cultural selfhood. I believe that cultural reciprocity answers their objections.

17. See Jawanza Kunjufu, *Developing Positive Self-Images and Discipline in Black Children* (Chicago: African-American Images, 1984), p. 94.

18. This list, adopted from Jawanza Kunjufu's description of the "Rites of Passage *(Simba Wachanga)* Program," was rewritten to apply to a larger audience. See Jawanza Kunjufu, *Countering the*

Conspiracy to Destroy Black Boys (Chicago: African-American Images, 1985), p. 34.

19. Rev. Nelson Copeland performs this as a four-weekend workshop session for teens or a two-weekend workshop training session for staff groups, which includes curriculum and follows the outline presented in Chapter 2. If interested inquire at:

> The Christian Education Coalition
> for African American Leadership (CECAAL)
> c/o Cultural Selfhood Workshop Director
> P.O. Box 31804
> Philadelphia, PA 19104

CHAPTER 3: YOUTH GANGS AND LEADERSHIP

1. To my preteen friends the term "blood brother" meant total dedication to each other—a relationship as strong as that of blood relatives. Other friends went a step further by pricking their index fingers and joining them together, symbolizing a blood mixture and their brotherhood.
2. See Edward F. Dolan and Shan Finney's definitions of youth gangs in *Youth Gangs: A Study of 1,313 Gangs in Chicago* (New York: Julian Messner, 1984), pp. 11–13.
3. Ibid., pp. 35–36.
4. For a complete listing of Thrasher's findings concerning the age of youth involvement see Frederic Thrasher, *The Gang* (Chicago: University of Chicago Press, 1927), pp. 72–75.
5. Ibid., p. 3.
6. Ibid., pp. 56, 57 and Chapter XI.
7. Dolan and Finney, pp. 30, 31.
8. See Copeland, Chapter 10.
9. Thrasher, pp. 37–41.
10. For an elaboration on each of these desires see William I. Thomas, *The Unadjusted Girl: With Cases and Standpoint for*

Behavior Analysis (Boston: Little, Brown, and Company, 1923), pp. 4–38.

11. See ibid., pp. 4–11.

12. Ibid., pp. 12–17.

13. Carol King, "You've Got a Friend," *Tapestry.* Columbia Screen Gems 34946.

14. Thomas, pp. 31–38.

15. See Thrasher, pp. 59–61.

16. Bette Orsini, "Dropouts: a Crisis for the Nation's Schools," *St. Petersburg Times,* November 16, 1986, p. 1Df. Reprinted in *Youth,* vol. 2 (Boca Raton: Social Issues Resource Series, Inc., 1986), Article 16.

17. See Thrasher, pp. 61–63.

18. Orsini, p. 1Df.

19. Ibid.

20. For further information concerning Whyte's findings on leadership see William Foote Whyte, *The Street Corner Society* (1943; reprint, Chicago: The University of Chicago Press, 1955), pp. 257–262.

21. See David Claerbaut, *Urban Ministry* (Grand Rapids: Ministry Resource Library and Zondervan, 1983), pp. 115.

22. See Whyte, pp. 257, 261–268.

23. Ibid., p. 261.

24. For an unsummarized explanation of this study concerning youth gangs see Dolan and Finney, pp. 63–68.

25. Ibid., pp. 68–72.

26. Ibid., pp. 72–76.

27. Ibid., pp. 76–78.

28. Vanessa Adams and Kevin Sessums, "L.A. Gangs," *Interview,* November 1986, pp. 135–138. The gang and graffiti paintings done by them are displayed in this article.

29. For further understanding of the Young Dillingers gang see Jennet Conant and Nikki Finke Greenberg, "Rebels Without a Cop," *Newsweek,* 1 July 1985, p. 45.

30. Neal Peirce, "The 'Guardian Angels'," *Nations Cities Weekly,* April 29, 1981, p. 9. This article is an excellent synopsis of the beginnings and goals of the Guardian Angels.
31. Ibid.
32. Listed are scriptures that will help lead a discussion on Jesus' Gang.
    - The initiation to join the gang—Matthew 9:9–13, Mark 1:14–20, Luke 5:1–11, 27–31, John 1:35–51.
    - The gang's training and initiation—Matthew 10.
    - The leader loves the gang as friends—John 15:15–17.
    - The wayward gang member—Matthew 26:47–56, Mark 14:43–52, Luke 22:47–53, John 18:1–11.
    - The gang's communal tradition—Luke 22:7–23, 1 Corinthians 11:23–33.
33. See Daniel 3.
34. See Romans 12:2.
35. For an expository of this theme see Charles Sheldon, *In His Steps* (Chicago: John C. Winston Company, 1937).
36. For further reading on justice as fairness see C. S. Lewis, *Mere Christianity* (1943; revised reprint, New York: Macmillian Publishing Company, 1984), p. 62.
37. See Galatians 6:2. Read 6:1–10 for a better understanding of the complete context.

CHAPTER 4: DISCIPLINARY INTEGRITY

1. Proverbs 22:6 is often used to express the laissez-faire view.
2. Proverbs 13:24 and 23:13–14 are often used to express the authoritarian view of discipline.
3. Kunjufu, *Developing Positive Self-Images,* p. 50.
4. See also Proverbs 29:17.
5. Kunjufu, *Developing Positive Self-Images,* p. 51.
6. For further understanding see M. Scott Peck, *The Road Less Travelled* (New York: Touchstone Books, 1978), pp. 18–69.

7. See Lawrence M. Brammer, *The Helping Relationship: Process and Skills* (Englewood Cliffs: Prentice Hall, 1988), pp. 66–94.
8. Kunjufu, *Developing Positive Self-Images,* p. 57. Also, for further understanding and examples of the communication theory see pp. 57–60.
9. John Santrock, *Adolescence: An Introduction,* third edition (Dubuque: William C. Brown Publishers, 1987), pp. 49–50.
10. Ibid., pp. 50–52.
11. Kunjufu, *Developing Positive Self-Images,* p. 61. For further reading see pp. 60–65.
12. These disciplinary procedures are from "Resolutions from Senior High Council Retreat," The Evangelical Association for the Promotion of Education, Philadelphia, November 11, 1989.
13. The word "lukewarm" is found in Revelation 3:16 describing those who call themselves Christians but practice mediocrity.

Chapter 5: Involving Older Teens

1. The term "late adolescence" refers to ages eighteen to twenty-one. See Santrock, p. 33. Although there is validity to the argument that adolescence ends at age twenty-five rather than twenty-one, I believe that the phase beginning at age twenty-one is qualitatively different from the one discussed here.
2. For more information on the age of youth in gangs see Thrasher, pp. 72–75.
3. See Dolan and Finney, pp. 93–96.
4. Some general resources which have proven useful for persons starting a peer counseling program are:
    Baldwin, Carol Lesser. *Friendship Counseling: Biblical Foundations for Helping Others.* Grand Rapids: Zondervan, 1988.
    Collins, Gary R., Ph.D. *Christian Counseling: A Comprehensive Guide.* Waco, Tex.: Word Books, 1980.
    Lawson, Leroy. *Friends Under Construction.* Cincinnati: Standard Publishing, 1984.

Sturkie, Joan. *Listening With Love,* 2nd ed. Resource Publications: 1989.

Sturkie, Joan and Siang-Yang Tan. *Peer Counseling in Youth Groups.* El Cajon, Calif.: Youth Specialties, 1992.

Sturkie, Joan and Siang-Yang Tan. *Advanced Peer Counseling in Youth Groups.* El Cajon, Calif.: Youth Specialties, 1993.

Please do further research to keep up with contemporary progress in this field.

5. Martin Buber, *I and Thou* (1958; reprint, New York: Scribner, Collier Books, 1987), p. 11.

CHAPTER 6: THE URBAN YOUTH INTELLECTUAL

1. For an excellent resource on the feelings of psychological inferiority experienced by oppressed people, see Na'im Akbar, *Chains and Images of Psychological Slavery* (Jersey City: New Mind Productions, 1984), pp. 20–23.
2. See Romans 12:2.
3. Washington, p. 46.
4. From Adrian Dove, "Taking the Chitling Test," *Newsweek,* July 15, 1968, p. 51.
5. Louis L. Knowles and Kenneth Prewitt, ed., *Institutional Racism in America* (Englewood Cliffs: Prentice-Hall, 1969), p. 35.
6. Ibid.
7. Santrock, p. 173.
8. Ibid., p. 178.
9. Ibid., pp. 178–9.
10. Ibid.
11. Ibid., pp. 172, 174–5.
12. Ibid., p. 186.
13. Ibid., p. 189–90.
14. Dove, p. 52.
15. Report released by the National Urban League. See James D. McGhee, *The Black Teenager: An Endangered Species* (Washington: National Urban League, 1981), p. 4.

16. Gerald Davis Jaynes and Robin M. Williams, Jr., ed., *A Common Destiny: Blacks and American Society* (Washington: National Academy Press, 1989), p. 338.

17. Ibid.

18. Cynthia Burton, "In Class of '88, Only 41% Got Diplomas," *Philadelphia Daily News,* March 20, 1990, p. 3.

19. Jaynes and Williams, p. 337.

20. Personal letter written October 7, 1991.

21. Santrock, pp. 624–5.

22. See Isaiah 1:18.

23. Malcolm X (Little), *Malcolm X Talks to Young People* (New York: Pathfinder Press, 1986), p. 3.

24. These first three types of intelligence were first stated by the chairperson of the Department of African-American Studies at Temple University, Molefi Kete Asante, in his book *Afrocentricity,* p. 37. The latter was created by the author.

25. Ibid., p. 85.

26. Woodson, p. xxxiii.

27. See ibid., pp. 17–25.

28. Ibid., p. 44.

29. National Center for Education Statistics, Office of Educational Research and Improvement, Department of Education, *Survey Report: Trends in Minority Enrollment in Higher Education, Fall 1976–Fall 1986,* CS 88-201 (Washington, 1988), p. 1.

30. According to personal tabulations of the data given by the National Center for Education Statistics (NCES), college enrollment for Blacks, Hispanics, Asians, Pacific Islanders, American Indians and Alaskan Natives totalled 2,059,000 in 1982. Four year later, these groups graduated 116,858 persons into the school year class of 1986–87, or 5.68 percent. This figure rises only to 7.76 percent with Caucasians added (not including non-resident aliens). See ibid. and NCES, *E. D. Tabs: Completions in Institutions of Higher Education, 1986–87,* NCES 90-322 (Washington, 1989), p. 7.

31. See article by Huntly Collins, "Retaining Culture and Students: Tribal Colleges Offer Native Americans Hope," *The Philadelphia Inquirer,* May 13, 1991, front page.
32. Ibid., p. 4A.
33. Ibid.
34. Ibid., front page.
35. See Huntly Collins, "Black Colleges are Booming: Rush to Get in Counters U.S. Trend," *The Philadelphia Inquirer,* April 15, 1991, p. 4A.
36. Ibid.
37. Ibid.
38. Jaynes and Williams, p. 346.
39. For more information, write CECAAL, c/o College Tours, P. O. Box 31804, Philadelphia, PA 19104.
40. For 1976 figure see NCES, *Survey Report,* p. 4. Note: 1988 figure received from an unpublished draft by the NCES.
41. NCES, *E. D. Tabs,* p. 7.
42. For 1976 figure see NCES, *Survey Report,* p. 4. Note: 1988 figure received from an unpublished draft by the NCES.
43. NCES, *E. D. Tabs,* p. 7.
44. The King James Version also adds "in spirit," making it a sixfold list.
45. This phrase is the title of a book by George Eldon Ladd concerning theology and eschatological hope. See *The Presence of the Future: The Eschatology of Biblical Realism* (Grand Rapids: Eerdmans, 1974).
46. See also Mark 12:30 and Luke 10:27.
47. This quotation was attributed to Malcolm X in a speech heard by the author.

Chapter 7: Producing a Practical Work Ethic

1. David Whitman with Joseph P. Shapiro, "The Forgotten Half," *U.S. News and World Report,* June 26, 1989, pp. 45f. Reprinted

in *Work,* vol. 4 (Boca Raton: Social Issues Resource, Inc., 1986), Article 53.

2. Ibid.

3. See Genesis 1:31.

4. Adam Smith, *The Wealth of Nations,* ed. Edwin Canaan (New York: Modern Library, 1937), p. 423.

5. James E. White, *Contemporary Moral Problems,* second edition (St. Paul: West Publishing Company, 1988), p. 198.

6. Acts 4:32, 34–35 (NIV).

7. Didache 1:6.

8. Anthony Campolo, Jr., *The Success Fantasy* (Wheaton: Victor Books, 1980), p. 9.

9. For a brief overview of the Geneva experiment see John Dillenberger and Claude Welch, *Protestant Christianity: Interpreted Through its Developments,* second edition (New York: Macmillian Publishing Company, 1988), p. 79–80.

10. This quotation is credited to the Reverend Dr. Martin Luther King, Jr.

11. For an excellent discussion of economic status and protestant religious affiliation see Max Weber's classic *The Protestant Ethic and the Spirit of Capitalism* (New York: Charles Scribner's Sons, 1958).

12. See Matthew 16:26.

13. The work ethic I utilize is a modification of the principles given by educator and lecturer Jawanza Kunjufu concerning the motivation of African-American teenagers. For the complete resource see Jawanza Kunjufu, *Motivating and Preparing Black Youth to Work* (Chicago: African American Images, 1986).

14. Ibid., pp. 21–22.

15. James E. Walsh, "Non-profit Can Profit," *Association Management,* July 1991, Volume 43, p. 65.

16. ***Resources to get you started!***
Joan Flanagan, *The Successful Volunteer Organization: Getting Started and Getting Results in Nonprofit, Charitable, Grass Roots, and Community Groups* (Chicago: Contemporary Books, Inc., 1981).

This resource is tops to know the full process of beginning an organization. Can be extremely insightful in beginning an entrepreneurial program.

Prentiss L. Pemberton and Daniel Rush Finn, *Toward a Christian Economic Ethic: Stewardship and Social Power* (Minneapolis: Winston Press, 1985). Needed to consider Christian business ethics.

Roger Fritz, *Nobody Gets Rich Working for Somebody Else: An Entrepreneur's Guide* (New York: Fodd, Mead and Company, 1987).

Julian L. Simon, *How to Start and Operate a Mail-Order Business,* fourth edition (New York: McGraw-Hill, 1987).

Spenser Johnson and Larry Wilson, *The One Minute Sales Person* (New York: William Morrow and Company, Inc., 1984). Excellent for teaching teenagers quick salesmanship skills.

The National Foundation for Teaching Entrepreneurship to Handicapped and Disadvantaged Youth Entrepreneurial Curriculum. This curriculum has already been put to the test. To secure write: NFTE, 64 Fulton Street, Suite 700, New York, NY 10038.

17. E. Digby Baltzell, *The Protestant Establishment: Aristocracy and Caste in America* (New York: Vintage Books, 1964), p. 122.

18. Interview with Frank R. Kennedy, Jr., September 22, 1991.

19. Ibid.

20. For a full explanation on the relationship of the "future-oriented" and "present-oriented" people of the upper, middle, and lower classes see Edward C. Banfield, *The Unheavenly City Revisited* (Boston: Little, Brown and Company, 1974), pp. 52–76.

21. Ibid., p. 61.

22. "Steve Mariotti," *Inc. Magazine,* April 1989, p. 66.

23. "Bonus! Entrepreneurship Can be Taught: Street Smarts," *Entrepreneur,* August 1991.

24. Elizabeth Greene, "Turning 'Street Smarts' Into a Way Out of Poverty," *The Chronicle of Philanthropy,* July 16, 1991, pp. 6–7.

25. Dot Yandle, "He Uses Hill's Principles With At-Risk Youth," *Think and Grow Rich Newsletter,* November 1990, p. 2.

26. The information concerning "Our Cookie Cart" was obtained via a telephone interview with Sister Thuerauf on November 21, 1991.

CHAPTER 8: RESPONDING TO TEEN PROFANITY

1. David A. Wiessler, "The Cussword Comes Out of the Closet," *U.S. News and World Report,* April 19, 1982, p. 88.
2. Ibid.
3. Hugh Rawson, *Wicked Words: A Treasury of Curses, Insults, Put-Downs, and Other Formerly Unprintable Terms from Anglo-Saxon Times to the Present* (New York: Crown Publishers, Inc., 1989), p. 114.
4. Sherry Suib Cohen, "When Kids Talk Dirty," *Women's Day,* January 16, 1990, p. 64.
5. Wiessler, p. 88.
6. Ibid., p. 87.
7. See Gary Collins, *Christian Counseling: A Comprehensive Guide* (Waco: Word Books, 1980), pp. 105–108.
8. It has been noted, however, that the Japanese and Native American do not use profanity as a construct of normal language. Wiessler, p. 88.
9. Cohen, p. 64.
10. For a sociological understanding of how primitive societies come to understand and order religious life around that which is sacred and profane see Emile Durkheim, *The Elemental Forms of the Religious Life* (New York: The Free Press, 1915), pp. 37–63.
11. *The Complete Works of William Shakespeare,* Masters Library (Minneapolis: Amaranth Press, 1987), p. 16.
12. The word *condemnation* as used in the New International Version texts is replaced with the harsher *damnation* in the King James Version. Compare Matthew 23:14, Mark 12:40, Luke 20:47, and Mark 3:29.

13. Robert Graves, *Lars Porsena; or, The Future of Swearing and Improper Language* (New York: E. P. Dutton and Company, 1927), p. 10.
14. For a few direct passages about God's power to cast the unrighteous into Hell see 2 Peter 2:4; Matthew 5:22, 29; 10:28; 23:33.
15. See Rawson, p.5.
16. For a parallel text see 1 Corinthians 3:16.
17. Rawson, p. 159.
18. Ibid., p. 43.
19. See ibid., p. 116.
20. The P-word has also been used as an affectionate name for a woman for "at least four hundred years." This meaning is not included here because the author has not recognized it in prevalent use in the city. Rawson, p. 315.
21. For an anthropological understanding of the incest taboo see Abraham Rosman and Paula G. Rubel, *The Tapestry of Culture,* second edition (New York: Random House, 1985), p. 50.
22. See Ashley Montagu, *The Anatomy of Swearing* (New York: The Macmillian Company, 1967), p. 313.
23. Rawson, p. 349.
24. Personal letter received on October 8, 1991.
25. The four personal responses to vulgarity were first printed by Dr. Edward Wakin. See Edward Wakin, "How to Cope with the New Vulgarity," *50 Plus,* April 1983, p. 42.
26. Ibid., p. 42.
27. See F. F. Bruce, ed., *The International Bible Commentary: With the New International Version,* revised edition (Carmel: Guideposts, 1986), p. 209.
28. Norman L. Geisler, ed., *Inerrancy* (Grand Rapids: Zondervan Publishing House, 1979), p. 290.
29. Although Proverbs 29:24 is better translated in the NIV, I specifically utilize the KJV for wording that alludes to a better discussion on profanity.

CHAPTER 9: HELPING TEENS CONFRONT CULTIC RELIGIONS

1. See Copeland, pp. 18–19.
2. See Robert A. McKay and John L. Smith, *Why Mormonism is a Cult* (Marlow, Oklahoma: Utah Missions, Inc., 1985), pp. 13–40. Some of the thirteen subtitles used for this section have been renamed in this book for clarity.
3. See 1 Corinthians 3:6.
4. The fifth point was added by the author. While alluded to by Reverend Lester Porter, it was not mentioned directly.
5. See Anne Cooper, ed., *Ishmael My Brother: A Biblical Course on Islam* (Kent: STL Books, 1985), p. 1.
6. Ari L. Goldman, "Mainstream Islam Rapidly Embraced by Black Americans," *The New York Times,* February 21, 1989, front page.
7. The information received can be found in a brochure by R. Max Kershaw, *How to Share the Good News with Your Muslim Friend* (Colorado Springs: International Students, 1990), p. 1.
8. See Goldman, p. B4.
9. Ibid., front page and p. B4.
10. See pamphlet by Carl Ellis, "How I Witness To Muslims," p. 1. Rev. Ellis is pastor of New City Fellowship, Chattanooga, Tennessee, and is an instructor for Prison Fellowship. This first appeared as an article in *Moody Monthly.*
11. Undocumented paraphernalia published on Islam in 1990 by *Jude 3 Ministries,* P. O. Box 923, Staten Island, NY 10314.
12. Ibid.
13. See Cooper, pp. 74–81.
14. M. H. Shakir, trans., *Holy Qur'an* (Elmhurst: Tahrike Tarsile Qur'an, Inc., 1986), p. 416.
15. *Jude 3 Ministries.*
16. See Cooper, pp. 78–80.
17. See Genesis 12:1–4, 15:2–6.
18. See Genesis 22:1–19 for the biblical account of Abraham with Isaac at Mt. Moriah.

19. See also Genesis 25:12–18.

20. Goldman, p. B4.

21. See Cooper, pp. 43–46 for a similar explanation of the five pillars of Islamic faith.

22. *Jude 3 Ministries.*

23. See Cooper, pp. 61–64.

24. Ibid., pp. 64–65, 68–70.

25. Shakir, p. 63.

26. Ellis, pp. 2–3.

27. *Jude 3 Ministries.*

28. Lester Porter interview on October 19, 1991.

29. Malcolm X [Little], as told to Alex Haley, *The Autobiography of Malcolm X* (1964; reprint, New York: Ballantine Books, 1984), p. 167.

30. *Jude 3 Ministries.*

31. John Hope Franklin and Alfred A. Moss, Jr., *From Slavery to Freedom: A History of Negro Americans,* Sixth edition (New York: Alfred A. Knopf, 1988), p. 377.

32. *Jude 3 Ministries.*

33. See Malcolm X, pp. 164–68.

34. Columbus Salley and Ronald Behm, *What Color is Your God?,* revised edition (Downers Grove, Ill. : InterVarsity Press, 1981), p. 74.

35. See Asante, pp. 2–7.

36. See Gerald Davis Jaynes and Robin M. Williams, Jr., ed., *A Common Destiny: Blacks and American Society* (Washington: National Academy Press, 1989), p. 193–194.

37. Malcolm X, pp. 339–40. His emphasis.

38. As quoted in Carl F. Ellis, Jr., *Beyond Liberation: The Gospel in the Black American Experience* (Downers Grove: InterVarsity Press, 1983).

39. Malcolm X, p. 319.

40. Undocumented paraphernalia published on Jehovah's Witnesses in 1990 by *Jude 3 Ministries,* P. O. Box 923, Staten Island, NY 10314.

41. Ibid.
42. Ibid.
43. From the movie *Witnesses of Jehovah* (La Jolla, Calif.: Good News Defenders, 1988).
44. This information is from a September 1982 circular by Leonard A. Chretien, "The Watchtower and the Generation of 1914," P.O. Box 8007, La Jolla, CA 92038, p. 2.
45. *Jude 3 Ministries*, Jehovah's Witnesses.
46. See Chretien, pp. 2–3.
47. From the one-page leaflet "Warning," published by The Watchman Fellowship, P. O. Box 7681, Columbus, Georgia 31908.
48. Ibid.
49. The following information on Jesus Christ was noted in the video presentation *Witnesses of Jehovah.*
50. Copeland, p. 167–8.
51. *Mormonism Researched,* Spring 1989, p. 6. This is a quarterly publication by the Mormonism Research Ministry, P. O. Box 20705, El Cajon, CA 92021-0955.
52. Undocumented paraphernalia published on Mormonism in 1990 by *Jude 3 Ministries,* P. O. Box 923, Staten Island, NY 10314.
53. *Mormonism Researched,* p. 6.
54. From the leaflet "As a Minister Do You Know What is: 'America's Most Successful Home-Grown Religion?'" Copies can be maintained through Honest History, P. O. Box 25771, Salt Lake City, UT 84125.
55. See ibid., p. 2, and *Mormonism Researched,* p. 6.
56. As quoted in McKay and Smith, p. 33.
57. Ibid., p. 9.
58. *Jude 3 Ministries,* Mormonism.
59. Ibid.
60. *Mormonism Researched,* pp. 5, 8.
61. *Jude 3 Ministries,* Mormonism.
62. From the Mormon *Articles of Faith,* as quoted in McKay and Smith, p. 27.

63. See *Mormonism Researched,* p. 2.
64. *Jude 3 Ministries,* Mormonism.
65. See McKay and Smith, p. 17.
66. As quoted by McKay and Smith, p. 20.
67. See ibid., p. 22.
68. *Jude 3 Ministries,* Mormonism.
69. For complete context read 3 Nephi 8, 9:1–15. Quote taken from 3 Nephi 9:15, *The Book of Mormon: Another Testament of Jesus Christ* (Salt Lake City: The Church of Jesus Christ of Latter-Day Saints, 1990), p. 425.
70. See McKay and Smith, p. 26.
71. Ibid., p. 25.
72. See F. F. Bruce, *Paul: Apostle of the Heart Set Free* (1977; reprint, Grand Rapids: William B. Eerdmans Publishing Company, 1986), pp. 236–7.
73. See John 4:10.

CHAPTER 10: THE HEROIC REVOLUTION

1. Cf. Larry Christenson, *A Charismatic Approach to Social Action* (Minneapolis: Bethany Fellowship, 1974), pp. 80, 94 and Matthew 3:2.
2. See ibid., p. 82.
3. Cf. Jonathan Edwards, "Christian Charity; or, The Duty of Charity to the Poor, Explained and Enforced," *The Works of President Edwards,* Research and Source Work Series, No. 271, vol. 5 (1817; reprint, New York: Burt Franklin, 1968), p. 399.
4. Ibid., pp. 400–401. Edwards' emphasis.
5. Stephen Charles Mott, *Biblical Ethics and Social Change* (New York: Oxford University Press, 1982), p. 4.
6. Ibid., p. 5.
7. Wendell Berry, "Manifesto: The Mad Farmer Liberation Front," *Collected Poems.*

8. Arnobius of Sicca, *The Case Against the Pagans,* vol. 1 of *Ancient Christian Writers,* trans. George E. McCracken (Westminster, Md.: The Newman Press, 1949), p. 58.
9. See Mott, pp. 10–15 for a full explanation of social reality.
10. Cf. Edwards, page not specified.
11. Ecclesiastes 2:11.
12. Ecclesiastes 12:14.
13. Walter Rauschenbusch, *A Theology for the Social Gospel* (1917; reprint, Nashville: Abingdon Press, 1987), p. 179.
14. Karl Marx and Friedrich Engels, *The Communist Manifesto,* trans. Samuel Moore, ed. Joseph Katz (1848; reprint, New York: Simon and Schuster, Washington Square Press, 1964), p.58.
15. See ibid., p. 116.
16. Term used by Robert Bellah to signify that America is based upon a constitutional civil religion. Therefore, a covenantal relationship is expected between the government and its subjects to ensure that democracy is enjoyed by all. See Robert N. Bellah, *The Broken Covenant* (Chicago: University of Chicago Press, 1975).
17. Thomas Jefferson, as quoted ibid., pp. 34–35.
18. Charles S. McCoy, "The Federal Tradition of Theology and Political Ethics: Background for Understanding the U.S. Constitution and Society," *The Annual,* Society of Christian Ethics, 1988, p. 114.
19. Cf. E. Clinton Gardner, "Justice in the Puritan Covenantal Tradition," *The Annual,* Society of Christian Ethics, 1988, pp. 91–111.
20. "I Have a Dream," *A Testament of Hope: The Essential Writings of Martin Luther King, Jr.,* ed. James M. Washington (San Francisco: Harper and Row, 1986), p. 217.
21. Excerpt from Maya Angelou's poem "On the Pulse of Morning," presented for the inauguration of President Bill Clinton, January 20, 1993. Reprinted in *Ebony,* March 1993, p. 125.
22. Benjamin W. Bacon, *Non-resistance: Christian or Pagan?* (New Haven: Yale University Press, 1918), p. 26.

23. Leroy H. Pelton, *The Psychology of Nonviolence* (New York: Pergamon Press, Inc., 1974), p. 16.

24. Nelson E. Copeland, Jr., "The Relevance of the Christian Tradition of Non-violent Resistance as a Strategic Premise for Implementing Social Change in Urban America," second draft (Master's thesis in Christian Social Ethics, Gordon Conwell Theological Seminary, 1993).

25. Bellah, p. 63. Emphasis mine.

26. Erich Fromm, *Escape From Freedom* (New York: Reinhart and Company, 1941). Quoted from David G. Gil, *Unraveling Social Policy,* Fourth ed. (Rochester, Vt.: Schenkman Books, Inc., 1990), p. 306.

27. Ernst Troeltsch, *The Social Teaching of the Christian Churches,* vol. 1, trans. Olive Wyon (1912; reprint, Louisville: Westminster, John Knox Press, 1992), p. 59.

28. "Society's soul" refers to that within every society which, if appealed to correctly, can cause guilt to fall upon the entire society and move it toward paradigmatic change.

29. Cf. Troeltsch, p. 107.

30. Drawn from Copeland, "Christian Tradition of Non-violent Resistance," unused portion of first draft, 1992.

31. Jeanne Larson and Madge Micheels-Cyrus, *Seeds of Peace: A Catalogue of Quotations* (Philadelphia: New Society Publishers, 1987), p. 177. Hugo's first quotation dates from 1877.

32. Phrase first used as the title of an essay by William James, written in 1910 for the Association for International Conciliation (Leaflet No. 27). Reprinted in *McClure's Magazine,* August, 1910, and *The Popular Science Monthly,* October, 1910. For the purposes of this chapter see *The Moral Equivalent of War and Other Essays,* ed. John K. Roth (New York: Harper and Row, 1971).

33. Larson and Micheels-Cyrus, p. 3.

34. S. J. Samartha, "Is Nonviolence Out of Date?" *Religion in Life,* No. 39, 1970, p. 393.

35. See Sidney Callahan, *In Good Conscience: Reason and Emotion in Moral Decision Making* (San Francisco: Harper, 1991), pp. 95, 97, 98.
36. See ibid., p. 99.
37. See ibid., p. 95.
38. Ibid., p. 103.
39. Francis X. Meehan, *A Contemporary Social Spirituality* (Maryknoll, N.Y.: Orbis Books, 1982), p. 9.
40. Cf. *Declaration of Independence of the United States of America,* paragraph 2.
41. Cf. Richard A. Horsley, *Jesus and the Spiral of Violence: Popular Jewish Resistance in Roman Palestine* (San Francisco: Harper and Row, 1987), p. 35.
42. Ibid., p. 22.
43. Cf. subtitles in Andre Trocme, *Jesus and the Nonviolent Revolution* (Scottdale, Pa.: Herald Press, 1973), pp. 145–146.
44. E. Clinton Gardner, *Biblical Faith and Social Ethics* (New York: Harper, 1960), p. 27. Gardner's italics.
45. See Trocme, p. 146.
46. "Good" is used in the Genesis account of creation to display God's pleasure with the harmony present in creation. Cf. Genesis 1–2.
47. Trocme, p. 180.
48. Ibid., p. 147.
49. Roland H. Bainton, *Christian Attitudes Toward War and Peace: A Historical Survey and Critical Re-evaluation* (Nashville: Abingdon Press, 1960), p. 18.
50. These principles were first presented in Copeland, "Christian Tradition of Non-violent Resistance," second draft, 1993.
51. See 1 Samuel 17.
52. See Acts 6:8–8:1.
53. See Daniel 6.
54. See Matthew 14:1–12, Mark 6:14–29.
55. See Daniel 3.

56. See Matthew 27:32–56, Mark 15:21–41, Luke 23:26–49, John
    19:16–37.
57. See Isaiah 6:8.
58. Cf. Daniel 3.
59. See Esther 4:16.

DATE DUE	BORROWER'S NAME

Top Notch Teacher Products, Inc.